SHOWS

Maxene Fabe

Photo Credits

CBS—1, 1a, 2, 3, 4, 5, 6, 9, 11, 13, 14, 16, 24, 25, 26, 28, 29, 30, 31, 32, 33, 33a, 34, 36, 38, 39, 40, 43, 45, 47, 49, 52, 55, 57, 59, 61, 66, 67, 68, 69, 71, 74, 75, 76, 77, 78, 79, 80, 81

Memory Shop—7, 8, 10a, 12, 20, 33b, 35, 37, 42, 44, 46, 48, 50, 51, 53, 54, 58, 58a, 60, 62, 63, 64, 65, 70, 72, 73, 82

NBC—10, 15, 17, 41

UPI—23, 56

DESIGNED BY MARILYN SCHULMAN

Library of Congress Cataloging in Publication Data

Fabe, Maxene.
  TV game shows.

  (A Dolphin book)
  1. Game shows. I. Title.
PN1992.8.Q5F27   791.45′5

ISBN: 0-385-13052-X
Library of Congress Catalog Card Number: 77-11390

791.455 F114t
FABE
 TV GAME SHOWS

FV

11.45

TV GAME

A DOLPHIN BOOK
Doubleday & Company, Inc.
Garden City, New York
1979

TV GAME SHOWS

Dedicated with love to Guy Davis Mulford III

"You can learn more about America by watching one-half hour of *Let's Make a Deal* than you can from watching Walter Cronkite for an entire month."

—Monty Hall's favorite quote

Contents

Introduction

Part One

Part Two

Appendix

INTRODUCTION

Confessions of a Game Show Addict

"Say the secret word and divide $100."

"Is it bigger than a bread box?"

"You have reached the first plateau. Think carefully. Will you take the money and stop, or go on for the $64,000 question?"

"You did not tell the truth, so you must pay the consequences."

"Would *you* like to be 'Queen for a Day?!' "

"Stop the music!"

"Heartline!"

"C'mon down!"

"Sign in, please!"

"From Hollywood, almost live . . ."

"Will the real game show addict please stand up?"

That would be me. Game shows and I go back *years*. I discovered them first in the days of radio, when I was in the second grade. Home from school with the sniffles, crosslegged in toast crumbs and crumpled Kleenex, the first buzzers and bells, the deep voices of those genial, fun-loving hosts, the peals of laughter from the throats of transcribed multitudes, crooned to me their siren song. *Queen for a Day, Strike It Rich, Break the Bank, Double or Nothing, People Are Funny* cheered me more than chicken soup, or back at school, the rigors of multiplication. Frequent cases of the "sniffles" followed.

Then, television! Its first flickering games and quizzes were all on in the evening, after dinner: *Twenty Questions, I've Got a Secret, You Bet Your Life, Pantomime Quiz, Masquerade Party, Beat the Clock*, and best of all, late on Sunday nights, *What's My Line?* Best, that is, until June of 1956, when *The $64,000 Question* bowed and suddenly the whole country went quiz-show crazy, and, when Charles Van Doren won his gladiatorial fortune on *Twenty-One,* crazier still. In three years' time we all were to know the awful truth: the glamorous big-money quizzes had all been secretly rigged. Boyish, beloved Van Doren became the John Dean of his day. "I was involved in deception," he testified.

You could look long and hard for a game show after that. Dozens were canceled. Those that survived were yanked from prime time and sealed in the ghetto of daytime, shackled with claustrophobic regulations, and over-run with police from the networks' standards-and-practices departments. The flashing lights flickered. And besides, I was growing up, going off to college, graduate school, entering the nine-to-five workaday world. Except during holidays that fell on weekdays, or when I had the flu, I rarely watched these exiled court jesters of my childhood. Seemingly, I had meta-morphosed into a normal, healthy adult. Who then could have predicted what happened next?

For the next scene finds the narrator abed at midday, crosslegged in toast crumbs, and not crumpled Kleenex but foolscap. The normally healthy adult has become a writer who stays at home to work during the hours of nine to five—but instead of writing, she is watching *Let's Make a Deal.* She is not watching judgmentally, she is not saying, "Tsk, tsk." She is not lament-ing the banality of her fellow creatures. Not at all: she is watching with delight. She is wishing that *she* lived in Los Angeles, where the show is taped, so that *she* could dress up like a carrot, not necessarily so that she might win A TRIP TO PARIS! A NEW CAR! AN AMANA RADAR RANGE! though that would be nice, but simply because the show looks marvelous.

"Take the curtain," a voice rings out. It is speaking to the television from the unmade bed. The voice is mine.

Game shows had survived. What is more, they were better than they had ever been before. Thank goodness I hadn't missed many. Games like *Let's Make a Deal, Concentration, To Tell the Truth, Match Game, The Price Is Right, Hollywood Squares,* and *Jeopardy!* had all been on the air before we'd parted ways. At least ten years old, they were still going strong. Immediately I set about effecting our sweet, sweet reunion.

I confess that at first I was as embarrassed by my afternoon love affair as a duchess caught with the dustman. You're not supposed to like game shows, you know. The critics say so.

Soon however, despite myself, certain telltale anecdotes began to steal into my conversations. "Did you know that California produces more plums and prunes than the rest of the country combined?" I'd mentioned over evening cocktails. "I heard it today on *Squares.*"

When bills arrived, I began demanding of my husband *à la The Price Is Right:* "Guess what the electricity came to this month?"

"Fifteen dollars?"

"Higher!"

"Twenty?"

"Lower!"

When *Family Feud* was on, I refused to take phone calls.

It got to be so bad, I even became a contestant. On *Jeopardy!* I came in second, winning $590, an encyclopedia, and a home game.

Eventually, when my infatuation failed to wear off, I became analytical. Something was drawing me, and millions of other people, to these shows every day, something that the critics, with their indictments, had failed to fathom.

It seemed clear to me that the critics could not possibly be watching the same game shows *I* was. For instance, they called the contestants greedy. But the contestants on the game shows I watched were not greedy. When they won, they did not gloat. When they lost, they did not sulk; they smiled and said what a good time they'd had. Moreover, some of the best game shows gave only small prizes and lasted years; some of the worst gave huge prizes, and disappeared before their thirteen weeks were up.

The critics were scornful of the squealing and jumping up and down they saw on the shows. It seemed to me, however, that the critics were *really* condemning the sight of someone (women, maybe?) acting spontaneous and uninhibited while participating in a competition. Why not, I wondered, the same opprobrium for sports fans screaming at a hockey game? Were the critics really trying to decide what fantasies, what stakes, it was proper to become emotional about: winning a mink coat, no; the Super Bowl, yes? It was a shame, I thought, shaking my head, about those critics; they were missing all the fun.

Having thus opened our hearts and minds to game shows, let us also be truthful. Most of them stink. Over the past thirty years, there have been, according to my count, nearly 700 of them. Most, deservedly, flashed and buzzed only a few times before being mercifully and permanently retired. Only the forty you'll be reading about in this book are worth remembering and commemorating for the classic shows they are. Why the disparate ratio? Blame the networks for that. To them the game show has always been regarded as filler, rather than the carefully crafted dramatic art form it actually is. Back in 1948, when TV was so new, people watched anything, even the test pattern. The big stars, safe in their niches in radio, were slow to brave the screen, so the infant networks offered a number of space-filling contests and games. For one thing, they were cheap to produce. All you needed for the set was a table and four chairs for a panel game; or a wheel of fortune borrowed from a carnival; a hopper full of postcards and a telephone for calling home viewers; a bunch of local actors playing charades;

or a disc jockey playing mystery tunes; a jovial host armed with a couple of hoary parlor games and a self-conscious audience full of church ladies. The games were easy to find sponsors for; what better public-relations gesture for a manufacturer than to donate a few percolators or savings bonds as prizes? Better still, because they were so inexpensive to mount, profits to the networks from game shows were always astronomical—at least 600 per cent, and usually higher. The networks could scarcely afford *not* to air them. When, from time to time, a game proved popular, the networks were pleasantly surprised. They upped the advertising rates and hastily launched a flurry of second-rate imitations. That these always failed only fed the networks' already low regard for the games, of course—until the next surprise hit came along. To this day, successful game shows, even the classic greatest of the great, tend to be regarded as happy accidents. "It's all a big crap shoot," one network vice-president shrugged to me not very long ago. She held a sheaf of statistics demonstrating that game show viewers are "fickle," not the discerning connoisseurs *I* might term us.

In fact, a good television game show is not an accident—and it never was. The classics, the ones you remember, were (and are) all painstakingly and lovingly crafted. "It's the greatest challenge in the world to invent a new game," says Mark Goodson, whose name is synonymous with game shows. "For every one you see, every concept that ultimately is refined and developed, a dozen are worked on and not worked on or almost worked on or dropped because they don't read any more. We test and hammer and test and hammer. When you finally get it down so that it looks very very simple, that one has had the most complicated amount of work."

Easier said than done, particularly in a medium as elusive as television. The first game-show pioneers, such as Mark Goodson himself, had a lot to learn. In fact, most of radio's biggest hit games and quizzes fell flat on TV. Exciting to listen to, they failed absolutely to make the visual transition. Yet, self-consciously playing to the camera—scooting contestants around the stage, dressing them up in costumes, using elaborate props, sets or gimmickry—did not automatically guarantee a television success either. Nor did the presence of glamorous celebrities, or the use of hilarious comedians as hosts, or even the offering of large sums of money as prizes. Game show pioneers discovered that while such frou-frou might provide extra bounce to a good game, it might actually sink a bad one. On the other hand, an early game-show hit like *What's My Line?*, which offered viewers a visually static format and never awarded more than fifty dollars in prize money, ran for seventeen years in prime time, longer still in syndication, and is *still* playing in foreign markets. Clearly for a game to be that magical, that memorable, it had to offer something more. That something is this: a game show has actively to involve the viewer. The TV game is a type of play that has never existed before. It elevates the role of the observer, the kibbitzer, if you will, to a position equal and often superior to the contestant. To achieve this feat, the creator of a good game seeks the simplest, sparest framework he can find, then builds into it a series of excruciatingly suspenseful dilemmas, the outcome of which is to the viewers so grippingly dramatic, so continually unpredictable, that the audience literally cannot contain itself. Put another way, if a game is any good, you the viewer will find yourself talking out loud to your television—involuntarily, helplessly, unashamedly.

So long as a game creates in the home audience this degree of involvement, its genius can take any form. Over the years, there have been dozens of different kinds of game show, no two ever quite alike. There have been word games, music games, charade games, love and marriage games, gossip games, bluff games, puzzle games, ESP-matching games, art games, merchandise and pricing games, stunt games, gambling games, physical games, sensory games, cerebral games, "hard luck" games and "most deserving" games. There are games played by one contestant at a time, or an entire audience, or an entire country, or two players, or three, or teams of two each or as many as six. There've been panel games; there have been celebrity games; games where contestants challenge celebrities and games where contestants and celebrities play side by side.

Indeed, if you would appreciate the inventiveness, the drama inherent in a modern game, merely compare a good one to one of its prehistoric cousins, the quiz. The quiz, as many producers were to learn to their rue, never quite worked. Even on radio it had seemed too static. One contestant stood up and tried to answer a series of increasingly more difficult questions. Because there is no true drama in that, producers had been forced, for years, to manufacture it. All radio quiz shows had routinely been manipulated a little, to inject the necessary suspense, the questions slanted, the contestants coached. Translating the radio quiz to television, even upping the stakes from $64 to $64,000 could only temporarily disguise the basic monotony of the question-and-answer format. Even before TV quizzes were unmasked as crooked, they were already afflicted with dipping ratings. In the fifties, it seemed, the viewers *had* been talking to their television sets. They had been saying, "Ho hum."

Still, if folks jabbering away at the home screen was all there were to game shows, I would not watch and neither would you. There's something more. The best hold out to us the golden ring. They makes it so achingly attainable.

* to be on television!
* to meet a real live star, if only for half an hour.
* to be flanked by "angels," judged by a heavenly "host." For you,

harp strings to thrum, the pearly gates to swing open, here, *now,* not in the dire hereafter.

Oh, I watch game shows all right. I watch riveted. I want to see how people act when it matters desperately how well they "play." And I ask, if it were *me* so tested and tempted and tried, could *I* cut it? Would *I* be graceful under pressure? If I won, would I be saved, changed, yea verily, born again?

Now, you see I've written this book, the logical manifestation of my mania. It's all about game shows, of course—the first book of its kind to embrace them affectionately, to take them seriously. It's not a history (fact—date, fact—date, linear and plodding). That would come nowhere near to doing them justice. Rather, it's meant to be read *like* a game show —to flicker and flash, to throw information and anecdotes at you zip, zip, zip, to have its varying textures and moods.

Like a game show, this book has its own carefully crafted internal organization. Part One takes you behind the scenes and tells you all about how the shows work, who works on them, and how you yourself can be a part of one. Part Two? After first setting the stage with a fond look at radio games, it commemorates the forty best—and the ten worst—game shows of all times. Interspersed throughout: photographs; questions and stunts from the games themselves; and a nice juicy section on the scandals of the Fifties. In the back, hard-core game show lovers will find a total chronological annotated listing of every game show ever.

Before we begin, you need to know one more thing—perhaps you've already guessed it. The people who work on game shows, from the fattest-cat packagers, to the producers, the directors, the hosts, the question writers, the "prize guys," the contestant coordinators, the celebrities, the celebrity bookers, the production assistants, the camera men and the stage hands, and the network people are *nice.* They take their craft seriously and work long, hard hours at it. On my trips to the studios in California and New York for numerous tapings; into the offices where the creative, behind-the-scenes staffs work; out on the lines and into the rooms where contestants are selected and cared for; into the very homes and dressing rooms of your favorite hosts, I could detect not one iota of the cynicism the critics of game shows imagine. What I received instead, particularly when it became clear that my mission was friendly and my enthusiasm genuine, was a generous outpouring of time and information.

Acknowledgments

Thanks are due to Jane Ahlquist, former contestant coordinator for *Jeopardy;* Paul Alter, Goodson-Todman Productions; Bob Bach, Goodson-Todman; Bob Barker; Bill Behanna, A. C. Nielsen Company; Bruce Belland,

Ralph Edwards Productions; Stu Billett, Hatos-Hall Productions; Bruce Burmester, Bob Stewart Productions; Edythe Chan, Bob Stewart Productions; Jerry Chester, Goodson-Todman Productions; The Columbia Oral History Library; Madeleine David, NBC; Richard Dawson, my backgammon partner; Geoff Edwards; Ralph Edwards; Howard Felsher, Goodson-Todman Productions; Bob Flaherty, CBS; Hy Freedman, writer, *You Bet Your Life;* Mike Gargiulo, Bob Stewart Productions; Alan Gerson, NBC; Jeff Goldstein, Merv Griffin Productions; Mark Goodson; Ray Goulding, NBC; Stuart Gray, NBC; John Guedel; Merrill Heatter; Cathy Hughart, Goodson-Todman; Joyce Jaffee, Goodson-Todman; Tom Kennedy; Larry Ketron, Bob Stewart Productions; Lincoln Center for the Performing Arts; Peter Marshall; Helen Manassian, NBC; Maria Martone, Mary Markham Associates; Ida Mae McKenzie, Heatter-Quigley Productions; Robert Noah, Heatter-Quigley Productions; John Rhinehart, formerly at NBC; Bob Rubin, formerly Merv Griffin Productions; Nipsey Russell; Ira Skutch, Goodson-Todman; Bob Stewart; Debbie Weiner Hefferan, Bob Stewart Productions; Jay Wolpert, formerly of Goodson-Todman, I only wish I could have spoken to everyone.

Extra special thanks to Roger Dobkowitz and to John Margolies for sharing with me their written research.

Houghtonville, Vermont
Winter 1978

Part One

BEHIND THE CURTAIN

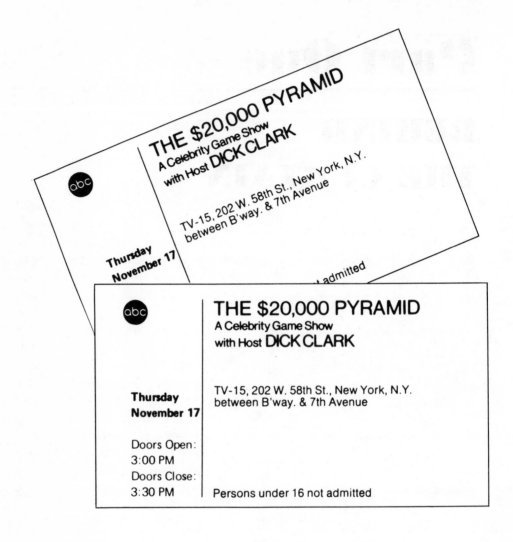

THE $20,000 PYRAMID
A Celebrity Game Show
with Host **DICK CLARK**

Thursday
November 17

TV-15, 202 W. 58th St., New York, N.Y.
between B'way. & 7th Avenue

Doors Open:
3:00 PM
Doors Close:
3:30 PM

Persons under 16 not admitted

Contestants!

You may never get that itch. But every year, hundreds of thousands of Americans do. One day, while sitting in their living rooms, they find themselves listening to those fleeting seconds a game show takes each day to inform home viewers how to get on the game. Each day, hundreds of viewers, maybe *you*, cross the threshold. They make the decision to become one of the contestants behind the screen they've watched so often from out front.

The odds are against you. When it comes to choosing contestants, game shows are very picky. They are looking for people with whom their viewers will feel comfortable; they are looking for people who will play the game with verve. Stated straight from the shoulder, they are not looking for contestants who are merely nice, or deserving, or even needy. They are looking for contestants who will boost their ratings. Each week, each game show interviews between two and three hundred hopeful contestants. Each week only 5 per cent will be selected. This is not a how-to book, but what the heck. Let's start off practically. If you have ever had the hankering to get yourself on television and possibly win yourself a refrigerator, here is how *you* can be one of them:

1. Be eighteen years old. That's a network rule.

2. Now, before you make a move, size up the show best for you according to your strengths. Games that require special knowledge or aptitudes like word games or music games will be easier to crack than the shows that ask nothing of their contestants but a nice personality; waiting lists for the latter kind of game are apt to be much, *much* longer.

3. If you live near Los Angeles or New York City, currently the only two places network game shows are taped, it is very much to your advantage to attend a taping first as a member of the studio audience. Write the networks for tickets. During breaks, members of the game show's staff will pass out application cards to the audience. If they are interested, they will notify you by phone or postcard within a few weeks.

4. If you are from out of town, prepare to vacation in Los Angeles or New York City. Then write a letter to the contestant co-ordinator's office of the packaging company airing the game show. Game shows announce their address every day on the show. To save you time, you'll find the information in the adjacent box.

Get Your Pencil . . .

Here, in alphabetical order, are the game show production companies likely to have a show on the air at any given time. Write to the Contestant Co-ordinator, care of the specific show, at:

Ralph Andrews Productions
10635 Riverside
Tolucca Lake, California 91602
(213) 980–8100

Chuck Barris Productions
1313 North Vine Street
Los Angeles, California 91602
(213) 469–9080

Barry-Enright Productions
1888 Century Park East
Los Angeles, California 90067
(213) 277–3414

Ralph Edwards Productions
1717 Highland Avenue
Los Angeles, California 91602
(213) 462–2212

Goodson-Todman Productions
6430 Sunset Boulevard
Los Angeles, California 90028
(213) 464–4300

Merv Griffin Productions
1737 North Vine Street
Los Angeles, California 90028
(213) 461–4701

Hatos-Hall Productions
6430 Sunset Boulevard
Los Angeles, California 90028
(213) 469–5821

Heatter-Quigley Productions
9255 Sunset Boulevard
Los Angeles, California 90069
(213) 461–4701

Hill-Eubanks Productions
P.O. Box 900
Beverly Hills, California 90213

Bob Stewart Productions
250 West Fifty-seventh Street
New York, N.Y. 10019
(212) 247–6300

In your letter stress that you are from out of town. Game shows can always find contestants from Los Angeles or New York. But players from other parts of the country are very much in demand, since they give a game show a wider regional appeal. No matter how many local people are on a game show's waiting list, contestant co-ordinators always give priority to visitors.

Say exactly when you will be in town and for how long. Include your home address and all relevant telephone numbers. It also wouldn't hurt to include your age, occupation, marital status, and anything else interesting about you that will make you memorable. Got a recent photo? Send it, too.

5. By now the game show has set up your preliminary interview. You have been called down to the contestant co-ordinator's office. Do not expect to see your favorite host, celebrities, or anyone else connected with the production of the game show. By network regulation, ever since the quiz-show scandals of the late fifties, even potential contestants are kept wholly segregated from anyone connected with the game show's questions or its prizes. Do not, in fact, expect to see anything remotely glamorous; the offices of the contestant co-ordinator are more than a little shopworn. After all, tens of thousands of hopefuls have preceded you.

When you arrive, behave as if you were on a job interview. Dress neatly and arrive on time. Be as personable and extroverted and naturally wonderful as you know how to be. From the moment you arrive, someone on the contestant co-ordinator's staff will be evaluating even your most casual gesture for televisibility.

You will first be required to fill out a questionnaire. Have you ever been on a game show before? Within two years? Do you know anyone connected with the show or its sponsors? Tell the truth. Game shows turn this information over to the networks; the networks keep computerized records. You will also be required to sign a statement at the bottom of the questionnaire, binding you to abide to all terms and conditions set by the packager and the network concerning the rules of the game and your receipt of any prizes. Sign. (And be prepared to sign again. Should you be selected, you will be handed a similar statement just prior to going on the air.)

Next, someone on the contestant co-ordinator's staff will take your picture. It will be stapled to your questionnaire and filed.

Some shows give a written qualifying test. How well you do on it is secondary, however, to the way your personality has come through on the interview.

6. Only half the potential contestants survive this preliminary screening. If you are one of them, you now meet with the game show's head contestant co-ordinator. You will chat; you will be briefed on the game's rules; you will

Big Brother Is Watching . . .

If the networks keep contestant files, so do the game shows. Room after room of them. Contestants are filed by age and by sex; then subfiled by "image" under such whimsical categories as "Swinging Single," "Young Married," "Uniform," "Grandmother," "Character," and "Mustache." Why? Not for security purposes. It's to achieve an audience-pleasing, rating-boosting balance on the show, as in "I've got a sweet little 'grandmother' here; find me a nice-looking 'uniform' from the file." The files also give game show packagers a ready-made contestant pool should they be lucky enough to sell another show.

By the way, should you be turned down by one packaging company, don't bother trying them again; you have become permanently *persona non grata*. Don't even try becoming a "Mustache." Thanks to those files, contestant co-ordinators have uncanny memories, and I'm afraid they had lasting reasons for rejecting you. Sorry, but that's show biz.

play a sample round of the game with her. If you do well on *this* round, one show, *Hollywood Squares,* goes so far as to give contestants an actual on-camera screen test. You will be seated in a square for one minute and asked to "be yourself."

Contestant co-ordinators are very nice people who like people. They also know exactly what they are looking for in a contestant.

"I look for people who think with their teeth," says Ida Mae McKenzie, a plump, white-haired, den-motherly former actress who wears muu-muus and slippers to work. Ida Mae McKenzie books contestants for the Heatter-Quigley shows, including *Hollywood Squares.* "Our show," she says, referring to *Squares,* "is a true 'walk-of-life' show. We look for anyone who might have personality; young and old, truck drivers, young housewives, grandmothers, attorneys, waitresses."

"I tell them all the decision to be on our show lies not with the producers, but with *you.* If you come up here with ENERGY! VITALITY! SMILING! THE FEELING YOU'RE GOING TO COMPETE!" (she really does talk like that), "you enhance your chances of being on the show ninety per cent. If you don't compete, what you come here to win ends up at the other guy's house."

Edythe Chan is the contestant co-ordinator for *The $20,000 Pyramid,* a show that is produced in New York. She is just as emphatic as Ida Mae. "We look for enthusiasm," she says briskly. "You've got to like this show and show it. If you're too slow, too quiet, forget it. If you're a dull tool, you're no fun to watch."

Obviously, contestant co-ordinators like to sound positive, but there are some unwritten rules. Save yourself the trip:

if you are very poor and needy and it shows;
if you are very rich and unneedy and it shows;
if you have an obvious handicap or a potentially unsettling occupation or a "disturbing" marital status;
or display uncontestantlike personality traits such as being argumentative, overbearing, blasé, or affected.

Expect to overcome some resistance:

if you are a senior citizen. The shows and their sponsors are looking to appeal to people with buying power, the housewives between the ages of eighteen and forty-nine; not *you,* I'm afraid.

if you are a male. Your problem is that you're culturally conditioned not to show your feelings. (If learning this makes you cry, disregard the above and get in line for *The Price Is Right;* they've been waiting for you.)

If you are from out of town and you pass your audition, you will be booked onto the game the next taping. If, however, you are a local resident, you will be sent home to wait until the show has run out of extroverted non-local candidates. Be prepared to wait a long time. *Hollywood Squares'* packaging company, Heatter-Quigley tells its hopefuls, "If you haven't heard from us in six months, burn three locks of your hair and try another packager." Game shows never bother to notify their rejects.

The Spoilers . . .

One ill-fated show, *Double Dare,* traced its early demise to having initially selected the wrong contestants. "At first we could only find bachelors with walrus mustaches," said a show staffer. "By the time we located good people, it was too late. Our ratings never recovered."

These game show folks certainly do have a fetish with mustaches!

7. You've made it! The show has called with the date of your taping. Bring a change of clothes. Though everybody knows by now that five shows are taped in one day, the game show wants it to seem to home viewers that twenty-four hours have passed between shows, not minutes. Should you win, be prepared to ad lib when the game's host winks and asks you what you did "last night." Hosts love to put contestants on the spot like that. Contestants like it, too.

8. Welcome backstage; it's taping day. Again from the moment you arrive at the studio, you will not just be segregated from the crew. You will be rigidly chaperoned as well, by a representative of the network's watchdog Standards and Practices Department, to insure that no one slips you any answers in advance. If you have to go to the bathroom, Standards and Practices will go with you.

In all probability you will not be on the air at all today. The reason, again, is security. The networks further insist that the game show provide twice the number of contestants that they will need for a taping to keep contestant selection random and unriggable.

"Lights! Camera!"

Sometimes, bringing an overnight bag and making a little small talk with the host isn't the *half* of it. During one taping of *Wheel of Fortune,* an overhead light blew out, temporarily stopping the show at an especially dramatic moment: the wheel had hit "Bankrupt," totally wiping out a contestant's winnings. Taping halted for fifteen minutes, whereupon the contestant could hear the voice of the director addressing her over the set's loudspeaker. "We got the shot of the wheel," he announced, "but we lost you. Look disappointed." Like a trooper, the contestant obliged with the appropriate groan of dismay.

Even though you won't be playing today, your time will not be wasted. For one thing, you'll begin to get a glimmer of just how complex a game show really is. You'll see that it takes literally hundreds of people to make it happen.

First, of course, there's the packager, who devised the show, sold it to the network, and hired the creative staff to execute it. Working for the packager are the game show's producer and his/her assistants, the director, the host, announcer, writers, the celebrity booker, and the contestant co-ordinator and her staff.

The game show's producer is responsible for the creative content of the show. During a taping, depending upon the format of the game, he sits at a table down on the shooting floor off to the side of the set. Or, if the game calls for complicated rulings, he may position himself directly behind the director in the control room. The producer makes the split-second decisions about whether a contestant's answer is acceptable within the rules of the game. In addition, he oversees the planning of each show down to the last detail. He hires the question writers, the script writers, and the advertising copy writers, then edits and approves their work. He specifies the prizes he wants with the network's contest co-ordination department, and plans the order in which they will be offered. He rehearses the content of each show with the announcer and the host. He checks the work of the celebrity booker and usually briefs all celebrities as to the rules of the game. And he is ultimately responsible for the contestants selected by the contestant coordinator; if *you* don't look good, his show doesn't look good.

Working under him/her are at least one associate producer and a large staff of production assistants. It is their job to type the script that will be used for a taping (see pages 61–64), to locate the props, to write the cue cards for the host and the advertising copy for the announcer, to prepare the color-still flip cards of the prizes for the cameramen, to co-ordinate the wardrobes of the models with the network wardrobe mistress, and entertain any manufacturer's representatives or media people present at the taping. During a taping, the production assistants cue the stagehands for any special effects buttons they'll have to push. They also keep written records of the scoring during the game, and which contestants win which prizes. After the show, they tally these results for the files of both the network and the packager.

The job of the game show's director is even more complex. He has participated in the planning of the game from its inception having helped the set designer stage the game, as to the number and placement of the cameras. He rules on the game's lighting and color scheme. On taping days, he arrives early to rehearse with the studio's cameramen and stagehands the order in which the routines, questions, and prizes will be shown.

During the taping, the director works in the control room, a dimly lit, glassed-in cockpit high above the game show's stage. Here he pulls together the many elements that comprise the picture on your screen. Intercom microphones connect him to each of the game's three to six cameramen. The pictures on each of their cameras are beamed by cable onto monitors, the closed-circuit TV screens in the control room that are banked in rows. Also on the monitors are any videotaped elements of the game show's graphics such as "the crawl" and the countdown clock that are to be super-imposed over the picture. It is the director's job, on the basis of his gut instinct and experience, to select the most dramatic shot available from each monitor, to keep the game going forward on schedule. He is usually assisted by an apprentice associate director.

The Crawl

All those names that whiz by faster than you can read at the close of the show, telling you who works on the game show? In television, this listing of credits is known as "the crawl." It's shot by having one camera focus on a special monitor containing the moving names on videotape. That shot is then superimposed on a shot of the game show's set. Network regulations allow the game show to broadcast the full listing, known as the "long crawl," only once a week.

Working with the director in the control room, are the video director, who is responsible for the proper color mix of the picture as well as all special visual effects; the audio director, who supervises the games micro-phones, the sound mix, special sound effects, recorded audience reaction tapes, and the game show's music; the lighting director, who works with the studio electricians to make sure the set's overhead lights and any special lighting effects are working properly; and the technical director who records the show on videotape, running it back if necessary for any controversial rulings, later editing the tape if a game has run long or a contestant has forgotten himself. Working with the technical crew down on the floor of the set is the game show's stage manager, who supervises the camera men and the dozens of stage hands. He is responsible for getting the prizes and props on and off stage on cue, for sliding the doors open and shut, and for rotating any props or podiums that need to be rotated. Finally, keeping the operation within its allotted budget is the network unit manager.

You will, of course, be only dimly aware of all of this, for your attention will be riveted upon the contestant co-ordinator and her staff. Throughout the long hours, they will brief and rebrief you with a barrage of advice on how to play the game better. They will patiently answer your questions. (Don't ask too many; if you're a pest or a whiner, you can *still* be cut from the show.) They will keep your spirits up.

By the end of the day, you and your fellow first-time contestants, have grown into a close and caring family. All competitiveness has vanished. You're all in this together. You want everyone to do well. When you return for the next taping, you will feel relaxed and confident. You will know the ropes. You know that, win or lose, you are among friends.

What the Well-dressed Contestant Wears . . .

The following instructions are issued to stand-by contestants on *Hollywood Squares:*

MEN: NO WHITE SHIRTS. No leisure suits. All jackets must be conventional. Two sport coats, suits or blazers and ties. No turtle necks or scarves. NO BRIGHT PLAIDS OR BLACK-AND-WHITE CHECKS, ETC.

WOMEN: At least two daytime dresses. YOU CANNOT WEAR: white, beige, black, hot pink or bright yellow. Avoid navy or dark colors. Good colors are BLUES, GREENS, GOLDS, ORANGES, PURPLES AND REDS. Dresses may be solid and trimmed with another color, but not trimmed in white, black, hot pink, bright yellow or print. Please bring at least three scarves, necklaces, beads or pins to "dress up" your clothing. REMEMBER: No hot pants, pants, or pants suits. No white collars. No long skirts or dresses. (You may wear a skirt and change solid color blouses only.) NOTHING SLEEVELESS PLEASE. NO HOOP OR DANGLING EARRINGS. No gauchos.

MILITARY PERSONNEL: NO white uniforms.

8. You're on! Only *you* will ever know what that feels like.

9. In a few brief seconds, the game is over. The bells and buzzers are silent. The squealed advice of the audience has stilled. The host has gone to his dressing room. The camera men, the production assistants, and the stage hands have left for their breaks. The hot overhead lights are dimmed. But the contestant co-ordinator remains. Whether you have won or lost, she pats your hand and has you sign for your prizes. Even losers win something, usually a small appliance or food product. You will not receive any of it now; it will be delivered by mail within ninety days of your show's air date.

Win or lose, you feel drained and wonderful. Finally alone, you know you were terrific to have come this far, to have tried at all. You will talk of it for years to come. "Yes," you will say, "I was on a game show once. I won a dining room and some carpeting, some Grease Relief, and an encyclopedia." Yes, you'll talk of it. For this has been one of the most unforgettable days of your life.

Come On Down!

Even the most spontaneous-appearing of shows, *The Price Is Right,* preselects its contestants. They use a method so secret the contestants never know until announcer Johnny Olson actually calls their name and sends them racing down the aisle. Here's how they do it.

About half an hour before show time, blue-jeaned producer Jay Wolpert,* accompanied by two clipboard-bearing assistants, emerges from the studio carrying a wicker basket. Waiting outside for him for the past four hours is the studio audience for the coming taping, lined up four abreast. Wolpert first addresses the line over a remote public address speaker. His aim is to energize everyone into a state of frenzied anticipation, and he succeeds. Soon, everyone is abuzz, no matter how much their feet hurt from waiting. Wolpert now chats individually with each of the 330 people in the line, all of whom carry perforated cards numbered according to their placement. "How are you today, Betty?" he'll say, eying her name tape. "What's going on with you?" As he passes, he has each person tear his ticket in half and drop the smaller piece into the basket.

---

* Or, these days, his successor Phillip Wayne.

C'mon down!

If Wolpert's banter seems light, it isn't. He is carefully evaluating everyone. "I hear you," he says enthusiastically from time to time if someone has appealed to him. "All right! I got it!" he'll say seemingly in response to their conversation. Off to the side, his assistants take down the contestant's number.

Halfway through the line, Wolpert and his staff retreat around the corner for a caucus over the numbered tickets they've gathered so far. They have another meeting when Wolpert has finished "doing" the second half of the line. In twenty minutes, the nine contestants for the taping have been selected. Wolpert will repeat the process two more times today, each with a fresh audience; three of the hour-long shows are taped a day. "It's draining," he says, "but if they ever try to take the line away from me, I'll quit. The people are fantastic."

Unlike most game shows, those who aren't selected the first time for *The Price Is Right* can try again. "The configuration of every line is different," Wolpert says. "Someone who isn't quite strong enough for us one day will be among the best contestants another. Some contestants have lined up seventy-seven times before getting on."

Wolpert would like to use as many men contestants as possible, but he says, "Men often fool me. They 'cheat.' They can be great in line, animated and enthusiastic. But once they're on camera, they start to think about their image. They become self-conscious. They just aren't able to show the way they feel inside the way women in our culture can.

"I couldn't, by the way, care less whether people jump up and down for me. But I *do* want to see someone who's genuinely pleased with our prizes, who's happy to be there. I want to see an honest manifestation of feeling."

You got it!

Some Contestants Get Excited; Then Again, Some Don't . . .

They squeal, they shiver, they jump up and down for joy . . . usually they do, anyway. Way back when, in the days before videotape, on the original *Name That Tune*, there was Mrs. August Jueneman of Rexford, Kansas. Mrs. Jueneman, a farmer's wife with six children whose husband earned $2,200 a year, had just answered the $2,500 question when that day's show came to an end. Did she want to come back for the next show to try for the $5,000 question? asked emcee George de Witt, benignly confident of the answer. It is the routine question asked by every host.

"No," said Mrs. Jueneman. "I have to be back tomorrow to sing in the church choir."

After the show, producer Harry Salter begged his decidedly unexcited contestant to change her mind. But to no avail. Still, even on game shows, the show must go on. Salter arranged for Phil Silvers to team with a substitute contestant, Louis Brugnolotti of Rockaway Beach. Together they earned an extra $2,500 for Mrs. Jueneman.

The Best Contestants

Ever since the scandals of the late fifties, the networks have gone out of their way to insure that individual contestants do not shine quite so spectacularly as the Charles Van Dorens of yore. CBS imposes a $25,000 limit on winnings, ABC a $20,000 ceiling. NBC has no ceiling, but like the other two networks, it limits the lifetime number of game shows on which a contestant can appear to two, and requires that these appearances be at least two years apart.

Despite these limitations, some contestants have managed to stand out.

Mrs. Pamela Brenner, a secretary in an insurance agency and the wife of a computer programmer, in 1975 won one hundred thousand dollars on NBC's Shamrock Sweepstakes, a special St. Patrick's Day promotion run by the network. Mrs. Brenner beat out four other competitors by answering the following questions with an Irish-American theme:

1. Who won a medal from Congress for "Yankee Doodle Dandy"? Answer: George M. Cohan.

2. Who ran for President with the campaign song, "Sidewalks of New York"? Answer: Al Smith.

3. What author immortalized the New York Telephone Company? Answer: John O'Hara in *Butterfield Eight*.

4. What ambassador's son criticized a foreign country for not being prepared for war? Answer: John F. Kennedy in *Why England Slept*.

No one but Mrs. Brenner knew the fifth answer, the name of "Mr. Dooley's" creator: Finley Peter Dunne.

Judy Bongarzone won $64,461 the next year, 1976, on NBC's week-long promotional competition. That included a Mercedes. Chuck (*Wheel of Fortune*) Woolery's hug came free, compliments of NBC.

When last heard from, Mrs. Brenner, the wife of a computer programmer, though $100,000 richer, was still working at her job as a secretary in an insurance agency.

On *Password,* the grand champion was Lewis Retrim of Boston. In the annual *Password* Play-offs, Retrim took all comers in 1972, 1973 and 1974.

The following were *Jeopardy!* World Champions from 1968 through 1974:
Red Gibson, South Ozone Park, New York
Jay Wolpert,* Glen Cove, New York
Gene Cheatham, New Orleans, Louisiana
Rock Johnson, Macon, Georgia
Ann Marie Sutton, Yorktown Heights, New York
Paula Ogren, Los Angeles, California
Denny Golden, Palisades Park, New Jersey

Oddballs

Using offbeat contestants is a tried and true game-show tradition, first used on the old Groucho Marx show *You Bet Your Life.* It was a full-time job for twelve people on that show to dig up the four contestants every week who would lend themselves to Groucho's wit. Memorable contestants:

Anna Badnovic, a divorcée who came from a town in Yugoslavia where *everyone* was named Badnovic;

Ramiro Gonzales Gonzales, a young laborer from San Antonio, Texas, who proved to be such a natural deadpan comedian on the show that he graduated into a successful nightclub career;

A skinny young housewife from Cleveland named Phyllis Diller;

And a young writer masquerading on the show as an Arabian sheik. During the course of the program, the beturbaned gentleman revealed himself to be one William Blatty. He and his partner won big: $10,000.

"What are you going to do with the money?" Groucho asked.

"Finish my book," he said. Blatty's book turned out to be *The Exorcist.*

---

* If the name sounds familiar, he's the same Jay Wolpert who until recently, produced *The New Price Is Right,* and is now developing new shows for an independent packaging company. Small world, isn't it?

One game, during the early sixties, *One in a Million,* leased an entire floor in New York's Hotel Buckingham to deal with its parade of ninety-five-year-old grandmothers who could chin themselves, Indians who could drag locomotives by their hair, and lumberjacks from the Bronx who could play the violin standing on their head while reciting *Hamlet* and tearing a Manhattan phone book first in half, then into quarters. Sound mesmerizing? Well, it was. Unfortunately the show ran out of one-in-a-million contestants before its thirteen weeks were up.

Today, the torch (or should we say, the gong?) has been passed to Chuck Barris. When it comes to the off-beat, *The Gong Show* brings them out of the woodwork. Still, things *do* come full circle. Today Phyllis Diller's wielding the gong!

The Audience

In Los Angeles, finding contestants is *one* problem. There's still the matter of coming up with audiences to fill the studios. Loudly vocal rooters on the scene are an important element in transmitting a game's excitement to the folks at home. The problem's so nettlesome that the networks actually hire a man named Bill McIntosh to round up busloads of church ladies, veterans, scout troops, and retirement villagers, and herd them into tapings. To sweeten the pot, some game shows have been known to pay the audience for rooting. One such show was *Tattletales,* which divided its seats into three sections represented on stage by three celebrity couples who won money on their behalf.

You can lead an audience to the studio, but you can't *make* them cheer. Why *do* the people present at game shows always sound so uninhibited? The warm-up man's been at work on them. On game shows, the warm-up man is the show's announcer. The techniques he uses to break the ice are as old as the hills, terribly corny, a little "blue," totally effective, and he repeats them word for word at every single taping.

Undisputedly, the best warm-up man in television is Johnny Olson. Goodson-Todman puts such a premium on his talents that when they used to tape shows on both coasts they would fly him back and forth across the country just to do warm-ups. When Olson works *The Price Is Right,* he has to be seen to be believed. The audience files into the studio to the finger-popping sound of Aretha Franklin. Suddenly, there is Olson, a short, balding, bespectacled man, wearing a suit and tie, doing the frug, the funky chicken, the bump, and a few grinds. Before the audience can recover, he has leaped down from the stage and into the lap of the nearest middle-aged woman. As he proceeds from person to person, his banter is carefully interlaced with important instructions: "Don't chew gum on camera; don't whistle; kiss Bob Barker if you want to, but don't kill him."

At the height of the hilarity, host Barker emerges and the taping begins. Electrifying? Just tune in and see: with Johnny O. around, *The Price Is Right never* needs the "Mackenzie." That's the technical name for the canned laughter machine many game shows *have* to use.

Olson is not the only treasured warm-up man in the business. Every game show packaging company has its own favorite announcer to do the job. In addition to Johnny Olson, Goodson-Todman also uses Gene Woods. Jay Stewart does the job for Hatos-Hall and Barry-Enright; Bob Clayton for Bob Stewart. Johnny Jacobs is Chuck Barris' warm-up man; Kenny Williams is Heatter-Quigley's. Charley O'Donnell is Merv Griffin's. John Harlan is Ralph Edwards'. And leave us not forget Don Pardo, the famed former voice of *Jeopardy!*

Hosts!

The game show host, that warm or rascally, friendly or fiendish best friend of yours on daytime television. He makes it look so easy. In reality, however, none of the popular names for him—master of ceremonies, emcee, host, or star—quite describes the breadth, or difficulty, of his job.

Most accurately, he is the game show's onstage producer. Everything that happens in front of the camera is the host's responsibility. He must monitor the game's pacing, tone, and flow. He must make the game look good; he must be certain that it plays as well as it can play. He must introduce the contestants to the audience, then draw these individuals out in a manner that is warm, clever, and completely off-the-cuff. He must make us, the viewers, care about the contestants as people. Then he must abruptly change the casual tone of the proceedings and briskly get the game rolling. He must explain the rules of the game succinctly, accurately, and without deviation. He must then be prepared to field any and all of the contestants' possible responses to the game during the course of play. The host must know when and how to wring every last measure of suspense from the situations posed by the game and by the personalities of the contestants. He must project genuine pleasure when he has a winner, disappointment when he has a loser to console. Throughout each game, he is in constant communication with the producer and his staff. The production assistants stand by the cameras, signaling him, flashing the score to him, holding up a listing of the contestant's winnings to date, cueing him to stretch the time or speed things up. In the event of an offstage ruling from the producer, he transmits the decision to the audience. During the specified time alloted each show, he solicits the home audience to write in for tickets to join the fun that he has so professionally engineered.

Says host Geoff Edwards about his job, "It doesn't matter how many teeth you have, or how big your smile. You have to be able to take charge."

But the "teeth" matter, too. The game show host must also be a personality in his own right, immensely likable without being overbearing, self-effacing with celebrities and contestants alike without acting weak or sycophantic. In short, he must be just the man you'd invite to tea, which is what you've done. You've invited him in—to your living room, and he's made *you* comfortable.

Thousands of home viewers write in every day to packagers. "I'm a salesman," they say. "Everybody likes me. I know I could host a game show if you'll give me a chance."

Getting the chance is not the problem. Hundreds of starry-eyed newcomers, many of them with home-town broadcast experience, line up for the auditions packagers hold in their search for new faces, but these hopefuls usually walk away empty-handed and overwhelmed. Dozens of well-known actors have tried and failed. They couldn't ad lib. They needed a script.

In the end, more often than not, the hosting jobs go to the pros, the very highly paid, very much in demand, small fraternity of men who, because they have become masters of their craft, you see on television game shows again and again.

Now on a More Serious (*Ha Ha Ha*) Note . . .

Hosting a game show takes concentration. Many a host takes his job *so* seriously that it's a constant temptation, indeed a time-honored tradition, for the game-show staffers to pull an occasional prank on him—*while* he's on camera. Slipping dirty words onto the cue cards, liquor into his off-camera water glass, making off-camera faces and distracting noises are a few of the tried and true.

The best are well aware of and most articulate about the skills they have. "I started in radio," says Bob Barker, who has hosted *The Price Is Right* for the past six years, and for fifteen years before that, *Truth or Consequences.* "That's the way most of the television game-show hosts got their start." Bob Barker continues, "I did everything on this little station in Springfield, Missouri: news writing, sportscasting, producing, announcing. And I did the man-in-the-street interview show. That's how I got the experience that I use every day.

"From the moment I come out on stage, during commercials, constantly, I talk to the audience. I try to create an atmosphere of fun. I want them to feel very much a part of things. *The Price Is Right* is an audience participation show. The audience is the most important ingredient. So what I do is create an atmosphere where *we,* the audience and I, can have fun. Because if we're having fun, genuine fun, then it's fun for the viewer, too.

"I'm *still* learning. But I started learning on the radio how to make different types of people feel comfortable in a situation which is completely foreign to them. On television, it's not so much the microphones that make them feel uncomfortable, the way it was on radio. It's the lights, the cameras, the cables, the stagehands. That's an uncomfortable feeling. So I must get them to relax by the way I talk to them and draw them out.

"You have to learn what to avoid. There are some subjects on a fun show you want to stay away from. You don't want to get into a really heavy discussion of politics. If they make a remark about a politician or some political situation, fine. They can make a remark. But you have to know how to handle it. Or religion can be fun to talk about. But if you feel that a remark could lead to something unpleasant, you have to know how to handle these things.

"The most important thing for a successful TV host is to know when to stop. When to move on to someone else. You can get a person and you can get a laugh . . . *laugh* . . . a BIG LAUGH, and if you stay too long, you begin to tail off, to go downhill with this person. You have to build . . . *build* . . . BUILD and then move on. You have to learn that. It's all part of timing

"Today, and this is one of the problems in the game show industry, there is no place to get the kind of experience I got. If you begin on a radio station today, you'll be a dj or read news. Or if you start out on a local TV talk show, you're dealing with an author or a celebrity with prepared anecdotes. That's quite different than going out into the audience and saying:

' "Hello."

' "I'm Mrs. Jones."

' "What do you do, Mrs. Jones?"

' "I'm a housewife . . ." '

"To bring her out, and she can very well be very interesting, requires some experience. And there's no place to get that anymore.

"Take a game on *The Price Is Right* like Double Prices. How much is there to it? Here's this chair. I'll give you this chair if you pick out the right price. Here's a price and here's a price. Now which one's right? The thing that's important to that game is the person standing beside me. You've got to make people want him or her to win that prize. Here's this girl, just

Bob Barker doing his thing.

married. She doesn't have furniture. Will she win it? Or here she is, she's sixty-five and just out here from New Orleans. She watches the show every day. Now *wouldn't* it be nice if she could take that back to her home in New Orleans?

Bob Barker's Biggest Compliment

"My job is to make other people funny. That's what it is that I do. One of the highest compliments I've ever received was from an elderly woman on my show years ago.

"Afterward she wrote me a letter. 'Thank you so much for choosing me,' she said. 'You made me feel wonderful. In all my life, I have never been that funny.'

"I want them to be glad they were on my show. I want them to enjoy themselves and I want them to look back on it with fond memories."

"Now for an emcee to do that takes experience. And if you're a packager today developing a show, one of the most difficult things to find is the emcee because there are no young men who are learning it. And there's no place to learn it except right on camera.

"You have to make it all look so easy. If it looks embarrassing or you are uncomfortable when you watch, then the host is not doing his job. You have to have a lot of things go wrong over the years to learn that."

Every game show host echoes Barker on the importance of having experience and the difficulty everyone had in first breaking into the business.

"I was a comedy straight man in vaudeville for twenty years before I became the host of *Hollywood Squares*," says Peter Marshall, winner of four Emmys for his superb emceeing. "All that time I was tucking away experience, knowing it would be here when I needed it, waiting for the break in which it would all come in handy. On *Squares,* that's what I do. I'm a straight man for other people. That takes experience. I know how to set up laughs. Being able to understand when a comedian is going through something; being able to lay back or move something forward—all that takes the experience I'd been storing away all the years before."

"I spent a lot of time in the early days just beating on the doors of producers," says Tom Kennedy. "I did I don't know how many run-throughs and pilots that never made it onto the air, before someone finally took a chance with me. But it gave me experience. My first show back in 1958 only lasted thirteen weeks, but at least I finally had a television credit. Since then, it's worked out pretty well for me. I've been working steadily ever since." It *is* working out well. Kennedy now has a long-term exclusive contract with NBC.

The Match Game's Gene Rayburn began his career as an NBC page. Geoff Edwards too, has been on endless rounds of auditions, runthroughs, and pilots. He mentions an extra problem to the host looking for his first big break. "It's when you do a pilot" (the tryout show the packager produces for network consideration) "that your career is most out of your hands," he says. "The networks can keep you on the shelf for a year." (To find out why, see pages 93–94). "That's a whole year when you can't really host any other game shows, just in case they should suddenly decide to buy the game and put it on the air." Edwards, like many emcees, has another career running to cover the dry spells. He has his own daily radio show in Los Angeles, and is putting together his own prime time packaging deals.

Other hopeful game show hosts circumvent their dependence upon the networks by attempting to break in through Canadian television or through the syndicated (ie: non-network shows sold by packagers to local stations for off-hour viewing) game-show market.

In another life. That's (top left) Jack Paar hosting *Bank on the Stars* . . .
Merv Griffin (top right) on *Play Your Hunch* . . . and none other than Mike
Wallace (below) host of *Who Pays?* Zippy the Chimp they paid in bananas

Host of Yesteryear. There was a time when Dennis James was synonymous with game shows. The first TV host ever, James dates back to 1938, when screens were 4 inches high. Over the years, he's hosted dozens, including *Okay, Mother, Chance of a Lifetime, High Finance, Can You Top This? Turn to a Friend, On Your Account, The Name's the Same, Judge for Yourself, People Will Talk, Haggis Baggis, PDQ, Your First Impression,* and *The Nighttime Price Is Right.* He's been on panels; he's announced. For being the spokesman of Kellogg's Cereals, he raked in $250,000 a year; for Old Gold Cigarettes, $350,000. And that was in pre-inflation times, twenty-five years ago. Remember the dancing Old Gold cigarette boxes that sashayed onto early quiz show commercials? James's job was to introduce them. Leggy Gloria Vestoff was "Regular," Dixie Dunbar was "King Size" and "Whitey" was the Little Matchbox.

Game shows are one of the most popular forms of syndicated programming. Most of these games (*Hollywood Squares, The Gong Show, The $25,000 Pyramid, The Nighttime Price Is Right, Match Game P.M.*) are specially made-for-syndication nighttime versions of concurrently running daytime network games. Such syndicated games usually use a well-known host, often the same host who appears on the daytime network show. Other syndicated games, though they no longer air on a network, are still popular enough, either as reruns or as freshly made productions to command a local market. Such games include *Truth or Consequences, Concentration, To Tell the Truth, Let's Make a Deal,* and *The Newlywed Game,* most of which also employ familiar hosts.

But many are new games seen exclusively in syndication. Filling this expanding new market are such independent packagers as Chuck Barris, Ralph Andrews, Ralph Edwards, Steve Carlin, and nowadays, one of the largest suppliers in this area, Barry-Enright Productions. It is through this conduit that such hosts as Wink Martindale, Jim McKrell, Art James, Jim Peck, Al Hamel, Clark Race, Jack Clark and others, first earned their spurs. Doing such shows can eventually earn a new face the coveted, greatly competed-for network berth.

Pale as a G(Host)

Once a host has made it onto the air, the heat's still on. Networks routinely survey their audiences not just to learn how well they like a given game show, but for how well they like its host. Usually, hosts aren't privy to this information, but there are ways of telling what the testing results were— like when the work stops coming your way.

Not all hosts have to scuffle, of course. Take the career of carefree Bill Cullen. From the time he entered broadcasting in 1944, when he was nineteen, Cullen has never been unemployed, and when he isn't hosting, he's guesting on panels. During one period in the sixties, Cullen simultaneously hosted shows on all three networks. Cullen is currently the host of the syndicated nighttime version of *The $25,000 Pyramid* for which, twice a month, he commutes to New York from Los Angeles to tape ten shows.

Why do so many hosts put up with all the stress and uncertainty? Because like everything connected with television, financially it's very much worth it. A good host makes between thirty-five hundred and five thousand dollars a week. A week, of course, in television terms, means one day's taping: five half hours.

Bob Barker, by the way, is in an entirely different league. The emcee of the daytime hour-long *Price Is Right,* as well as the nighttime version of the show, Barker signed with Goodson-Todman for a five-year, three-million-dollar contract for the daytime version alone—and that doesn't include the money Barker gets for his other enterprises: *The Pillsbury Bake-Off,* the *Miss Universe Pageant,* his guest appearances, and his own independent TV packaging company. "He makes $11,000 every time he steps before a camera," estimated one *Price Is Right* staffer. The price *is* right!"

The Young Studs

Back in 1973, a young woman named Lin Bolen blew into the game show sweepstakes. She was the vice-president of NBC Daytime Programming, and, some say, a dead ringer for Diana Christiansen, the Faye Dunaway character in *Network*—she was that hard-driving and ambitious. Bolen is no longer vice-president of NBC Daytime Programming; and only one (*Wheel of Fortune*) of Bolen's shows survives today. Still, she is credited with permanently changing the *look* of game shows.

To Bolen, in 1973 game shows looked old and tired. The sets seemed dated, the hosts the same faces that had been on the screen for twenty years. So she set about to *do* something. It especially annoyed Bolen that older women watched NBC's games. To lure young housewives with advertising-money buying power, Bolen went out and recruited a whole new breed of host. Then she groomed them to convey what she called the "young stud" image. According to insiders, she commanded Geoff Edwards to get his hair permed, then clothed him in light-colored leisure suits and open-necked Continental shirts. She cultivated in Alex Trebek a threatening, brooding look. Trebek she instructed never to wear plaids, but a dark suit and tie instead. Jim McKrell's image conveyed a subtle slightly dangerous double message: that nice boy who just might become crazy when drunk," in the words of one insider.

New breed of host.

Bolen's biggest find was *Wheel of Fortune*'s cowboy host, Chuck Woolery, well-known to his fans for his enthusiasm over the show's prizes and his casual approach to cue cards. Woolery it seems is "just plain folks" to NBC's viewers.

Still, when Lin Bolen left NBC to go into the game show business on her own, which of her young stud newcomers do you think she picked for her first show? None of them. Bolen's host for her show *Stumpers* was veteran emcee Allen Ludden, who, with other experienced professionals like Bill Cullen, Tom Kennedy, Jack Narz, Peter Marshall, Bob Barker, and many others, are surviving just fine.

HOST QUIZ

Old breed, new breed, do you know enough about the careers of your favorite hosts to pass this quiz?

First, some questions about some old-timers.

1. Like many hosts, Jack Narz started out as an announcer. Name his most famous off-camera credit; now name his famous hosting brother.
   ANSWERS: Narz was the voice of infant TV's *Space Patrol;* his brother is Tom Kennedy.

2. Early TV game shows host Clayton "Bud" Collyer is best remembered for emceeing early game shows *Beat the Clock* and *To Tell the Truth.* But he, like Narz, first scored with the public in a famous off-camera role. Name it.
   ANSWER: Collyer was the radio voice of Superman.

3. Speaking of the days before television, can you think of two ex-radio hosts who went on to score in two popular TV dramatic series?
   ANSWERS: a) Ben Alexander, formerly host of such radio quizzes as *Anniversary Club, Heart's Desire* and *Watch and Win,* played Jack Webb's sidekick on *Dragnet.* He also hosted one TV game, *About Faces,* seen in 1960; b) Does the name Marvin Miller ring a bell? Well, it did once. TV's generous go-between "Michael Anthony" on *The Millionaire* began his career on radio's *Stop the Villain.*

4. Several long-running game shows have had a succession of hosts.
   a) *Concentration* has had seven. Name them.

ANSWER: Jack Barry, Hugh Downs, Art James, Bill Mazer, Bob Clayton, Ed McMahon, and Jack Narz.

b) *The Big Payoff* is best remembered for its host Randy Merriman. Now name three more.

ANSWER: Bert Parks, Mort Lawrence, and Robert Paige.

c) *Masquerade Party* had at least seven. Name them.

ANSWER: Bud Collyer, Eddie Bracken, Peter Donald, Bert Parks, Robert Q. Lewis, Doug Edwards, and Richard Dawson.

d) Of late, Tom Kennedy's been hosting the syndicated revival of *Name That Tune*. Can you recall the original show's three hosts?

ANSWER: Al "Red" Benson, Bill Cullen, and George de Witt.

e) When most people recall *What's My Line?*, they think of its host for seventeen years, John Daly. At least two other people subsequently hosted the syndicated version of the show. Name them.

ANSWER: Wally Bruner and Larry Blyden.

Temporary Breakthrough

Only one game show to date has had a black host. Do you remember him?

His name was Adam Wade and he was the singing host of CBS's short-lived *Musical Chairs* which aired between June and November 1975. The game had a musical format. Contestants were required to guess the last line of a given song. Having Wade was a great idea, but as for the show: tra la la . . . flop!

---

5. By now, everybody knows that before he took over the *Tonight Show* from Jack Parr, Johnny Carson hosted *Who Do You Trust?* Now,

a) Name the other game show Carson hosted.

ANSWER: *Earn Your Vacation.*

b) Name the host who replaced Johnny on *Who Do You Trust?*

ANSWER: Woody Woodbury.

c) Name the original name and the original hosts of *Who Do You Trust?*

ANSWER: *Do You Trust Your Wife?* with ventriloquist Edgar Bergen and Charlie McCarthy.

d) Now name two other ventriloquists who hosted game shows in the fifties.

ANSWER: Paul Winchell and Jerry Mahoney hosted *What's My Name?;* Jimmy Weldon and Webster Webfoot hosted *Funny Boners.*

e) Finally, name the game shows Jack Paar hosted.

ANSWER; *Bank on the Stars, Place the Face, It's News to Me,* and *Up to Paar.*

6. What famous comedian-host picked his very name as a result of an audience-participation contest?

ANSWER: Thomas Garrison Morfitt is better known as Garry Moore thanks to the creativity of a woman in the audience who won a hundred dollars for her selection.

7. The late Ernie Kovacs served on many celebrity panels. He also hosted four game shows. Do you remember any of them?

ANSWER: *One Minute Please, Take a Good Look, Take a Guess,* and *Time Will Tell.*

Trying to Live it Down

He gets the dirt on everybody else, so we can surely turn the tables. Mike Wallace was once a game-show host, only he hates to be reminded! A few years back, Wallace did a particularly negative segment about game shows on *60 Minutes.* As part of his research, he interviewed the dean of the elegant and tasteful games, Mark Goodson.

"I must say," said Goodson dryly, "that I'm not terribly happy to be talking with you knowing that you're going to go back to New York and edit this any way you choose. Suppose I had said something about your being the host of *The Big Surprise.* Would you have left that in or taken it out?"

"I would have taken it out," said Wallace.

Wallace was also the host of *Who Pays?, I'll Buy That,* and *Guess Again* back in the fifties. For proof, see photo, page 25.

---

8. Which of the following never hosted a game show?

Jacqueline Susann	Basil Rathbone
John Cameron Swayze	Vincent Price
Rod Serling	Don Ameche
Walter Cronkite	Melvyn Douglas

ANSWER: They all did but one, and he almost did. Swayze hosted *Guess What Happened, Chance for Romance,* and *Nothing But the Truth;* Serling hosted *The Liar's Club;* Rathbone, *Your Lucky Clue;* Price, *ESP;* Susann, *Your Surprise Store* with Lew Parker, and *Ring the Bell;* Ameche, *Take a Chance;* and Douglas, *Your Big Moment.* Walter Cronkite was all set to host *It's News to Me* until his image-conscious bosses at CBS hauled their star anchor back to ship.

Reluctant host. The late Herb Shriner was a hit on comedy quiz *Two for the Money,* but after three years he wanted out. "Too limiting," he said. Shriner was unsuccessfully replaced by Sam Levenson.

9. A Chip Off the Old Block Department. Art Linkletter was the long-time host of *People Are Funny* and *House Party*. But do you remember either of the two games hosted by his son Jack?

ANSWER: *Haggis Baggis* and *The Rebus Game.*

10. The Canadian Connection. There's a slew of game-shows up in Canada, most of which haven't found favor with American audiences. The opposite has been true of Canadian-born hosts. Name at least two:

ANSWER: Monty Hall, Alex Trebek, Art Linkletter, Al Hamel.

11. In the late sixties and early seventies, after Chuck Barris' successes with *The Dating Game* and *The Newlywed Game,* it became fashionable for game shows all to have a similar "nuclear family" format and for their hosts, who all seemed to be named Jim or Clark, to be cut from the same mischievously boyish mold. I dare any reader to run the following gauntlet and match the hosts in column A with the games they hosted. Warning: some hosted more than one game. Answers are below.

A	B
1. Art James	a. *Spin-Off*
2. Jim Peck	b. *The Object Is . . .*
3. Jim Lange	c. *The Cross-Wits*
4. Jim McKrell	d. *Second Chance*
5. Dick Clark	e. *Diamond Head Game*
6. Jack Clark	f. *Honeymoon Game*
7. Clark Race	g. *Celebrity Sweepstakes*
8. Bob Eubanks	h. *The Dating Game*
9. Richard Hayes	i. *The Parent Game*
10. Tom Kennedy	j. *The Mother-in-Law Game*
11. Al Hamel	k. *Who, What, and Where Game*
	l. *Dealer's Choice*
	m. *The Baby Game*
	n. *The Game Game*
	o. *Big Game*
	p. *Big Showdown*
	q. *The Newlywed Game*
	r. *The $20,000 Pyramid*

Answers: 1-k; 2-p,d; 3-h,a; 4-n,f; 5-b,r; 6-c,l; 7-i; 8-q,e; 9-m; 10-o; 11-j.

12. Last question. Here's a little sexist quiz. Cover column B. Now see if you can match the "lovely assistant" with the game show.

A	B
Lynn Dollar Wendy Barry	*The $64,000 Question*
Janice Gilbert	*Break the Bank*
Evelyn Patrick Patricia White	*Dollar a Second*
Carolyn Stroupe	*The Big Surprise*
Renee. This *is* sexist, I don't even have her last name!	*Masquerade Party*
Dorothy Hart	*Pantomime Quiz*
Marian Stafford	*The Original Treasure Hunt*
Marilyn Burtis—she appeared with the "secret word" when they didn't use the duck	*You Bet Your Life*
Lisa Wiss Lisa Loughlon	*The $64,000 Challenge*
Liz Gardner	*Play Your Hunch*
Jackie Dougherty Millie Sinclair	*Earn our Vacation*
Ruta Lee	*High Rollers*
Susan Stafford	*Wheel of Fortune*
Gypsy Rose Lee	*Think Fast*
Elaine Stewart	*Gambit*
Siv Aberg	*The New Treasure Hunt*
Jane Nelson Joey Faye	*The Gong Show*
Beverly Bentley Toni Wallace June Ferguson	*The Original Price Is Right*
Anitra Ford Janice Pennington Dian Parkinson Holly Hallstrom	*The New Price Is Right*
Vivian Farrar	*Sense into Dollars*
Virginia Graham	*Strike It Rich*
Carol Merrill	*Let's Make a Deal*

Temporary host,
Ed McMahon.

Cosell, Are You Listening?

Over the years, in their search for new faces, game shows have made occasional raids into the sports world. Does anybody remember:

Joe Garagiola's *Memory Game; Sale of the Century; He Said, She Said;* and the syndicated version of *To Tell the Truth;*

Sportscaster Dick Enberg as the emcee of *Baffle, Three for the Money,* and *Perfect Mate;*

Bill Mazer as the host of *Reach for a Star* and *Concentration;*

Vince (a.k.a. Vin) Scully on *It Takes Two;*

Frankie Frisch and Lefty Gomez as the panelists on NBC's *Are You Positive?*

Most struck out, and quickly returned to the more familiar footing of the press box.

Still, others have been more successful. Dennis James began his career as a wrestling sportscaster, and Monty Hall covered New York hockey, soccer, and wrestling.

Bert Convy of *Tattletales* played professional baseball as part of the Philadelphia Phillies' farm system.

Art James (born Artur Simeonvich Elimchik) and one-time host of *Say When, Temptation, It's Academic, The Who, What, and Where Game, Blank Check,* and the *Magnificent Marble Machine,* was almost a New York Yankee.

If the trend continues, Peter Marshall's son Pete LaCock has a career in game shows all laid out for him. He's a first baseman for the Kansas City Royals.

Emshees, Anyone?

Why, the question is often raised, don't women ever get to emcee game shows? Why are there only men up there? In fact, there have been a sprinkling of women game show-hosts over the years.

In the early days, back in 1948, Arlene Francis, with Jan Murray, hosted a local New York show called *Blind Date,* where a contestant's phone manner won a college boy a date with a model at the Stork Club. (Sound reminiscent of *The Dating Game? They* thought so too. There's a lawsuit circulating somewhere.)

In 1953, Vera Vague coaxed her contestants to *Follow the Leader.* The following year, Denise Darcel invited contestants to *Gamble on Love* over the Du Mont Network. Then there was *Quick on the Draw* with Eloise McElhone and *On Your Way* with Kathy (Arthur's sister) Godfrey.

Alas, most women, for cultural reasons, have been cast in the role of the sexy assistant who slinks across the stage to giggle or wink. Some game-show assistants (see sexist quiz) have been models; some, like Elaine Stewart and Carol Wayne, the producers' wives. Few were ever heard from more than once.

There is, of course, no real reason more women can't host game shows. The dean of game shows, Mark Goodson, agrees. "Finding the right woman to host a game show is very difficult for societal reasons," says Goodson.

Upward mobile host, Johnny Carson, flanked by Jackie Dougherty (l.) and Millie Sinclair (r.), relaxing backstage of *Earn Your Vacation.*

"So far it's been tough to get a woman who has the necessary control, who can say 'all *right,* that's enough fun, let's *play!* without sounding like a third-grade teacher or a gym coach. Often," Goodson says, "if you get a woman who's soft and pretty and feminine, she comes over as mousy or saccharine or like a B-girl. And when you consider a woman celebrity to host a show, most of them are actresses. Acting is not good preparation for hosting, since it's all ad lib, without a script in sight.

But times are changing. In Sarah Purcell, Goodson was able to find the charm and strength it takes to host. She co-starred with Bill Anderson on *The Better Sex.* Purcell came to game shows from ABC's *AM in Los Angeles* Show. Before that, she hosted the *Sun-Up Show* in San Diego.

And Then There Was Roxanne...

Her real name was Dolores Rosedale and she was *the* quintessential game-show assistant, the tall, statuesque blonde.

Roxanne was a model so much in demand in the early days of television that she appeared on not just one but two of the games: she photographed stunts on *Beat the Clock* and was the Miss Mennen girl on *Twenty Questions.* Roxanne more than any other woman on early TV game shows emerged as a personality in her own right. She was a featured part of the Macy's Annual Thanksgiving Day Parade. Her diet and exercise plan made the pages of *TV Guide.* Bud Collyer, host of *Beat the Clock,* was rumored to be jealous of all the attention she received.

Roxanne also let it be known that she had more creative aspirations. "I want to be an actress," she said. I wonder where she is today.

Roxanne.

Celebrities!

It's a marriage made in heaven: celebrities and game shows. Celebrities agree. The impact of a game show on an entertainer's career—if he or she is telegenic and likable to begin with—can be immeasurable.

"Nowhere else," says comedian Nipsey Russell pragmatically, "can an entertainer attain the same instantaneous recognizability with the public as on a game show. On television, your face is there in a person's living room for a full minute at a time, far longer than in a movie close-up, and at a far more intimate range than in a nightclub. That allows people to develop a warm feeling toward you that is absolutely impossible anywhere else."

Other celebrities may claim other motives for doing games. They're the ones who appear only during the weeks some shows turn their stakes over to charity. And others can afford to be purely hedonistic. "If someone asks me what I do," says Richard Dawson, "I tell them. I play games, and they *pay* me! Isn't that marvelous?"

Still, after strolling down a New York street with Nipsey Russell after a taping one Sunday afternoon, I can report that Russell is right. When he is spotted, people from every social stratum flock around, begging him for one of his poems they've heard him recite on the dozens of game shows he plays. Gracefully, he obliges, accepting their hugs and handshakes.

Of course, a game show's definition of a celebrity may not be everybody's. Ever since the early days of television, game shows have been a special sanctuary for the second banana, the star whose career peaked early yet who was too good an ad-libber, too clever a conversationalist, too nice a person, really, to be allowed totally to vanish from public view. Put those celebrities to work playing a game, intersperse them with someone trendy, whose TV movie of the week or new series was coming up, or whose act was rolling into Las Vegas, and it might do something for a game show's ratings.

Poet-Laureate

It was on a game show that Nipsey Russell stumbled across the special talent that has become his trademark. The show was *Missing Links;* the year was 1963. Host Ed McMahon liked an impromptu verse of Nipsey's so much that he asked for a new one each day that week. Nipsey accommodated him and has been reeling them off ever since.

So easily do the rhymes come to Russell that another packager tried to base an entire program, *Rhyme and Reason,* around him. It's fate: it didn't rate.

In the beginning they sat on panels. Oh, did they sit on panels! Four celebrities behind a desk being brittle, arch, and oh so clever. On the radio, a quiz called *Information, Please* had proved that audiences would listen to famous people being erudite. Now, in the early days of television, it seemed only natural to plunk four people down and have them discuss something—or better still, play a little guessing game.

There were dozens of panels in the early days, now forgotten in a blur of monotonous sameness: *Who Said That?* was only one of several celebrity news games. There was as well: *Headline Clues, I Made the News, It's News to Me, I've Got News for You, Quizzing the News, What Happened, Guess What Happened,* and *What's the Story? What's It Worth?* and *Treasures or Trash?* invited celebrity art appraisers to evaluate artifacts. *The Big Idea* and *What's It For?* turned their attention to inventions, *What in the World?* to archaeology. *Who's Whose?* had celebrities guessing which contestant was married to which mystery spouse. *Who's the Boss?* had them hazarding which secretary worked for which mystery boss. Then there was *Anyone Can Win, Celebrity Time, It's About Time, Keep Talking, Ladies Be Seated, Ladies Before Gentlemen, Penny to a Million, Put It in Writing, Down You Go, QED, One Minute Please, Quick on the Draw, Twenty Questions, Masquerade Party, Pantomime Quiz, What Happens, The Name's the Same, Where Was I?, Take a Guess, You're Putting Me On, Make the Connection, Liar's Club, What's in a Word?, Where Have You Been? Think Fast, Time Will Tell, Split Personality, Take a Good Look, What Do You Have in Common? What's Going On? What's the Pitch? Who's My Parent? Why?* and *Your First Impression.* To name a few.

The Above-It-Alls

There are some celebrities who never ever appear on game shows. They are Hollywood's superstars, such as Paul Newman,* Robert Redford, Faye Dunaway, Frank Sinatra, Steve McQueen, Barbra Streisand. Image conscious? Too elitist to pick up a mere $750 a day when they command a million or more dollars per movie? Too much to lose if they forget themselves or play poorly? Or is it simply because they consider game shows *déclassé?*

It might be any of the above reasons—except the last. Though superstars may not ever venture onto a game show, they are all avid fans. "Loved you on *Squares,*" Paul Newman will tell a celebrity pal. *Family Feud* is Sammy Davis Jr.'s favorite game. Though superstars may not show their faces on them, rest assured, they're all sitting at home watching . . . just like you.

Vintage celeb.

* Before Newman hit it big, he did appear on one game show. It was *I've Got a Secret.* See page 150.

Then as now, the celebrities of the early days seemed virtually interchangeable, shameless in their panel promiscuity. Arlene Francis, Garry Moore, Henry Morgan, Kitty Carlisle, Ernie Kovacs, Hermione Gingold, Robert Q. Lewis, Morey Amsterdam, Roger Price, Peter Lind Hayes and Mary Healy, Ilka Chase, Jayne and Audrey Meadows, Steve Allen, Larry Blyden, Una Merkel, Polly Bergen, Betsy Palmer, Hans Conreid, Buff Cobb, Conrad Nagel, Nina Foch, and everyone's favorite, Faye ("cleavage") Emerson, did scores of the things. Never huge forces in the entertainment world,* here they flourished, the way that their modern incarnations, Orson Bean, Betty White, Peggy Cass, Soupy Sales, Tony Randall, Charo, Loretta Swit, Peter Lawford, Rose Marie, Dick Cavett, Jaye P. Morgan, Arte Johnson, Jamie Farr, Charles Nelson Reilly, Zsa Zsa and Eva Gabor, Phyllis Diller, Bobby Van, Jo Ann Pflug, Nipsey Russell, Luci Arnaz, Dick Martin, Rex Reed, Buddy Hackett, and perhaps two dozen others do today.

As surely as celebrities need limelight in which to preen and make their playful pronouncements, game shows need ratings. In theory, it works like this: the audience loves to see famous people; hence, game show places famous person on panel; ergo, the audience is supposed to love the game show. In reality, of course, things often work out differently. Celebrities remain famous; the many game shows they grace come and go. It took the two early game-show practitioners Mark Goodson and Bill Todman to figure out how to bridge the theoretical gap: how to use famous people on game shows *and* get good ratings. The secret, they discovered, was not in the fame, it lay in the game. Today it is easy to take the precept for granted. But what Goodson-Todman did had never been done before. "For the first time," says Mark Goodson, "we dared to make the contestant the puzzle. What was that woman's occupation on *What's My Line?*, that man's secret on *I've Got a Secret;* which contestants were lying on *To Tell the Truth?* Observing the thought processes of four people trying to solve the problem became the focus of attention for the audience. That the four people on the panel were famous became incidental. In fact in our early games, we created our own celebrities.

Nor, even if the panelists were celebrities, Goodson-Todman discovered, could they be just *any* four people dragged on stage and seated behind a table. A good panel did not just happen. "We cast them carefully, the way a Broadway director casts a play," says Goodson. "It takes a lot of trial and error, but when we get our 'family,' when a panel is finally working, each member possesses his or her own unique problem-solving talents that blend with and complement the personalities of the others."

* Celebrity exceptions reading this, you know who you are!

BIG BIRD Feathered celeb.

Though *What's My Line*, *I've Got a Secret*, and *To Tell the Truth* are gone, the celebrity game is still a Goodson-Todman hallmark. Today, however, it has been greatly expanded and modified. Take for example, G-T's *Match Game* with its two-tiered panel of six celebrities seated three and three. *The Match Game* carefully arranges the seating of the celebrities according to the ability of each to provide entertaining chitchat. In the lead-off seat on the top tier to the left sits a male guest celebrity, whom producer Ira Skutch tellingly refers to as "the new kid on the block." (At other times this seat is occupied by semi-regular panelist Gary Burghoff). Seated to the right of the "new kid" are two of *The Match Game*'s veteran regular panelists, strong-willed and acerbic Brett Somers and fey, sophisticated Charles Nelson Reilly. If the response of the "new kid" to a question is not quite entertaining enough, Brett and Charles together can improvise something witty to ease the conversational flow down to the second row. There, to the far left, sits "the sexpot," as Skutch calls her, the pretty starlet, who like the "new kid" above her, is not apt to be as strong a player. She, however, can be bailed out if necessary by the show's anchor, its ablest player, Richard Dawson.* In the last seat sits another "strong" character, a woman celebrity with an offbeat imagination whose function on the panel is to conclude with an original remark. Semi-regulars Patty Deutsch, Marcia Wallace, Betty White, Joyce Bulifant, and Fanny Flagg all work well in this position.

---

* Though, of late, Dawson's departed.

Best Buckeroo

As a celebrity panelist, Richard Dawson's clearly doing *something* right. On *Match Game,* the former star of *Hogan's Heroes* was single-handedly responsible for giving away over three million dollars!

Equally skillful casting enables the celebrity panel to survive in other modernized forms. *The Gong Show* invites a panel of celebrity entertainers, three at a time, to pass judgment on its acts. *Celebrity Sweepstakes* used to have the studio audience vote electronically on the odds that the celebrity panel would know the correct answers. *Tattletales* invited the audience to root on three celebrity husband-and-wife couples' knowing intimate facts about each other.

The most complex and entertaining panel game ever devised is *Hollywood Squares,* the three-storied, star-studded tic-tac-toe board of nine celebrities. Paul Lynde reigns in the most-called-upon center square, where he has collected three Emmys for providing some of television's most

Flock together celebs.

All in the *Hollywood Squares*. In the X, left to right: Joanne Dru (she's Peter Marshall's sister), Anson Williams, Earl Holliman, Mike Connors, Demond Wilson, Anthony Newley, Paul Lynde, Theresa Merritt, Peter Marshall, Sandy Duncan, Karen Valentine, Ernest Borgnine, Edward Asner, Loretta Swit, Florence Henderson, Roddy McDowall, Shirley Jones, Richard Crenna, Peter Graves, Redd Foxx, Milton Berle, Vincent Price, Karen Grassle, Michael Landon, McLean Stevenson. In the O, left to right: Zsa Zsa Gabor, Marty Allen, Kent McCord, Art James, Alex Trebek, David Groh, Robert Fuller, Marcia Wallace, Adrienne Barbeau, Elke Sommer, Ruta Lee, Robert Blake, Art Linkletter, Vince Edwards, Jessica Walter, Robert Goulet, Rose Marie, Janet Leigh, and Jo Ann Pflug.

sustained funny moments. Rose Marie sits directly above him, and George Gobel now occupies the seat of the late Cliff (Charlie Weaver) Arquette at the bottom left. Semi-regulars on the show include Joan Rivers, Tony Randall, Vincent Price, Pearl Bailey, Rich Little, Elke Sommer, and Harvey Korman. Non-regulars are seated in positions less strategically important to the game.

Having the same famous faces on a game show panel lets the viewer feel he is tuning in to old friends. *That* boosts a show's ratings. And *that* is such a nice idea to a packager that it is very much to his advantage to sign good celebrity players to exclusive contracts. The regular celebrities on both Goodson-Todman's *Match Game* and Heatter-Quigley's *Hollywood Squares* are barred from appearing on other packagers' games. In exchange, the packager pays celebrities handsomely. A celebrity regular can realize at least fifty thousand dollars a year to sit in that seat one evening per week, for five half-hour tapings; that's just for the daytime version of the game. Up that figure if the show has a syndicated nighttime version, then throw in a nice fat residual check every time a show is repeated.

Still, there are fewer hit shows than there are celebrities, and on even a classic show like *Hollywood Squares,* not everyone can be a regular. Among celebrities, it creates what you might call a pecking order.

To deal with the exigencies of that, the game show employs a person known as the "celebrity booker." Most of the week hers is a telephone job. Celebrity bookers spend hours on the phone trying to get through to agents of "hot" stars to convince them that the game will be good for the star's career. At the same time, the celebrity booker must field—or shun— the calls of the lukewarm-popular celebrity, the actor or comedian who needs the game show more than the show needs him or her. The celebrity booker must schedule stars months in advance and have a reserve of stand-by talent to call upon in case of inevitable last-minute cancellations. Her day does not end at five, nor does her week finish on Friday. The celebrity booker must be present at all tapings, usually done in the evening or over the weekend. During a taping, she must make sure that the stars are comfortable, which means that she must be prepared to run a variety of errands for them and perform any necessary ego-stroking. She must dine with the talent at the starchy buffet of cold cuts provided by the packager during the tape breaks. Then she must be sure that each celebrity receives his or her fee. Non-regular celebrities on the West Coast collect $750 per taping for a daytime show, and more for the syndicated nighttime version.

The job of coming up with good celebrities, then keeping them happy, can be so taxing that *Hollywood Squares* has solved the problem by hiring an outside booking agency. All non-regular celebrity panelists used by

The Feeding of a Celebrity

Four stars (not the celebrity kind, the rating kind) to *Hollywood Squares'* intra-taping buffet. Unlike other game shows where cold cuts reign, the food is hot, delicious, and endless: thick roast beef, juicy ham, rich and creamy beef Stroganoff, fresh fruits and vegetables, four different kinds of salad, and five different kinds of dessert, including chocolate mousse served from a large chilled bowl. Guess that's the mark of a hit show.

Heatter-Quigley are booked exclusively by Mary Markham Associates, a Hollywood talent procurer. Each show, Markham tries to balance older stars with "nostalgia" appeal with rising new faces. And she tends to be choosy. Celebrities often have to wait several months until Markham feels they are "ready." "My career had been coming along all right," said a relieved Burt Reynolds, "but I knew I really had it made when I was asked to do *Squares.*"

More white knuckles lie ahead once a new celebrity has been booked onto the show. He is on probation, carefully judged by Markham according to how well he plays the game. Big-name actors, Markham feels, are especially risky as players, needing as they so often do, to have a script in front of them in order to shine. "Some of the people with the biggest box office draw just don't get invited back," explained Maria Martone, a spokeswoman at Markham. "They just didn't play well; they created an enormous lull."

Other celebrities are too anxious to put themselves across rather than to play the game. According to Richard Dawson: "Some of the worst celebrities on game shows are the stand-up comics. They're getting big laughs with an ad lib," he says, "and the contestant's ten thousand bucks is going down the drain. All someone has to do on *Match Game* is to try that once and they're *never* invited back. There's just too much at stake for our contestants for one wise guy to blow it all on a joke."

Panels are the safest games celebrities can play. Back in 1961, another, riskier, far more exciting form of game show evolved, one that left no possible room for lulls or large egos. The new game seated celebrities together with "civilian" contestants, as equals, and pitted them against an evenly matched celebrity-contestant team. The first game with this format was *Password,* and the sight was electrifying. For the first time, viewers could watch a celebrity agonizing and exulting, triumphant or thwarted, competing and suffering every bit as intensely as any contestant. You no longer had to wonder," What's he *really* like?" You *knew*.

Why is this man laughing? He's just collected the check he gets for sitting there year after year.

Richard Nixon

Richard Nixon was once a guest on a game show. The show was *Your First Impressions;* the year was 1962. According to Monty Hall, owner of the show: "Richard Nixon was a guest on the show when he was running for governor of California. He had lost his bid for the Presidency to John F. Kennedy two years earlier, and he was waging a losing battle to beat Pat Brown. He was highly, explosively nervous, and we had to lay everything out for him very carefully. He was worried about his television image, which had been criticized in his campaign against Kennedy, and he was worried he would say something he shouldn't. But he got through the program all right. He even came up with a clever line: 'I wish that I . . . had become a P.T. boat captain.' That wowed the audience, and he was very pleased with himself."

Today, after two incarnations and a run of over ten years, *Password* is gone; so are a lot of its celebrity-civilian imitations: *Baffle* (first known as *PDQ*), *You Don't Say, The Magnificent Marble Machine, Stumpers, Get the Message, The Cross-Wits, Shoot for the Stars, To Say the Least,* and others. But *Password's* direct descendant, *$20,000 Pyramid,* is still very much alive. It is no accident that *Password* and *Pyramid* in some ways resemble each other. Both are intense word-association games that pit two celebrity-civilian teams against each other and the clock. Both games were created by Bob Stewart. *Password* was developed while Stewart worked at Goodson-Todman; *Pyramid,* an even more exciting game—in that it is possible to see people win as much as $25,000 in sixty seconds— Stewart perfected after he had gone into game show packaging on his own.

Because *The $20,000 Pyramid* is taped in New York, the packaging company sweetens the pot for California-dwelling stars by picking up the cost of a celebrity's airfare, hotel, and meals, and paying a higher rate to celebrities for playing the game than they could receive for most games in California.

Once they arrive, celebrities who have never played the game before are given just as full a briefing and rehearsal before a taping as the civilian contestant. At ABC, a special network liaison practices the game beforehand with the celebrity. When he has finished, a member of the game show packaging company, usually Bob Stewart himself, takes over and puts the celebrities through more paces. Helping celebrities win the most possible money is everyone's goal, so celebrities do it over and over and over again until they get it right.

If the preshow briefings and runthroughs that celebrities get are similar to those given their civilian teammates, there *is* one big difference. Celebrities are furnished with their own dressing rooms for their five glamorous costume changes. They also get their own wardrobe mistresses, hairdressers, make-up artists, and, if their egos require, entourages. They are stars, after all!

Fetish Games

Americans are so star-struck that over the years there have been several games that have attempted to capitalize upon the "mana" of celebrities' personal possessions.

Does anybody remember *Personality Puzzle?* The show, which aired over ABC back in 1953 and starred John Conte and Robert Alda, required that four celebrity panelists guess the identity of a mystery celeb from an article of clothing or one of the tools of his or her trade.

Another show, *Who's There?* enjoyed a short run over CBS back in 1952. On it, a panel of celebrities sized up apparel and props of famous people to hazard a similar guess. The panel included Arlene Francis, Bill Cullen, Paula Stone, and Robert Coote.

Who Pays? a panel game with Mike Wallace hosting, trotted out the mystery celebrity's valet, gardener, and chauffeur for the consideration of the panel.

Other shows have attempted to lure viewers by displaying the pictures of famous people in their games. Over the years, there's been *Are You Positive?* which aired celebrity baby pictures, *About Faces, All About Faces, Bank on the Stars, Broadway to Hollywood, Everybody's Talking, Hold It Please, Make a Face, Place the Face, The Face Is Familiar, The Movie Game, Personality, The Reel Game,* and *Dotto.*

The Name's the Same capitalized upon the glamour of a famous person's name, *Let's Play Post Office* delved into his mail, and *Name Droppers* dragged in his relatives.

Even juicier have been the following celebrity gossip games in which stars tattled on themselves or their spouses. *Answer Yes or No, The Celebrity Game, Funny You Should Ask, The Game Game, He Said, She Said,* later known as *Tattletales, Hollywood Connection, Hollywood's Talking, People Will Talk, Tell Us More,* and the recent *All Star Secrets.*

Questions!

The first thing you notice about the questions on a game show is that they are easy. "Oh, I know the answer to *that*," you say. You are meant to. The networks remember the days when questions were hard and the stakes so astronomical that bank officers carried the questions on stage (flanked by armed security guards) to be answered from soundproof booths. Even more vividly do the networks remember the year the truth came out: all those security measures had been sham, the gripping suspense orchestrated: the bank vaults empty, the questions "controlled," the contestants coached.

Now That's Going Too Far...

Right after the scandals, game-show security was even more fanatical than it is today. To keep snoopers away from the show's questions, Norm Blumenthal, former producer of *Concentration*, believed that locking the answers in a suitcase and posting a sign reading SECURITY AREA—NO LOITERING was an adequate preventative measure.

The man from Standards and Practices disagreed. He insisted that the answers to each puzzle be encased in a box, wrapped with 3-inch-wide masking tape, affixed with red sealing wax in four places and stamped with Blumenthal's ring. *Then,* each box was to be placed inside a thick envelope, which in turn was taped and wax-sealed. Finally, the envelope was placed in a strong box and secured with three locks!

N

NBC   National Broadcasting Company. Inc   Thirty Rockefeller Plaza
                                                    New York, N Y 10020   212 664 4444

·   ·

·   ·

TO: <u>Compliance and Practices Department</u>

PROGRAM: <u>"TO TELL THE TRUTH"</u>   KNBC AIR DATE:_____

1. How were you selected as a participant?
   Please explain on reverse side.

2a. Are you or any member of your family an
    employee or related to an employee of
    NBC, RCA or Goodson-Todman?   YES ☐   NO ☐

 b. Are you a member of AFTRA, SAG or AGVA?   YES ☐   NO ☐

3. Have you ever participated as a contestant
   on this or any other game show <u>prior</u> to
   your above noted appearance? If so, please
   give the name of the program(s) and the
   date(s).   YES ☐   NO ☐

4. Were you induced to refrain from winning
   by anyone or to engage in any conduct
   contrary to the object or rules of the
   game? If so, please explain on reverse
   side.   YES ☐   NO ☐

5a. Did you know or ever meet any of the panel
    members prior to your participation?   YES ☐   NO ☐

 b. Did you have any contact with any panel
    member on the day of taping prior to your
    participation on the program?   YES ☐   NO ☐

    If your answer to either of the foregoing
    questions is "Yes", please explain on the
    reverse side.

Every contestant's paperwork, courtesy of the network standards and practices
office.

Since that day, the networks have taken steps to guarantee that never again would the viewer have to doubt the honesty and integrity of their games. They formed their standards and practices departments to monitor down to the minutest detail the security surrounding the contestants, prizes, and, especially, the questions. Before a game show ever goes on the air, the packager must submit to the network a detailed written account, known as "the bible," limiting and defining who on its staff shall have access to the questions and under what, if any circumstances, exceptions can be made. On a taping day, the game show is required by the network to have on hand four times the number of questions that could possibly be used. To further guard against possible cheating, a master list, all of the host's question cards, and the game's electronic or cardboard "read-outs" are kept under lock and key in a guarded security area. During a show, in the event that a question can be answered more than one way, the contestant is always given the benefit of the doubt and called back for a future show if necessary.

Southern (DUH!) California

The aftermath of the scandals is not the only factor that keeps game show questions so homogenized. According to many producers, the proliferation of easier questions is one of the consequences of the game shows' westward move.

"It's not that contestants are less intelligent in California," said one. "It's just that they don't seem to care about certain kinds of information. In New York, what you know and what you talk about is provided for you by the New York *Times*. If you haven't read the paper that day, you won't be able to show your face in public. The competitive social pressure to be "up" on things is that great. It definitely makes for sharper, more intellectually combative contestants than we find out here. We have to get players, so we gear our games and our questions to who's available."

To avoid such confrontations over whether a question is right or wrong, game shows today have preferred to shy away from what's known in the business as "the hard quiz." Instead, they have developed a whole new type of question in a whole new sort of game, where there *is* no right or wrong, just hunches and happinstance. At issue on *Hollywood Squares,* for example, is not who's right, but who's bluffing. On *Family Feud,* it's can you match the top answers taken from a poll of one hundred people? On many other shows, wheels of fortune, rolls of dice, the turn of a card, determine the game's outcome. Sometimes contestants are asked only to rely on gut instinct: "to take the curtain or to take the box?"—that is the question.

When game shows do ask contestants to come up with the right answer, the questions always draw upon common knowledge ("geared to the level of a fifth-grader," one producer confided.) —facts about Benjamin Franklin and Abraham Lincoln are favorite subjects. So are such "pop" culture events as movies, TV series, sports, and recent headlines. "Deeper" information may be drawn from the topical psychology and sexology found in the "how to" books on the best-seller lists, in *Cosmopolitan, Reader's Digest,* and "Dear Abby" columns.

Below the Belt...

The following Famous Quotation was once asked on *Jeopardy!* during one of the show's championship playoffs:

"What Jim Jeffries' manager said to him before the Bob Fitzsimmons fight."

"Boo! Hiss!" went the audience. Even in a tournament of champions, the question seemed too obscure. The Jeffries-Fitzsimmons bout is hardly one of boxing's best-known events.

The correct question? "What is 'The bigger they come, the harder they fall?' "

"Ahhhh! Well!" went the audience, obviously pacified. *That* they'd heard of!

If coming up with such fare sounds easy, it is not. In the words of John Rhinehart, former staffer on *Jeopardy!* and ex-producer of *Wheel of Fortune,* "Thinking up the questions for a game show is an art form. It takes a long time to learn to be a question writer. Question writers are very, very special, unique people, and they're hard to find. They have a

MATCH GAME 78

TOM SAID:
"I THINK I
HAVE THE
RUSSIAN FLU.
I KNOW IT'S
RUSSIAN BECAUSE,
I HAVE AN
UNCONTROLLABLE
URGE TO
_____."

THE BETTER SEX

A SURVEY OF JURY MEMBERS SHOWS THAT, IN
THEIR DELIBERATIONS, ONE OF THE SEXES
GENERALLY GIVES MORE INFORMATION, OPINIONS,
AND SUGGESTIONS THAN THE OTHER SEX. WHICH
SEX IS IT?

THE JURY MEMBERS THAT GIVE MORE INFORMATION ARE
MEN

FAMILY FEUD

V (5) - 1   TOP 4 ANSWERS
TRY TO FIND THE MOST POPULAR ANSWER.

NAME SOMETHING PARENTS SAY TO THEIR
DAUGHTER BEFORE HER FIRST DATE.

TATTLE TALES

LADIES-- CAN A
WOMAN BE IN
LOVE WITH TWO
MEN AT THE
SAME TIME --
YES--OR NO?

Ever wonder what the questions look like to the host?

sense of the dramatic, and they understand the level of difficulty a question can be for the contestant and the audience at home. The questions must build in intensity from round one of the game to round two, when the stakes are double, to the last round, the end game, which will determine the winner if any, that day, of the big money prize. Question writers must keep in mind the game's commercial breaks and plan cliff-hanging questions to coincide with them. Most important, the questions they write must be understandable, interesting, fun, readable, informative, and entertaining." The former producer of *Jeopardy!,* Bob Rubin, was a master of it, says Rhinehart. "He'd cock his head to the side and say, 'Let's see, a question about the Chicago Fire is a thirty-dollar question; the Boer War is worth eighty.' He had a feeling for it in his fingertips."

Question writing on a game show does indeed fall under the jurisdiction of its producer. He (or she) writes the question himself or hires a staff. Traditionally question writing used to be one of the best ways to break into the game show business. These days, however, it's not as easy as it once was, as a growing number of game shows now farm their questions out to freelancers. "Go home this weekend and write me a hundred questions on history," a producer will say. "I need them on Monday." Of these hundred, the producer may select ten. The freelancer is paid only for the questions that are used.

Singing the Blues

Having to "resort" to writing the questions for a game show may harbinge the arrival of hard times for some. Doing the job for *Name That Tune* is Terry Kirkman, brilliant song writer for now-defunct sixties rock group "The Association." Kirkman is the composer of "Windy" and "Cherish."

To the best, the most experienced go the plum jobs. *Hollywood Squares* has a permanent staff of eight question writers on salary. Jay Redack, Harry Friedman, Harold Schneider, Gary Johnson, Steve Levitch, Rick Kellard, and Rowby Goren are so good at tailoring entertaining questions for the show's celebrity players, they've been singled out for Emmys two years in a row. At their disposal are two hundred magazines to which *Hollywood Squares* subscribes for their needs.

Question Writing . . . The Easy Way

There's an even easier way to write questions than subscribing to two hundred magazines. Sometimes the game show invites an encyclopedia publisher to donate his tomes to the show as consolation prizes. In exchange, the show announces that all its questions came from the encyclopedia. The implication, of course, is that if *you* owned that encyclopedia, you too could be smart and rich.

Before each taping, the show's writers prepare nine sets of questions they've tailored to the personalities and interests of each of the celebrities. The questions are then placed in packets, affixed with the star's name, and placed in individual slots on host Peter Marshall's podium. Celebrities never actually know the answers to the questions, but before each show, the writers brief them about the general areas the questions will touch upon and supply them with suggestions for amusing bluffs.

Family Feud thinks up the questions for its polls, then mails them out at random to one hundred of the people whose names it keeps on file. The show obtained the names its first week on the air when it requested home viewer volunteers and thirty thousand people responded. For special questions, *Family Feud* polls children in local Los Angeles schools.

The $20,000 Pyramid used to have a staff of question writers. Now that the show is so established, producer Ann-Marie Schmitt does the job herself. During odd moments she can pull topics from the hundreds of categories she keeps on index cards in her office in huge cross-referenced file boxes. It takes her only a few minutes to put together questions for a whole week of shows.

Four professional joke writers are employed by Goodson-Todman as consultants to write *The Match Game*'s unique questions. According to producer Ira Skutch, "The fellows, Dick de Bartolo, Joe Neustein, Patrick Neary, and Elliot Feldman, sit around and make up questions singly and together. Then they come in for a conference and go over them. We then throw some out, rework them, and polish them. What these questions are, are actually little jokes within themselves. But it is a very narrow, specific joke form. You have a joke where the punchline has a hole in it. The questions have to be wide enough to allow the possibility of a match. They also have to be carefully constructed so they don't have too many elements in them. Take the example of 'The millionaire Japanese dwarf came to the

United States and bought a BLANK.' There you have too many elements that can affect the answer. The question should lay a field for funny or amusing answers, but not so wide that there is no chance for a match.

Ooh! That's Too Hard!

Not all game show questions are easy, especially when a game show is a little over the budget for a given week and has given away a few too many prizes. Have you ever noticed, for example, that a certain percentage of the questions asked during the course of a week on *The $20,000 Pyramid* are too frustratingly amorphous, well, for *words?* *Hollywood Squares* has its trickier Secret Squares; *Name That Tune* its more obscure melodies; and even *The Price Is Right* its share of "forget it" games.

Game shows want to give away all the money allotted to them in a week; that keeps the ratings high, and what they don't give away reverts to the network. Nevertheless, when a show's been too generous look for "curves" from the question-writing department.

"The material we have selected is then tested around the office to see whether the answers we think we're going to get are actually the answers we do get. Then we arrange the questions to avoid conflicts in subjects. Even while the show is on the air, we are constantly doing last-minute checks for new conflicts that might arise."

Tattletales producer Paul Alter prided himself on the philosophical depth of the questions asked of its celebrity couples. Like *The Match Game,* they were written by free-lance professionals. Explored on the show were such issues as ethics, loyalty, attitudes toward children, and other open-ended dilemmas. *Can* a woman be in love with two men? Goodness! *That's* a far cry from Benjamin Franklin and Abraham Lincoln.

Finally, though the content of most game show questions might make some folks pessimistic about the future of Western civilization, others know better. Even back in the days of the big money quizzes, the questions game shows asked were *never* particularly highbrow. Said Bergen Evans, once the professorial question writer for *The $64,000 Question,* "Viewers don't like experts; they're too elitist." What they *do* like seeing is the drama of a nice person struggling to emerge triumphant from a difficult ordeal. Which on a good show is just exactly what they get!

PROPS: Jay tray: on it the
open, a large box of
Creamettes. Hidden in
it -- $400. Also on
tray, a lift-off box
to hide a Polaroid
Camera, from Coley.
(Camera catalog number
-- V55W4353 --
$169.88. Case number
-- 55W4315-M $18.98.
Both are on Page 336
in Spiegel catalog.)
In it -- $400.

Coley flip in limbo.

Rollaway box hides the
G.E. Stereo and Porta-
Fi Speaker.

Behind Curtain #2, a
flock of 4 little
steers.

MAN AND WOMAN

"SAME CIRCUMSTANCES"

                MONTY

I'm going to find out how a man
and a woman trade under the exact
same circumstances!

(PICK A MAN AND WOMAN. NAMES)   _____

(MEANWHILE JAY ENTERS WITH HIS   _____
 TRAY)

Let's see how you do with this
box of macaroni, and what's under   MS JAY'S TRAY.
this box on Jay's tray.

But first listen to Jay.

MUSIC: APPROPRIATE

          JAY (MONTY'S MIKE)

This is a two-pound box of Creamettes,   CU BOX OF CREAMETTES.
the quick cooking macaroni.
Creamettes are of the highest quality
and finest texture -- selected from
special Durum wheat, formula enriched
and made into macaroni.

This box sells for... 47¢!

There's more than one kind of writing on a game show. While the shows aren't exactly scripted, the producer plans down to the last second the order in which contestants will be approached, games played, and prizes revealed. A typed log for each day's taping is then made available to the host, announcer, director, technical staff, and network watchdogs. . . .

MONTY

Now, you can trade what you brought
today for either one of these items.
If you both take the same thing,
I'll duplicate it.

What do you want to trade for?

(WHICHEVER WAY THEY GO, REVEAL THE
JAY BOX)

(COMMENT ON HOW THEY TRADED)

Jay, what's in the box?

(JAY REVEALS CAMERA)   MS JAY'S REVEAL OF CAMERA.

It's a Polaroid Camera and Case!

(APPLAUSE)   CU REACTION.

MUSIC: APPROPRIATE

JAY (MONTY'S MIKE)

This is the exciting Model #250   CU POLAROID CAMERA AND CASE.
Polaroid Camera and case. It was
chosen from the wonderful selection of merchandise
of the well-known E.J. Coley Company CU COLEY FLIP IN LIMBO.
of Chicago, Illinois. The E.J.
Coley Company is known for its
quality and value.

The camera and case sell for...
$~~100.86~~ $198.86!

MONTY

(IF BOTH TRADED AWAY SAME ITEM,
REVEAL MONEY HIDDEN IN IT.

OTHERWISE, REVEAL HIDDEN MONEY
ONLY WHEN ITEM IS TRADED AWAY OR
HELD AT END OF DEAL.

CAMERA REVEAL

(WITH APPROPRIATE COMMENTS, SHOW   FOLLOW THE ACTION.
THAT THERE'S $400 INSIDE)

CREAMETTES REVEAL

(OPEN BOX AND SHOW THIS WAS A RICH   FOLLOW THE ACTION.
STRAIN OF WHEAT -- $400 IN HERE)

Who knows what unsung genius brought forth this collector's item: the actual text containing succulent advertising copy, for announcer Jay Stewart to read, props, camera shots, and all, of Monty Hall's first deal of the day, Monday, June 9, 1969. Time of the "Same Circumstances" deal: 4 minutes; 35 seconds. . . .

         MONTY

Again, let's see how a man and
woman trade under the same
circumstances.

Either or both of you can trade
what you now own for what's in   WS MODEL AT BOX ON DISPLAY
that big box on the Display Floor!   FLOOR.
Whaddya say?

(WHICHEVER WAY THEY GO, YOU'RE
GOING TO REVEAL THE DISPLAY FLOOR
BOX.

BUT IF EITHER CAMERA OR MACARONI
IS TRADED OFF -- FIRST REVEAL MONEY)

DISPLAY FLOOR BOX REVEAL

Now -- let's see what's in that
box! Carol?

(BOX ROLLS TO REVEAL STEREO)   WS BOX REVEAL OF STEREO.

It's a Stereo Console!

(APPLAUSE)   CU REACTION.

MUSIC: APPROPRIATE

        JAY (MONTY'S MIKE)

Here's the General Electric Console   SHOTSA G.E. STEREO.
Stereo with exclusive Porta-Fi that
lets you enjoy music from anywhere
in your home. Plug the Porta-Fi   CU PORTA-FI.
Receiver into any wall outlet.
Sound convenience with no custom
wiring necessary. From General
Electric.

This unit sells for... $399.85!

         MONTY

Here's the final test! Wanna keep
what you now own...

Or would you rather trade for what's
behind the curtain Carol Merrill is   WS MODEL AT CURTAIN #2.
now pointing to?

KEY:

    MS = medium shot
    CU = close up
    WS = wide shot
    "Limbo" = a camera shot, done off to the side, of a color photo "flipcard"
of a prize, in this case a camera from the Coley Merchandise Catalog.

                    MONTY

(IF ANY UNKNOWNS REMAIN, REVEAL
WHAT THEY KEEP LAST)

CURTAIN #2 REVEAL

Let's see what's behind that
curtain!

(CURTAIN #2 OPENS ON THE STEERS)   WS OF CURTAIN #2 OPENING
                                          ON STEERS AND CAROL.
It's a small herd of small steers!

(APPLAUSE)   CU REACTION.

MUSIC: APPROPRIATE

You can now start your own beef   CU STEERS.
trust!

But don't trust them -- they're
quite young and haven't any
manners!

(COMMENT ON THE DEAL)

Believe me it's been fun -- and
that's no bull.

(APPLAUSE)   STAY ON TRADERS.

Sets:

The things that flash and buzz!

Game shows look and sound different from any other kind of television program: they flash and twinkle; they glide and slide; they sink and rise; they buzz and ring and dance to spritely "think" music; their colors come from an unearthly palette. Lately, the beeping of the computer, the hum of sophisticated electronic technology, and the lilt of the disco is heard in game show land. The best, most successful game shows create their own unique, self-enclosed fantasy world.

The people who know games best, packagers like Mark Goodson, Bob Stewart, producers like Robert Noah of Heatter-Quigley and Stu Billett at Hatos-Hall, will tell you that the set and special effects on a game show are just the window dressing; that how the game plays comes first. Still, you will not catch them skimping. The set is the largest single expense on a game show.

Which shows how times have changed. In the early years of television, game shows were low-budget, to say the least. All you needed was a table and four chairs for the celebrity panel and a cardboard logo with the sponsor's name on it. *The $64,000 Question,* with its gilt and glitter, IBM technology, and ornate isolation booths, introduced lavishness into set design; with the idea apparently for the show to look as ostentatiously *nouveau riche* as the contestants themselves hoped to become.

That was only the start: higher budgets and still higher electric bills were to follow. If having an idea is commonly depicted by a lightbulb, then by the late fifties, game show sets began to resemble a massive, incandescent brainstorm as thousands of them flashed at once. Then came color. Game shows rose to the occasion with the aquas, salmon pinks, chocolate browns, intense vermillions, the royal blues, the gold and the silver, the mosaic mirrors and the glitter that exist nowhere else. And, of course, it became

TILT!

de rigeur for game shows to have yard upon yard of matching wall-to-wall carpeting. By the late sixties, the electronic breakthrough called chroma-key enabled game shows to superimpose one camera shot over another to produce such special effects as the split screen used on *The Price Is Right.* Chroma-key is also what enables stars to peer out of their "secret" squares on *Hollywood Squares* and to wave good-by on *The Match Game.*

In their westward migration to Hollywood, game show sets have realized their full flamboyant potential. New York's studios, originally designed for radio broadcasting, had been closet-sized. Now that there's room, no game show can be without a burnished, gliding, sliding, open-widing hydraulically-powered two-story plinth bearing its name. There is room for bigger prizes, too. "When we taped in New York," said one producer, "we had to cart them up slow, creaky, freight elevators that moved one foot an hour. Sometimes, to get a car on stage, we had to saw it in half and reassemble it in the studio. Out here in California, the studios are all on the ground floor. We can wheel in boats, vans, trailers, even airplanes, if we want to—and we do." In California, that's not all that gets wheeled in. Typical of the Los Angeles mobile mentality, there, contestants no longer walk on stage, they are borne by turntables.

As game show sets have grown more and more spectacular, packagers have come increasingly to depend on specialists to design them, specialists who have advanced degrees in computer technology. Most respected in this new craft is a former Broadway designer named Theodore Cooper who serves as the "creative consultant" at Goodson-Todman. Cooper does not construct the physical arena in which the game will be played; that task he farms out to men like Ed Flesh, James Agazzi, or Henry Laquel, specialists in their own right in a subsphere that involves drawing up and executing the highly detailed blueprints of the game's floor plan. At Goodson-Todman, Cooper oversees their work. Rather, his main job is to figure out such essentials as how the game will be scored, where the game's mechanical and electronic elements will be positioned, both in and out of camera range; and how many people it will take to operate them. Such calculations take months to perfect and hundreds of thousands of dollars to implement, yet when Cooper has finished, his work will be so seamlessly integrated into the game it will be taken for granted by the viewer. As a representative example of the amount of work that goes into orchestrating a game show, let's explore in detail Cooper's work on *Family Feud.*

Cooper must first work from the game's rules of play handed to him by the producer and his staff. On *Family Feud,* for example, two families of five contestants each vie to match the top-ranking answers in a poll previously given to one hundred people. The families compete in several rounds to be the first to amass two hundred points and earn the right to play an end game called Fast Money. Fast Money is played by two members of the family, each of whom must, against the clock, attempt to give the best answers to five questions without duplicating each other. If this combined total also reaches two hundred points, the family wins five thousand dollars and the right to face a new family the next day.

To follow the game, the audience must be able to take in at one glance the *two families, the central podium* at which they play the face-off round to determine which family controls the question, *the scoreboard* on the back wall of the set which graphically reveals the most popular answers in the poll, and two smaller *score indicators* placed behind each family's station to show the number of points the family has accumulated after each round. Once set designers solved the problem of what the set would actually look like, and the game's director figured out what the cameras would actually show on the home screen, Cooper had to solve the logistics of those parts of the game that would always be in flux. How, for example, should the results of a poll be revealed? More important, since there were going to be several polls revealed in the course of a game, how could the answers to the next polls be gotten swiftly into place without slowing things down? By what device should the contestants learn that an answer hadn't made the survey?

Bulb Snatching

Game show sets are constructed so that they can be easily dismantled and stored between tapings. You know all those flashing lights on *The $20,000 Pyramid*'s set? To avoid breakage between tapings, each one of those lights has to be tediously unscrewed, stored, and then of course, resocketed. Just that alone takes the efforts of *four* stagehands.

Cooper's solutions requires the manpower supplied by nine production assistants and nine stagehands (by union decree, no member of a game show production company is permitted to push buttons or touch any part of the set; production assistants give signals, stagehands throw switches); and the purchase of a Jacquard computer and the type of information read-out mechanism, known as a Ferranti-Packer, used in airports. These two

elements alone cost $150,000. Cooper stationed the first production assistant–
stagehand team behind the scoreboard. Their job: to load the answers for
three games onto the triangular swivel he devised for its capacity to be
rotated into place automatically without slowing down the game.

Cooper's plan for executing the rest of the game is an operation that
might leave Rube Goldberg slack-jawed. Say, for example, the topic of a
poll is "Name something salty," and a contestant answers, "Herring." If
the contestant's answer has made the survey, the production assistant standing behind the scoreboard gives the signal to a stagehand to push a button
that magnetically lets the "herring" card drop into view, revealing as well

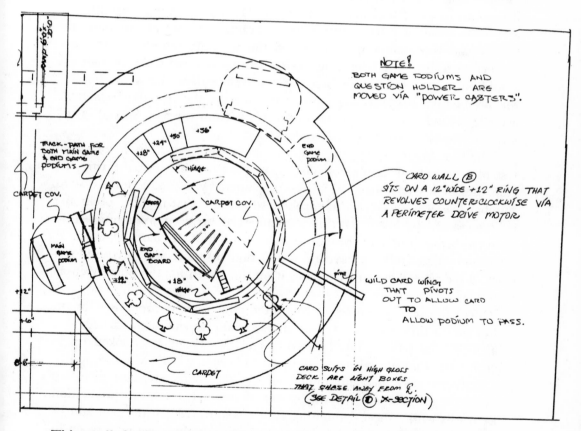

This small detail taken from the actual blueprinted floor plans of Goodson-
Todman's *Card Sharks* gives you an insider's view of the mechanical complexity
of the modern game show. Full of pivots, power casters, and perimeter-drive
motors, they are.

that twenty-three people in the poll gave that answer. Simultaneously, the second production assistant–stagehand team, who mans the game's sound-effect system, activates a chime that is electronically connected to its own microphone. They and the rest of the production assistant–stagehand teams operate from a command center off to the side of the set where they can see both the action of the game and the rulings made by producer Howard Felsher sitting in the front row of the audience. Meanwhile, the third stagehand, directed by a production assistant, electronically flips the score (23), into a computer memory bank and presses a button to indicate on the family's scoreboard that they now have twenty-three dollars in the till. If the contestant has not matched the survey with his answer, a fourth team whose job it is to control the game's special visual effects, presses a button creating the electronic impulse of "X" on the screen, registering a "strike" against the contestant. At the point when one family has amassed 200 points to win the game, the visual effects team also presses a button to activate a series of intervening lights, a dramatic visual aid to show the money and the victory going over to the winning family's scoreboard. Cooper worked out this lighting device because otherwise the human eye would move too slowly to register the win. While these lights are flashing, the production assistant–stagehand team over at the sound effects table activates a louder series of chimes to audibly register the win. Special "win" music is also activated from the control room.

The Fast Money end game is even more complicated. In it, one contestant is placed in earphones offstage to prevent him from hearing the responses of his teammate. He is accompanied by a production assistant number five, wearing identical earphones to insure that nothing occurring on camera can be heard. During a commercial break, a sixth production assistant brings the Fast Money questions to host Richard Dawson. A stagehand, directed by a seventh production assistant sets a countdown clock; a special camera superimposes it on the screen for the home viewers to follow.

Off to the side of the set, a computer programmer, supervised by an eighth production assistant, sits at an electronic typewriter attached to a small television screen. The typewriter and the screen are hooked up to the computer that has been programmed to keep track of the score, multiply, type, center, erase, and remember. As the first contestant gives his answers, the programmer types them out. Beside her, the ninth production assistant sits with a sheet containing every answer given in the poll and its numerical worth. In a separate operation, these numbers are now typed in by a second programmer to become the contestant's score. As soon as Dawson says "Turn around," to the first contestant, the keyboard operator presses a button. One by one, the contestant's answers, automatically centered, are typed across the computer-interfaced yellow-on-black Ferranti Packer readouts, followed, in a separate operation, with their numerical value. Designed to look like lights to the home viewer, these readouts are actually highly reflective hard material which, unlike lights, will not fade out in the intensely lit studio. As the answers are revealed, the sound effects team activates a chime if an answer 'has made the survey, a buzzer if it has not. At the same instant, the ninth production assistant hits a button on the computer to automatically add the contestant's total numerical score to the family's bank, and then a second button to show this total on the overhead scoreboard.

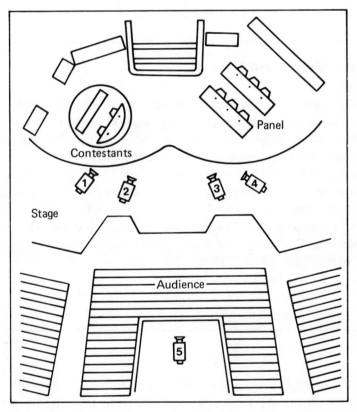

This is *Match Game*'s tidy floor plan. Note that two cameras cover the contestants, two cameras cover the celebrity panel, and a fifth one in the back captures a long view of the entire stage. Contestants enter the set through the broken wall to the left, but they are carried onto the stage via the circular turntable. Host Gene Rayburn emerges down the carpeted stairs in the center to greet the celebrity panel, all of whom are already seated at the start of the show. The small dots on both the contestants' and the panelists' desks are microphone positionings. Rayburn wears a remote radio frequency mike.

Before the second round of Fast Money begins, the first computer key-board operator now wipes the first contestant's answers from the screen but leaves the score. Now the second contestant answers and has *his* answers recorded. Finally, to determine whether the family has reached its two-hundred-point goal, the second keyboard operator pushes a button on the computer to bring forth the first contestants' answers from the memory bank. Total time of the Fast Money round: three minutes.

While Cooper works out his complex choreography and the set designer his, other elements of the new game that are also part of the set begin to fall into place: the music is commissioned, the contestant name tags are ordered, the decorative question cards are designed for the host to hold.

Music Maestro!

When they want the tinkling, light, upbeat music distinctive to games, most game show packagers have to hire outside companies like Score Music Productions to compose it. Not so on the Merv Griffin and the Chuck Barris games. Merv and Chuck compose their own.

Griffin, it's said, tends to get touchy when his is tampered with. Once when staffer Stu Billett was searching for a piece of "think music" for a new game, he found the effect he wanted by speeding up one of Griffin's more stately compositions. Ecstatic over his discovery, he called Merv and played it for him. Billett found his inspiration greeted with gales of icy silence. "Merv?" he asked. "Merv? Are you there?" Billett's an ex-staffer now, thanks to the incident.

Now the game is ready for its first "light and set" rehearsals, as they're called. In the studio, everything that has looked so good in theory must now be put into practice. How will the game actually look when first seen through the television cameras? Will the set work in miniature, the size at which it will appear on the home screen? No matter how experienced the producer, director, and the creative consultant, once the game is finally "up," there are many adjustments to be made. Here is a light that has been awkwardly placed and appears to be sticking out of a contestant's hair; there, the contestants are tripping over a raised decorative lip on the set.

(At this stage, the experimental run-throughs are played by veteran contestants drawn from the game show's files.) As the rehearsals proceed, the set may be radically redesigned, lights rehung, lettering enlarged, and colors repainted to be more effective or less strident. The designer and the director analyze each shot the game's five (sometimes six) cameras will see at any given moment of the game, much as a motion-picture director uses a storyboard to block out scenes in a drama. What will be showing in the background of each close-up, medium, or wide shot? The important opening shot is carefully planned for dramatic impact: on *Family Feud* it is the two families formally posed as if for a homespun family portrait.

Even now, one of the most complicated elements of the game show's set is still to be tackled: its sound system. "Dramas are easy to wire for sound," says Mark Goodson. "They need only one or two microphones. Game shows, on the other hand, have by far the most complicated audio engineering in television, and the audio engineer who works on a game show is the most skilled in the entire industry." Each contestant has his or her own standard microphone. (On Goodson-Todman's *The Better Sex*, there were twelve). The host wears the delicate radio frequency remote microphone that allows him to move freely about the stage. Public-address microphones are hung so that the studio audience can hear the game. Additional microphones are strategically placed to capture the audience's response to the game for the home viewer. All of the microphones—sometimes there are as many as eighteen—must function without feedback.

At last, the set is finished, a twinkling and colorful fantasy haven for our hopes and dreams. Sure it was expensive to build, costing somewhere between two hundred thousand dollars and three hundred thousand dollars. No matter; the network cheerfully foots the bill, considering such costs part of the research and development expenses that go into creating a pre-air pilot show. But more about that and other head-spinning financial matters anon!

All That Glitters

Credit Lin Bolen, former NBC vice-president of daytime programs for many of the innovations in game show set design. For better or for worse, she smashed all traditional notions of what a game show set should look like. Reportedly highly disenchanted with the static sets that prevailed when she took over, Bolen called in a prime-time variety show director.

His name was Marty Pasetta and his credits included the 1973 Elvis Presley Special and the Oscar and Emmy presentations that year.

According to reporter Thomas Thompson, writing in *Los Angeles* magazine:

"Pasetta dropped the traditional backstage curtain giving the set a from-here-to-infinity look. Floors were constructed out of shiny material, polished enough for Fred Astaire to tap dance across. Set pieces were designed to fly in and out and revolve on turntables like Broadway musicals. And lights as gaudy as those which bejewel the billboards outside Las Vegas strip hotels were added. Extensive use was made of computers, both as integral parts of the games themselves and as dramatic visual aids.

"For *Celebrity Sweepstakes,* $250,000 was spent on a computerized tote board which allowed the audience to establish racing odds on whether a celebrity could answer a certain question. For *Wheel of Fortune* and *High Rollers,* a cameraman was positioned in mid-air, shooting down onto the playing area."

Thompson continues, ". . . Bolen reached her apex, or her nadir, more claim, with a 1975 disaster called *The Magnificent Marble Machine,* which required contestants to answer questions flashed at them via a Broadway marquee computer. Then the end game required contestants and celebrities to grapple with an enormous pinball machine, including unwieldy flippers, a giant steel ball and lame sound effects. The total effect was deadly. The show," says Thompson, "became the joke of the business."

The high-gloss Glo-coat look of daytime games has outlasted Bolen. Resident guru in game show set design these days is Pasetta disciple Ed Flesh. They say he's so busy, he doesn't know whether he's flashing or buzzing.

The Worst Sets Ever

Sure there was *The Magnificent Marble Machine,* but do you remember any of *these?*

Top Dollar. "Rife with gadgets," snickered *TV Guide* of this 1957–1958 CBS game, "flashing scoreboards, and electronic flimflammery. Even Bergen Evans looks confused. The human element has been wholly overlooked," they lamented. The game was based on the old parlor game of "Ghosts" played by three contestants. Any eight letter words became translated into digits. If contestants at home could match them with serial numbers on their dollar bills, they could win big bucks.

Reach for the Stars. Merv Griffin originally wanted this comedy stunt show to feature a curtain hung with stars that contestants could reach up and pluck for prizes. And he told his staff so. Then he left town on an extended business trip. When he returned, he found that instead his staff had constructed an elaborate space ship full of dials and lights, with the stars hung outside of portholes. "This isn't what I wanted," shrieked Merv. Too late. The show was scheduled to go on the air the following week. Come to think of it, maybe the set wasn't so terrible. Perhaps it was all the contestants required to chew crackers and then whistle "Dixie." *Reach for the Stars* aired briefly in the early sixties over ABC. Bill Mazer was the host.

Singled out for opprobrium, the set of *Money Maza.*

Video Village. Contestants on this first Heatter-Quigley game trekked through this larger-than-life board game to the roll of a die, carrying special pocketbooks in which to stash their winnings. Airings over CBS between 1960 and 1962, the show featured Kenny Williams as The Town Crier, and lovely assistants Eileen Batton and Joanna Barton. *Video Village* did not pass go.

Diamond Head Game. In the endgame of this mid-seventies' show, contestants clambered up a huge papier-mâché volcano erected on the beach of Waikiki. Bob Eubanks hosted this short-lived show that aired over ABC.

Money Maze. This unbelievable game placed wives into a large maze and sent them scurrying, rat-like, through it for cash and merchandise while their husbands stood on a raised platform calling out directions. The show aired over ABC in 1975.

Double Dare. Even Goodson-Todman falls down on the job occasionally. This show encased its contestants in adjoining twin isolation booths only letting them out to face "spoilers" also so encased. The device gave the show a cold, sterile look and prevented any rapport with the contestants. Cold-fish host Alex Trebek didn't help. The show aired briefly early in 1977 over CBS.

The Better Sex. Another Goodson-Todman disaster. Although the game concept was sound, the set was full of gadgets operated by remote control which leaped into place with a jarring thud, and podiums that rose and sank into the wall-to-wall carpeting like will-o'-the-wisps. *The Better Sex* was almost totally redeemed by its end game with neat red and green light-up cricketlike vote indicators.

Prizes!

As sure as Broyhill makes dining rooms, Z-Brick makes wall tiles, West Bend makes cookware, and Herculon makes carpets, game shows give prizes. What they give away is pretty generally wonderful: money enough, literally, to change your life—pay off your college education, make the down payment on a house, enable you to get married—or divorced; out of hock, or out of town. Day in, day out, it's Christmas, a bottomless cornucopia of cars, furs, boats, trips, all the things you've ever wanted. "Ooh," you say to your screen, your eyes moist for the lucky person who's won. "Ahh, if only that were *me*."

Still, it has been demonstrated time and time again, game shows cannot buy or bribe their audiences into watching merely because they offer lavish luxury items or astronomical sums of money. "The prize must be a pure extension of the format," says packager Ralph Edwards, who grandfathered the giveaway show back in 1940 with his long-running *Truth or Consequences*. "It cannot be indiscriminately given. To be meaningful to the contestant, and more important, to the audience, it must be fairly won or lost." And so there must be small prizes for easy questions, middle-sized payoffs for questions of medium difficulty, and finally, dramatically, for the contestant who has beaten out all competition, taken great risks, fought the great fight to stand at last alone victorious, the most splendiferous of spoils. And spoils they are: *The $20,000 Pyramid* gives away a million dollars a year. Airplanes fly into people's lives, one-of-a-kind antiques, Rolls-Royces and Porsches, trips around the world and on and on and on. How *do* those game shows afford it?

As a matter of fact, they *don't*. It's the networks who actually provide the loot you see on game shows, by strict Federal Communications Commission regulation. As soon as a network buys a game show from a packager, that show is assigned a member of the contest co-ordination department to handle prizes. If a game show's format requires the awarding of cash prizes, the co-ordinator's job is very simple. The network provides the game show with a fixed prize budget of, let's say, $15,000 a week. It is now up to the packaging company to devise questions for the show in a way that will allow it to stay within this budget. If a game show gives away more money one week than its prize budget allow, that amount gets "averaged out" over a thirteen-week quarterly period, known in television as a "cycle." If at the end of that time, the show continues to be in the red, the packaging company must pay the difference out of its own operating expenses. If a game show is under budget, the money reverts to the network.

On a game dispensing merchandise prizes, the contest co-ordinator's job becomes immeasurably more difficult. As on the shows dispensing cash prizes, the network allots a budget to the game show offering merchandise prizes. Does the game show then go out and use its allowance to purchase the products it uses as prizes the way you or I would, outright, at a department store? No. Over the years, the networks have provided any manufacturers interested in televising their wares with two alternatives. They can produce an expensive thirty-second commercial *and* in addition pay the network $15,000 (on the average) each time it airs the commercial during the day. Or they can offer their product as a prize on a game show by paying to the network a $500 promotional fee each time it is shown or mentioned.

In practice, it's a bit more complicated. The FCC allows game shows to break down the merchandise it offers into three categories: small, medium, and large. The manufacturers of the small prizes, such as the Chapstick used as props on *The Price Is Right's* grocery game, or the slow cookers given to losing contestants as consolation prizes, must pay the network's $500 promotional fee each time such products are shown on the screen. Game shows are permitted to show no more than five such "fee items," as they're known, per half hour. In exchange, the game show reads a short piece of advertising copy which the networks strictly limit to eight seconds. This time limit is the reason game show announcers always talk so fast; each taping, the networks are actually standing by with stopwatches. The small fee items are the bread and butter of every game show, even the ones that give cash prizes. During the final forty seconds of the show when the announcer races through the listing of the manufacturers who have paid such fees, $3,000 a day, or $15,000 a week, gets collected; *voilà*, the game show's weekly cash allowance. Merchandise shows use this money to purchase their trips, furs, and other luxury prizes. Because medium-range prizes such as refrigerators are worth approximately $500 in and of themselves, the FCC permits their manufacturers to waive the payment of the promotional fee and donate such products outright. The cars given away

Major heart-throb name in game shows: Dicker and Dicker of Beverly Hills. Mac Dicker himself's ushering a befurred model past his plate glass window.

on game shows constitute a special category. The game show may choose to purchase the car out of its budget, but it may arrange its game in such a way to show the car on camera as often as it can, and collect $500 for each titillating appearance, hoping to pay for it in this manner before a contestant wins it.

Payola

Such elaborate network supervision wasn't *always* the case. Back in the fifties, games and quizzes had to scrounge their prizes from manufacturers in any way they could while the networks studiously looked the other way. The usual practice was for the game show to receive two of everything from a manufacturer. The game show would then display and praise an item on the game show, providing the manufacturer with clandestine free exposure and the game show with more prizes in the future. This was called "payola." The game show would then sell the "duplicate" prize to raise money to purchase other prizes. This was known as "sleazy."

The network contest co-ordinator's job has just begun. He must see to it that the merchandise, with the manufacturer's descriptive promotional copy, arrives at the studio on time for a taping. If a prize is physically unavailable, he must then make sure the manufacturer provides a properly mounted full-color photograph of the prize to display on camera. After a taping, the contest co-ordinator must follow through to make sure that the prizes promised to the contestants are actually delivered. Even if they have won cash, contestants never leave the studio with their prizes. All merchandise must be ordered by the network from the manufacturer and independently shipped from his warehouse. Delivery usually take ninety days from the show's *air* date, as opposed to the date the show was taped and *that* wait can be as long as six weeks!

Getting all of this taken care of can be such a chore that over the years, an entire industry has grown up to spare the networks the bother. Prize brokers, also affectionately known in the business as "schlockmeisters," make their living by approaching manufacturers on their own and signing them to exclusive contracts. The brokers then approach the networks with the prizes, advertising, and paperwork in tow. For their trouble, they collect from the network a commission of 40 per cent of the retail value of the prize. Sometimes brokers also collect a commission from the manufacturers. Edward Finch, Incorporated, is the largest game show prize brokers which claims, among other accounts, Broyhill Furniture. Not by coincidence are Finch's Hollywood offices located on the same floor as Hatos-Hall, the producers of *Let's Make a Deal,* and downstairs from Goodson-Todman.

Fond Memories . . .

In the mid-seventies, one short-lived game gave its contestants prizes that still linger in memory. The show was *Gambit,* a game for married couples, and it was based on the casino card game Twenty-one. "Our prizes weren't particularly flashy in terms of cash value," says producer Bob Noah, "but we did work hard to make them special." For instance: $100 a month's free groceries at the supermarket of the contestant's choice; $1,000 toward a shopping spree at Georgio's on Beverly Hills' Rodeo Drive; and the anniversary dinner: the show would fly a couple to a variety of exotic settings, such as Paris, Rome, London, Tokyo, or Mexico City, put them up in a hotel for the day, and buy them dinner to celebrate the anniversary of their nuptials.

Other prize brokers are TV Marketing Consultants, which among other products handles Dentyne Chewing Gum; Video Enterprises, which handles American Tourister Luggage, Westclox, and Good Humor Ice Cream; Video Merchandisers, which has a corner on Foster-Grant sunglasses; Norm Checkor and Jerry Bender, who supply the Ralph Edwards' games with prizes; and Jan Victor, who has carved her empire out of Zenith Products and Amana Radar Ranges.

Prize brokers also work closely with non-network-affiliated syndicated game shows which otherwise would have to find prizes on their own.

Prize brokers save work for everyone, but there are drawbacks to using them. They do tend, after all, to provide the same tired old prizes over and over. The result of that can be the deadly sound of millions of bored viewers simultaneously reaching for their channel changers. The scenario is so naggingly real to some game shows that many are relying less and less on prize brokers.

The Spiegel Catalog

("Over 50,000 quality items . . . Chicago, 60609.") It's how game shows let their fingers do the walking. Using the Spiegel mail order catalog enables game shows to get prizes in quantity or out of season. In exchange, game shows have made Spiegel another one of those household words.

The New Price Is Right, for example, never relies on prize brokers exclusively, not when they've got CBS's Bob Flaherty working with them. "I pride myself on searching the world to find prizes that have never been seen on television before," Flaherty says. His finds are stored in a huge warehouse behind the CBS Studio in Hollywood, which at any given moment contains an inventory of prizes worth one-and-a-half million dollars. Parked outside the warehouse, under guard, are a row of boats, another row of trailers and vans, and a row of new cars—all to be given away on the show. Inside, the array of goodies seems to stretch for miles: beautiful and tasteful furniture from W. & J. Sloane's and Hammacher-Schlemmer; redwood hot tubs; six-foot wine storage cabinets and saunas; a greenhouse; a working merry-go-round; a sedan chair; a hot-dog wagon; a round bed; an English sword encrusted with gems worth six thousand dollars; a circular shower that dispenses heated towels; a child's bed in the shape of a racing car; and on and on.

Flaherty, who has a staff of three, visits the furniture markets around the country four times a year. He also shops at Tiffany's, Gucci, Hermès, and Dunhill. *The Price Is Right* has given away airplanes and trips to Nepal, Lord Byron's autograph, and a table of solid gold dinnerware. The show waits two weeks before offering the same item twice. It does not offer any medicinal product or any food products to which a contestant might be allergic. Some "safe" food items are protected from harm by the warehouse cat.

Once Flaherty has found and stored his merchandise, each prize is

You see their dining rooms all the time on TV. But how often do you get to see the Broyhill *factory?* That's it sitting right smack dab in the middle of Lenoir, North Carolina.

logged into a thick inventory book which the show's associate producer consults when lining up the hundreds of prizes she needs each week. Her job is so complicated she must plan one month in advance what she will need for each show's six one-bid games, and each of the six preliminary prize games full of cars, appliances, novelty items, and inexpensive props. It's a job too big for one person, so two more, the show's producer and production assistant write the show's two showcases and plan the prizes for them. Their frequently offbeat ideas pose special challenges to Flaherty. He's up to them, though, and it shows. The prizes on the daytime *The Price Is Right* are far and away the best on television.

Taxes and Other Strings

All prizes, from the boat that sleeps six down to the year's supply of ravioli are taxable according to their *retail* value. When it comes to prizes, the IRS does not allow for the fact that the discount store around the corner is selling something you just won for 30 per cent off. Moreover, your prize is taxable not as a capital gain but as income. Say you make $15,000 a year and win big on a game show. You may conceivably owe more in taxes than you make.

If you hate your prize, the networks will make every effort to substitute another piece of merchandise of equal value, or to accommodate you by providing a color or model you might prefer. But as for giving you cash instead, no. The world saw you win that yacht, and that's what you get. Should you try to sell your prize and not find a taker at your price? That's your tough luck, says the IRS.

Trips are the prizes toughest on contestants. Going around the world may sound glamorous, but few people can afford the time off to take them, let alone the clothes they'll need or the spending money to enjoy them. Game shows require you to take your trip within one year, provided it's not during a peak vacation time or a holiday. Nor are airline tickets negotiable—it's a felony to trade them in for cash.

Those who protest their lot are often directed to a clause in the statement they signed before ever going on the air, "Contestants," it reads "are not obligated to accept prizes." Or as they used to say on one game show many years ago, "Take it or leave it." Between 5 and 10 per cent of game-show winners do leave it, with trips being the prize most frequently bypassed.

The Cupboard Was Bare

Then there was the show that ran out of prizes. Back in 1954, before the networks regulated such matters, a show called *Be My Guest* had to leave the air when Brooklyn contestant Rose Schmetterling won her choice of jewelry or toys for her children, only to learn that *Be My Guest*'s till read tilt. The bankrupt daytime quiz offered her instead a gift certificate worth her winnings in delicatessen cold cuts. To add insult to injury, when she tried to make good on her marker, no market would honor it. Guess what Mrs. Schmetterling's famous rejoinder was to that empty promise? "Baloney."

"A fortune in fabulous prizes"—from the studio audience's vantage point. Don't bid on model Anitra Ford.

The Megaprofits!

They may just seem like little games to you, but to the networks who air them and the packagers who create them, game shows are big, big business. They are one of the least expensive forms of television programming to produce. At the same time, they are among the most lucrative; the profit margin to the network from a game show is always, even with a flop show, at least 600 per cent. The profits from daytime television in general (and game shows comprise 40 per cent of the daytime schedule) are so enormous that they finance all of prime time television. In the days when ABC was foundering far behind NBC and CBS, it is said that the profits from two daytime shows alone kept the entire network in the black. Those two shows were *Let's Make a Deal* and *The Newlywed Game.*

The networks make their profits from the game show's commercials. During daytime hours, the Federal Communications Commission permits the networks to sell six minutes of commercial time per thirty-minute show, double the number of commercials the networks are allowed at night. To determine how much to charge for this time, all three networks employ the A. C. Nielsen Company, an independent rating service whose job is to determine the number of people who are watching a given program at a given time. In addition, Nielsen also makes demographic computations to determine viewer income and age, information which is of great interest to advertisers wishing to target their messages precisely. Nielsen calculates its daytime ratings differently than it does at night. The nighttime ratings are based upon the *total* estimated number of households owning televisions. Since during the daytime most people who use televisions are at work or at school, it makes more sense to calculate the *available* daytime audience at a given time, a figure that will always add up to 100 per cent. This figure is known as the audience "share." If, for example, a daytime show has a thirty share, it means that 30 per cent of the available daytime audience is watching that program, even though its rating may be a low 5 or 6. Because advertisers would rather sell their products on a program that commands the larger number of viewers, the networks charge more for commercial time on a hit show than they do for a marginal one. These days, the daytime advertising rate for a thirty-second commercial costs a sponsor between $12,000 and $22,000, probably higher by now.

To get some idea of the size of network profits, let us first look at the network's cash outlay when it purchases a game show from the packager, whom we'll be meeting in a moment. On the surface, after all, game shows sound expensive to produce. The network, as we've seen (see The Things That Flash and Buzz!), has paid as much as $250,000 for the game show's initial pilot. Each quarter a network generally underwrites three such pilots. That amounts to over three million dollars a year in research and development alone. Moreover, when the network purchases a game show, its cash outlay to that show is $100,000 a week for the duration of its run. Half of that figure, known as the below-the-line costs, pays for studio time, and includes the salaries of the network technical personnel necessary to produce the show. A game's prize budget is also a below-the-line expense. The other $50,000 a week, known as the network's above-the-line expenses, goes to the packager who uses the sum to pay *his* salaries and make his profits.

So $100,000 goes out of the network's coffers. Now, what comes in, by way of advertising revenue? First, let's assume that the network is airing a game show that is only marginally successful, with a correspondingly low advertising rate of $12,000 for a thirty-second commercial. Multiply that figure by twelve to come up with the six minutes. That comes to $144,000 in advertising income for just one half-hour show. Even when you subtract advertising agency commissions, it is easy to see that the network has more than made back its *weekly* cash outlay by the time just *one* show is in the can. What you have left is almost half of Monday, all of Tuesday, Wednesday, Thursday, and Friday of pure network profit with the cost of that "expensive" pilot easily amortized over the show's first thirteen weeks. By the end of the week, this marginal show has brought to the network, free and clear, between $400,000 and $500,000. Now assume that the network has latched onto a hit, and can now charge $22,000 for the thirty-second spot. Subtracting the weekly $100,000 cost of producing the show, the network is realizing more than a million dollars of *profit* every single week that show is on the air! Twice what it makes on its flop.

Profitable though even flop game shows may be, the networks are not interested in airing these marginal shows. They're bad for the network's image; they're harmful when it comes to attracting packagers and advertisers for other daytime and prime time shows as well. To make sure it only airs hit shows, the network employs daytime programming personnel whose job it is to orchestrate an impregnable schedule, one that will (at the expense of the other two networks) contain nothing but shows with high shares. Their job is to look for ideas for new shows, develop them into pilots, test their potential drawing power through market research, put the show on the air for a thirteen-week period, known in the business as a "cycle," and, with luck, build a block of equally strong shows preceding and following the hit show to keep the viewers—and advertisers—glued to that network all day long. At the end of the thirteen weeks, the network programmer must decide whether to renew the show, strengthen its format, change its time period, or cancel it altogether. The programmer has to be right. His or her shows *have* to shave a point or two off the competition and show a gain of their own—or else. Just as bad game shows come and go on television with blinding speed, so do daytime programming network vice-presidents.

For the daytime programmer to do his or her job with some semblance of science, all three networks have top-secret research departments whose job it is to predict the tastes of their forty-two million viewers. Huge notebooks full of statistics independent of the A. C. Nielsen Company's detail the age, marital status, number of children per household, and incomes of their viewers. Perhaps because their predictions are notoriously spotty, the networks are very closed-mouthed about their specific findings. They are more willing to offer the following general observations:

* Game shows are easier to develop than a serial, but their audiences are more fickle. Once developed, a soap opera audience remains more loyal.

* Game show audiences are older and less "up scale" socioeconomically than soap opera viewers, who are supposed to all be young housewives.

* Mornings are better for scheduling game shows because games don't require as much concentration. A housewife can do her chores, enter and leave the room while a game is in progress. In the afternoon, all the housework done, she can settle in front of the set and immerse herself more deeply in her favorite serial.

If young, intelligent adults do not fit the networks book full of statistics, neither do the hit game shows that sneak up on them. In point of fact, when a good game comes along, it breaks all the network's rules and always comes as a surprise. Still, so long as the money to be amassed in games is so astronomical, the real question will continue to be: Will the next solid-gold show be on Network #1, Network #2, or Network #3?

Into this cynical jungle comes the game show's packager, the seller from whom the networks must buy. Theoretically, anyone can dream up a game show and sell it to the networks. In practice, it doesn't work that way. Oh, independent packagers may sell the network an occasional game; other packagers may have one long-running hit but prove unable to develop another; but only a small corps of packaging companies have the proven track record of being able to mount success after success.

Such hard facts deter few, for if you are fortunate enough to have developed just one successful game show and sold it to a network, you may consider yourself wealthy. *How* wealthy? Well, remember the $50,000 a week the network hands over to the packaging company for its above-the-line costs? Let's see where it goes. First we have to pay our staff. Let's be very generous. We'll give our producer and his associate producer $2,500 a week. (That *is* generous, but let's say they won an Emmy for our last game show. Most producers make *far* less; when Nancy Jones first became the producer of *Wheel of Fortune,* Merv Griffin was paying her $900 a week, and she was thrilled.) We'll give our director and his assistant director $2,500. (This, too, is very generous. Directors' salaries are set by the guild to which they belong. At the time of this writing, $1,500 a show is the top rate.) Our host's a big name. Pay him $5,000. The show's got two celebrities a week to pay; give them $1,000 each for a taping. (If the show doesn't have celebrities, maybe it's got models to pay. They come a lot cheaper.) We'll pay the contestant co-ordinator and her staff a total of $1,500 a week. To the question writers and researchers, we'll give a combined figure of $2,500 a week. Then we'll spread $1,500 around to the associate producer and the production assistants. One thousand dollars to the celebrity booker. Feeling magnaminous, we'll pay our announcer $2,500 a week; he was with us on our first show back in radio and we're sentimental. Twenty-five hundred more dollars to pay the clerical staff and the switchboard operator and to cover all conceivable office supplies. To our loyal lawyers, $5,000 a week. So far, we have spent $28,500. We'll bring that figure up to an even $30,000 by springing for a nice catered dinner for the gang when we tape the show. Now we'll pay ourselves $10,000 a week and go out and buy some nice designer suits and a shiny black limo. We deserve it. All that done, depending on how generous the packager really feels like being with everybody's salary, what's left over are profits, free and clear, in the neighborhood of $5,000 to $15,000 a *week!* With a hit show, one that runs for years, the packager has, not counting the $520,000 a year salary we're giving him, made an additional *minimum* $250,000 profit. And that's just for daytime.

If the game show is strong enough, there isn't the slightest reason it cannot be sold in syndication. To do so, the packager absorbs all the game's below-the-line costs himself, then sells it to a commercial distribution company such as Viacom or Jim Victory, which, in turn, for a commission, sells the show to local stations across the country on an individual basis, charging whatever the traffic will bear. Usually a local station agrees to buy fifty-two weeks of tapes, thirteen weeks of which are repeats, thereby defraying some of the packager's expenses. Once a local station has aired one episode, it then sends the videotape cassette onto another. Profits to packagers airing successful syndicated games are practically unlimited. *Hollywood Squares* grosses $8 million a year in syndication alone. Goodson-Todman's *The Nighttime Price Is Right* grosses $3½ million; Chuck Barris' *The New Treasure Hunt* $2 million. Preferably, a packager can have one game show airing on the network during the day and the same show in syndication at night. But, thanks to syndication, a packager can even make do without the networks if he has to. Many a game show canceled from the network's schedule still has a large enough following to justify dozens of local stations buying it for viewing in off hours. Or, a packager can mount an all-new production for syndication the way Barry-Enright Productions is successfully doing right now with shows like *The Joker Is Wild, Hollywood Connections, Tic Tac Dough,* and *Break the Bank.*

Perhaps the packager can sell his show abroad. Canada, England, Australia, Germany, France, Italy, and many countries in South America all purchase the rights to American game shows.

Collecting royalties for the home board-game version of the show can be most lucrative. Perhaps Milton Bradley, Hasbro Toys, or Western Publishing will be interested. Money from a good home game like *Password* or *Jeopardy!* often outlasts the show itself.

Maybe Sarah Coventry would like to design some jewelry for the game the way she has for *Hollywood Squares:* more royalties.

Owning one good game show is guaranteed to make you rich. If, however, your name happens to be Goodson-Todman, let us put it bluntly: you are very, very, very rich indeed. You usually have, after all, five hit shows airing on all three networks during the day and six more running in syndication. Even then, things can be rough. "Quite frankly," says Mark Goodson, "we can't satisfy the network's demand for our games."

Running second in the profit sweepstakes is Heatter-Quigley Productions, the owner of *Hollywood Squares. Hollywood Squares* is currently in its thirteenth year on network television. It is also in syndication. Heatter-Quigley is the most profitable division of publicly—held Filmways, Inc. Third comes Chuck Barris, whose company packages *The Newlywed Game, The Dating Game, The New Treasure Hunt,* and *The Gong Show.* Barris' production company was, at last look, worth three million dollars on the New York Stock Exchange.

The trick is, of course, dreaming up a hit show. "I think almost no one has any appreciation of how difficult these shows are to do—to devise, to get into shape to go onto the air," says Robert Noah, of Heatter-Quigley.

"Game shows look easy and they are traditionally looked down upon by everyone. But it is very tough to come up with a format that is merely workable—forget about successful—just let it *work*. If it were easy, we'd *all* be millionaires. We all make the same mistakes, endlessly. All of our formats end up being far more simple than when they start out. And the process of getting these shows ready is endless simplifying. Really, it just never stops. The biggest thing is clarity. The rest, the set, the flashing lights and the buzzers come later."

The godfather of game shows, Mark Goodson, says, "To do game shows, you need two equal and opposing forces. You need wild imagination, which means you have to go at it with almost a free association technique. Otherwise, all you do is imitate. Then, once you've gotten an unfettered looseness, which leads you to the concept, then you have to approach that idea with Germanic logic, because games are a mixture of emotion and logic. The game has got to be theatrical; you have to enjoy watching. But you also have to be able to play along. To do that it has to be very solid, yet at the same time, very simple.

That Was a Very Bad Year . . .

The game show business isn't all gravy. There was the year 1969. To mention it in game-show circles is to draw a shudder. That was the year none of the networks bought any new games, and canceled many that were still on the air to make room for sitcom reruns. The impact was devastating. Goodson-Todman, which had held three floors in New York's Seagram's Building, shrank from three floors to a third of a floor.

"We survived through syndication," Goodson says. One show, *He Said, She Said,* the syndicated prototype for *Tattletales,* pulled them through.

Over the years, Goodson-Todman has suffered other kinds of headaches. Some of their shows have made *too much* money! Clobbered by huge capital-gains taxes, Goodson-Todman has on occasion had to sell some of their shows to the networks to keep their accountants happy. In 1958, CBS took *What's My Line* off their hands for $2.5 million; *I've Got a Secret* went for a cool five mil. And that was twenty years ago, before inflation.

"Some games have a great concept but are weak on execution, and succeed. Others have a very ordinary idea but succeed on execution. When you get the two together you have an enormous hit. When you get it, when it's found, it instantly touches a nerve in the audience, and they go right for it. You get a *To Tell the Truth*, a *Password*, a *The Price Is Right*, a *Family Feud*. Games with 'textures,' with 'thicknesses.' "

All successful game show packagers, like Goodson-Todman, Heatter-Quigley, Merv Griffin, Bob Stewart, Ralph Edwards, and Chuck Barris, employ a full staff of people whose job it is to develop new games for possible sale to the networks. Chuck Barris' organization is perhaps the least structured. "Chuck will listen and encourage anyone to work on an idea, no matter how way-out," says a former Barris staffer.

Goodson-Todman, on the other hand, is perhaps the most formally structured packaging company. Within its ranks are an inner circle creative producers, many of whom have been with the company for over twenty years, men like Bruno Zirato, Jr., Chester Feldman, Howard Felsher, Ira Skutch, Paul Alter, Frank Wayne, Robert Sherman, and, of course, Mark Goodson himself (William Todman is semi-retired; Jerry Chester handles the business details Todman used to). When not taping their current hits, all of them daily find time to work on new ideas, confer, play the games, iron out kinks, bounce new ideas off each other. Some they reject; others they salvage. If one or more of the producers is able to sell Mark Goodson on a new idea, and he in turn is able to sell a network, that producer now owns a piece of the new show. If he has also helped develop any shows still on the air or in syndication, he also receives a share of their profits. A producer like Frank Wayne, who has been with Goodson-Todman since *Beat the Clock*, who has worked on a dozen of shows since, and who is currently the executive producer of both the daytime and nighttime *Price Is Right*, makes at least $250,000 a year, and in a good year much more.

Once a new idea is ready, the next step is to call upon the daytime program development department of a television network and make a pitch. All three networks have both East Coast and West Coast personnel whose sole job it is to weigh new game show ideas.

"There are perhaps one hundred new ideas submitted to each network every quarter," says John Rhinehart, former NBC West Coast representative, and producer. "These proposals can and do come from anyone—the major packagers like Goodson-Todman, the independents who have managed to sell one or two shows over the years, and the layman who thinks he's got a great idea. I wade through them all. Then I show the best twelve or thirteen proposals to my boss."

In the words of former *Jeopardy!* producer Bob Rubin, here's what happens next:

"If they like your idea," says Rubin, "the networks will pay you 'x' thousand dollars as development money. Then you have six weeks or two months to do runthroughs, change ideas, write it, the whole works. There is no pay. Everyone works on spec. Say you get two thousand dollars' development money. That goes to paying guinea pig contestants ten dollars, twenty-five dollars, whatever, to play the game, for typing paper, telephones. You usually lose money.

"When you think the show is ready, you call the network in and say 'Here is my presentation.' That's called a demo. The network comes and looks at it and they tell you one of three things: 'We hate it. Thanks a lot. Good-by.' 'We like it a lot, but we have other shows we like better this quarter, so we'll give you holding money; we'll option it for another thirteen weeks. Maybe we'll give you a pilot next quarter.' Or 'We love it! Let's do a pilot.'

"To do a pilot means the network pays everything but there is no profit involved. You do it as if it were an air show in terms of staff and everything, but there is no profit built in. Everyone works on reduced salary. Everyone makes half. You need half-a-dozen people or so exclusive of writers—clerical, secretarial, production, whatever. You have to make all your deals as if you were going on the air: you sign your contracts with your emcee and your announcer and for your music if you have any. All that has to be done up front. Because when you go to pilot, everything has to be laid out. All prices are built in for ten years. You make a ten-year deal. All escalators are built in.

"Of course, in reality, if the show is a big hit, your agent goes in and renegotiates after a year, which the network fights and complains about, but that's what happens. Similarly, if your show is marginal, the network can come back and say, 'Hey we don't want to do five cameras any more. Figure out a way to shoot it with four to save us some money.'

"Once you have your pilot green light, you have four to six weeks to shoot it.

"Now, if the show goes on the air, the cost is amortized over the first thirteen weeks, which makes it reasonable for the network. If the show doesn't go on the air, the network has to swallow it. So that's their gamble.

"So now you make your pilot. And of course, you do the best you can and you hope. The pilot is in competition with the other pilots being made that quarter. Next the pilot goes out to a test market. They feed it onto a cable—they have cables all over the country for people who are inveterate daytime watchers. And they research them—with very deep research. 'What parts do you like best? What parts do you like least?' They also do qualitative testing: fifteen people sit around a table, are given coffee, shown a videotape cassette and then asked to guide the network in their responses. Now the programmer comes back and tells the packager one of two things: 'We love the pilot, the testing was good. You're going on the air in such and such a time period.' Or they will come back and say, 'It was okay, but were not putting you on this quarter.' If they say that, you as packager can't do anything. Now they own your property for one year. So you move on to another project.

"The best thing is, though, there is no other business that gives you as much fun or as much gratification. The people are wonderful. The camaraderie is fantastic. And if you're good, the sky's the limit. You can be a network producer at thirty, at twenty-eight. But you have to be the right person. If someone comes in looking for a job and says 'What are the hours? Do you give benefits?' they're in the wrong business."

So You Want a Piece of the Action?

Hypothetically anyone can dream up a game show and present it to the networks. Because, however, of the financial risk involved to the networks, few if any amateurs get very far. Most packagers will not even consider an idea offered to them by an outsider, because, in the agitated words of one packager, "You could get sued! If someone mails me an idea, it goes back by return mail . . . unopened." If you would like to develop and own your own game show one day, realistically there are two ways:

1. Work your way up. You'll start at the bottom, as a production assistant, or go-fer, as they're called. The pay is low, perhaps $150 a week, but the opportunities for learning and advancement are wide open. Says one producer at golden Goodson-Todman, "Anybody who cares enough to keep trying, who keeps offering suggestions, will break through in this company."

2. Be the boss's kid. The following sons and daughters of game show producers are currently on the payroll of various packaging companies: Jonathan Goodson and Andrew Felsher at Goodson-Todman; Mae Quigley

and Peter Noah at Heatter-Quigley; Sande Stewart at Bob Stewart Productions; and Della Barris at Chuck Barris Productions.

In either case, be prepared. Game shows are not a particularly secure place to be. Your job may only last thirteen weeks. Even if your father *is* the boss.

The Killing of a Classic

Unlike the soaps, which the networks will often allow a full year to develop an audience, a game show has only thirteen weeks to pull the numbers. In daytime television, thirteen weeks can be a l-o-n-g time. Usually the handwriting is on the wall in three: that's when you can see the desperation seeping through the forced smile of the host.

If a game is ailing, sometimes the network will try to fix it. The rules of the game will be altered; sometimes the host will be replaced. Sometimes the game itself will vanish only to pop up in another time slot against weaker competition. But usually not: there are plenty of other games where that one came from, and if the public doesn't like this one, perhaps they will the next. And the public *is* the judge. There are on television no *succès d'estime,* no games are left on the air to be aesthetically admired by an elite few, a cabal of cognoscenti. A game makes it with the "masses" or it is yanked.

Only occasionally is a truly good game killed before its time. The show was the original *Jeopardy!* (see graph) a game that claimed the allegiance of college students everywhere. The original *Jeopardy!* ran for eleven years. It had been going well in the noon spot all during its run. Then, according to Carol Kramer, writing in The New York *News* Magazine on May 4, 1975.

"But its share dropped from 33 to 12," said Lin Bolen, then head of NBC daytime.

Just a minute. In 1973, its share at noon went from 33 to 29.

"I gave *Jeopardy!* a fair chance," said Bolen. "I moved it to two different time periods."

The first new time period was 10:30 A.M.

"*Jeopardy!* demands too much of the viewer. You can't put it on that early," said producer Bob Rubin.

Next she gave it the 1:30 slot, known familiarly to everyone in daytime television as the "graveyard." CBS is at that time running *As the World Turns,* the most popular serial on television. ABC was then running *Let's Make a Deal,* a top 20 show. *Jeopardy!*'s share at 10:30 was 22; at 1:30, it dropped to 12.

"She was playing the executive game," said Rubin. "She wanted to put her stamp on things. She needed a good slot for a pet project of hers."

Jeopardy! was killed at Christmas 1973. No daytime game on NBC has had ratings nearly so high since.

Share figures deleted at the request of A.C. Nielsen Company.

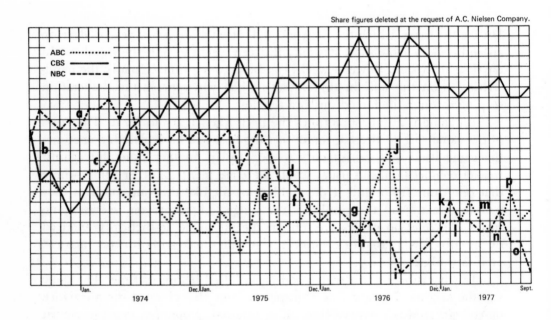

This graph tells a tragic tale: how, in 1973, NBC committed a fatal scheduling error, from which it has *never* recovered in its noon to twelve-thirty time slot. At the end of 1973, NBC decided to move *Jeopardy!* from the noon spot it had held for eleven years, to 10:30 A.M. The excuse was that the game had begun to slip a few share points; television insiders (see page 95), insist the real reason was that NBC's new head of daytime scheduling, Lin Bolen, wanted to introduce her new game, *Jackpot!* (a) NBC's timing couldn't have been worse: CBS had just launched a new soap opera, *The Young and the Restless.* (b) Although viewers initially balked at watching it and CBS's ratings dipped dangerously in the first quarter of 1974, *Jackpot!* was nowhere near as intellectually satisfying a game as *Jeopardy!* Disaffected game show fans shifted their allegiance to ABC, where *Password* (c) began to edge up a bit. But *Password* was old and tired. Dials across America began to turn again, this time to CBS. The ratings of *The Young and the Restless* began to climb. Indeed, CBS's rise was not even offset during the summer when vacationing school children, well known to prefer games to serials, showed obvious preference for *Password,* to the marked disadvantage of NBC.

While CBS maintained a steady hold, the two other networks began a frantic scheduling shuffle. NBC's new audience share continued to plummet into mid-1975. Its new game, *The Magnificent Marble Machine,* (d) proved to be a disaster, driving CBS's share to an unprecedented high. At the same time, ABC's *Show-offs,* (e) its *Password* replacement, attracted only a temporary following. Now in late 1975, NBC dipped below ABC, an alarming position from which it would be unable to rise. NBC desperately adjusted its schedule, switching its early morning show *High Rollers* (f) briefly to noon, then tried once more with *The Magnificent Marble Machine.* (g) In June of 1976, NBC tried *The Fun Factory* (h) then in October sank to an all-time low with *Fifty Grand Slam.* (i) ABC's *Hot Seat* (j) enjoyed a brief fling at NBC's expense, but the scuffling for second place continued when NBC temporarily rallied with *Name That Tune* (k) ABC countered with a variety show, *Don Ho,* (l) then pinned its hopes on a new Goodson-Todson game, *The Better Sex.* (p) While it was being readied, ABC aired a game called *Second Chance.* (m) NBC sank even lower when first *Shoot for the Stars* bombed, then *To Say the Least.* (o) Meanwhile, over at CBS, *The Young and the Restless,* now mature and sedate, settled into an unassailably commanding position of domination. Its audience share: only a little higher than *Jeopardy!*'s had been in 1973 before NBC made its fatal move.

Part Two

SIGN IN, PLEASE . . .

The Best, the Worst,
and the Rest

But First, There Was Radio . . .

A time before game shows? For that we must travel back to 1936, to the golden age of radio, when no home was without the huge wooden console in the parlor, the small Bakelite table model on the kitchen shelf or nightstand. There came that year a modest little show called *Uncle Jim's Question Bee*. "Uncle" Jim McWilliams, it seemed, simply invited members of the studio audience to approach the radio microphone, then rewarded them with cash for possessing the simplest of common wisdom, or lacking that, merely for being such good sports. Instantly dubbed a "quiz" show, the Uncle Jim program was diverting enough, nostalgically recalling the school room, and it proved popular enough to spawn two other McWilliams' quizzes, *Uncle Jim's Ask-It Basket* and *Correction, Please*. Nothing particularly earthshaking here. Then, hard on its heels, the very same year, came another even more popular question-and-answer show known as *Professor Quiz*. Up to the stage of a local movie house, located each week in a different city, would stride the plump, Oliver Hardyish professor, Craig Earl, posing an easy question and calling for a show of hands. The selected contestant would then join the professor up on stage and submit himself to a long circumlocutional exchange more reminiscent of the vaudeville hall than the classroom, before getting his chance to answer the question and collect a prize of five whole dollars. Soon all of America was tuning in to laugh, play along . . . and demand more.

There had been prototypes. Throughout the early thirties, *The Major Bowes Family Hour* and his *Original Amateur Hour* had brought members of the studio audience up on stage to participate in humorous interviews before taking part in a talent contest. Winners on the Major Bowes hours were determined by the spin of a wheel of fortune; losers dismissed with a gong. Assisting the Major had been a promising young vocalist named Belle "Bubbles" Silverman, later to be known professionally as Beverly Sills. There had been *Vox Pop*, a man-in-the-street (and factory) interview program dating back to 1932, that had thanked its participants with small merchandise gifts. Back in 1924, *Time* magazine had once sponsored a news quiz called *The Pop Question.* Local radio stations had long held contests to boost their ratings during their quarterly "sweeps," as radio stations still do today. For years, sponsors had staged jingle contests demanding from participants nothing more than a mountain of boxtops. But these two new shows marked the beginning of a coming avalanche, and for the next fifteen years, radio's most inventive producers would turn every form of radio programming they could think of, from the beloved big-band show, to the panel discussion, to the sportscast, the mystery hour, to the soap opera, into a prize-giving game, quiz, contest, or jackpot. By 1940, there would be more than fifty quizzes on the air; by the end of the decade nearly two hundred, some more memorable and permanent in impact than others. (For a full listing see pages 295–318.) And even as they proliferated on radio, a few experimental quizzes in the late thirties and pre-war forties, the pet projects of local college professors and teachers with access to NBC, CBS, and Du Mont-owned equipment, found their way onto a handful of primitive television sets. Though seen by few, the early television quizzes made a point not lost on early producers: the sight of contestants straining and exulting for prizes would translate well to the new medium.

But for now, the future was very much in radio, where producers at first seemed content to imitate *Professor Quiz.* Soon there were *Dr. Dollar, Colonel Stoopnagle, Professor Peter Puzzlewith,* with the pinnacle of the *Professor Quiz*-lookalike shows coming in 1939 with *Dr. I.Q.,* the "Mental Banker" with the jingle of silver dollars about him. Like *Professor Quiz, Dr. I.Q.* built a broad base of popularity by traveling to local theaters around the country for its broadcasts. But unlike its predecessor, contestants did not come up on stage to be quizzed by the Doctor, Lew Valentine. During *Dr. I.Q.*'s broadcasts, Valentine's assistants came to the contestants. Circulating about the theater with hand-held microphones, they would approach those with upraised hands. "Doctor, I have a gentleman in the balcony," an assistant would call. Then Dr. I.Q. would reply, "I have ten silver dollars for the gentleman if he can tell me the name of our third President." Winners collected their silver dollars on the spot to the sound of heavy clinking. In addition, each week, Dr. I.Q. offered a contestant a Biographical Sketch question mailed in by a listener at home. If a contestant could guess the identity of the mystery personnage from the first clue, he won seventy-five dollars. The size of the prize diminished with each subsequent clue, with the balance going to the author of the question. In addition, each week, Valentine offered a Memory Thought Twister

It's Professor Quiz, Craig Earl himself (center), transmitting one of America's first radio quizzes.

which the Doctor would say "one time and one time only," for the designated contestant to repeat. Besides Valentine, during the show's long run, there were two other Doctors, Jim McClain and Stanley Vainrib, and a *Dr. I.Q., Jr.,* for children. Mars Candy was the long-time sponsor of both shows which aired Monday nights over NBC.

Soon more innovative quizzes began to be heard. Bandleader Harry Salter's *Melody Puzzles* in 1937 was the first to add music. Then out of Chicago, in 1938, came a music quiz with an even more successful format, *Kay Kyser's Kollege of Musical Knowledge.* Essentially a showcase for Kyser's orchestra, the show also featured an instantly popular comedy quiz. Wearing a cap and gown, Kyser would administer questions to members of the audience during the "midterm" and "final exam" segments of the show. The questions were easy and Kyser's hints so broad that no one ever walked away empty-handed. Whenever a contestant (inevitably) answered correctly, Kyser would shout, "How'd he get that?" The show, which aired over NBC on Wednesday nights, enjoyed a fifteen-year run including a stint on television in the early fifties. Nineteen thirty-eight was the year as well of NBC's popular *True or False; Battle of the Sexes,* an early comedy panel game; and Mutual's *What's My Name?* the show which marked Arlene Francis' quiz show debut. The quiz show was here to stay. Even staid *Vox Pop* shifted its format. And still *Professor Quiz* continued to dominate the airwaves.

Nevertheless, not everybody that year found *Professor Quiz* amusing or the common practice of making fun of the contestants during the quiz-master's preliminary interview, certainly not one formidably independent producer named Dan Golenpaul. Offended by the low comedy of *Professor Quiz* and its imitators, in 1938 Golenpaul countered with a quiz of his own, which quickly proved to be one of the most intelligent, erudite, and entertaining programs ever on radio. *Information, Please* did not, as did the others, put the contestant on the spot. Instead, it called upon the home audience to mail in questions of their own device and try to stump a panel of experts which included book critic Clifton Fadiman, columnist Franklin P. Adams, and the show's most popular panelist, sports writer John Kieran, whose gravelly longshoreman's voice could wax particularly eloquent on the subjects of nature and poetry. "Wake up, America," the show would exhort each week as a rooster crowed in the background. "It's time to stump the experts." Stumping them wasn't easy, but when, infrequently, the panel was indeed buffaloed, home listeners heard the sound of a cash register, and the successful home questioner received a set of *The Encyclopaedia Britannica. Information, Please* aired for fourteen years, until 1952. Over the years, panelists came to include playwright Russel Crouse, pianist Oscar Levant, and historian Hendrik Willem van Loon, Though it was unsuccessful on early television, *Information, Please* influenced the look and content of every television panel game and quiz throughout the fifties.

Information, Please was influential in another way. It impressed upon all prospective producers of the day the importance of a producer's controlling his own show. Dan Golenpaul owned *Information, Please,* and he ran the program his way, with integrity, and without meddling from sponsors. At the time, radio programs came onto the air two ways: either they were underwritten by one single, very much involved advertiser or they were self-"sustaining," in which case, the show's owner-producer assumed its costs. Because at first advertisers considered *Information, Please* too intellectual for the average listener, Golenpaul himself paid the show's expenses. Luckily for his bank account, *Information, Please* immediately claimed large ratings: the very first week it aired, 25,000 listeners mailed in questions. Still, it continued sponsorless for the first year until it was "discovered" by a member of the board of the Canada Dry Ginger-Ale Company on a business trip to Syracuse. To his amazement, when the local NBC station pre-empted the show by airing the Minor League World Series, thousands of local residents that evening angrily jammed the switchboard in protest. Suitably impressed, Canada Dry hastily signed the program, cheerfully paid its expenses, and had the wisdom to grant Golenpaul complete autonomy, enjoying in exchange a healthy boost in sales. When, however, Canada Dry could no longer afford Golenpaul's asking price, *Information, Please* reluctantly took a new sponsor, the Reynolds Tobacco Company. Reynolds swiftly ran afoul of Golenpaul when they first tried to dictate that panelists smoke its brand of cigarette, then tried to foist on the country a series of irritating and obviously untruthful commercials. Finally, in 1943, in a gesture that made him a national hero, Golenpaul fired his sponsor. The message was not lost on many a would-be producer waiting in the wings.

One such producer was Ed Byron. Already successful in 1939 with *What's My Name?* Byron reasoned that if the sound of silver dollars, roosters, and cash registers could boost listenership, perhaps the sound of the telephone could be even more mesmerizing; and his new show, *Pot O' Gold,* the first quiz with a cumulative jackpot, proved mesmerizing indeed. While the orchestra of Horace Heidt and his Musical Knights played a popular tune, the show placed a call to "some lucky person somewhere in America." If the contestant could answer a question correctly, he or she won all the money that had been accumulating in the pot since the last correct answer. Sometimes the pot held as much as $100,000. Rush Hughes was *Pot O' Gold*'s first announcer, but his successor, Ben Grauer, coined the phrase that entered the language so completely it actually became the name of *Pot O' Gold*'s biggest rival ten years later. "Hold it, Horace," Grauer would shout. "I've got an answer. Stop the music!" *Pot O' Gold* proved so popular that in its heyday, movie theaters tried to combat droop-

This expert doesn't look stumped. Clifton Fadiman's moderating John Kieran and F.P.A. (Franklin Adams) on one of America's most beloved radio quizzes, *Information, Please.*

ing attendance on the night it aired by promising to match the *Pot O' Gold* jackpot should a patron subsequently learn he had been at the movies when the show called his home. A safe bet: the odds against a given person's being called, let alone winning, were one in twenty-eight million.

For a time it looked as if nothing would stem the jackpot craze created by *Pot O' Gold* and its dozens of imitators. In 1940, however, the Federal Communications Commission raised the question of just how sacrosanct a producer might actually be, especially if it could be shown that the jackpots actually constituted a form of illegal gambling. Government test cases clouded the horizon for both quiz show producers and networks alike, until 1954, when the Supreme Court finally ruled that tuning into a quiz did not constitute wagering no matter how high the stakes. Still, to protect itself, *Pot O' Gold* had Grauer take special precautions whenever he reached a contestant. If a child answered the phone, Grauer could not ask to speak to the head of the household; such soliciting would imply that participation in the quiz was not voluntary.

Despite such limitations, listener and sponsor enthusiasm for quiz shows showed no sign of cresting. Thirty new quizzes bowed in 1940, including a handful so brilliant that special phrases from them have permanently entered our vocabularies. Nineteen forty marked the year, for example, that advertising executive Milton Biow created a quiz for his sponsor, Eversharp Pencils. The quiz was called *Take It or Leave It,* and it posed "the sixty-four-dollar question." *Take It or Leave It* started off with "the two-dollar question," then asked four more. With each question the stakes doubled. At each level a contestant could take his money and quit. But if he missed even one question, he left with nothing, a consequence repeatedly impressed upon the contestant by *Take It or Leave It*'s beloved master of ceremonies, accordion-playing comedian Phil Baker. *Could* a given contestant answer the two-, four-, eight-, sixteen-, thirty-two-, and sixty-four-dollar questions without missing? Would he choose to? This dramatic dilemma, more than the actual questions themselves, commanded faithful listeners for the next ten years as the show ran through five other quizmasters, including Bob Hawk, Tom Breneman, Garry Moore, Jack Paar, and Eddie Cantor.

Still, good ideas for quiz shows did not just happen to men lucky enough to own an advertising agency, and in 1940 in New York City, a tall, blond Californian named Ralph Edwards was just about to prove it. A farm boy from Merino, Colorado, who had grown up in Oakland, California, Edwards first broke into radio in 1930, while he was still a senior in high school, with his own local quarter-hour program. Even then, he had begun to dabble in the contests that would make him world famous: he ran a "Name the black goat" contest, playing the part of the goat himself. Edwards graduated from the University of California at Berkeley and Merritt Business College, and then in 1935, took a job at local station KFRC in San Francisco. Nonetheless, it was not radio but the lure of the Broadway stage that initially drew him East, and when a friend promised him a role in a play, Edwards, then twenty-three, borrowed a hundred dollars to make the trip. When he arrived, the show had already closed and Edwards, down to his last quarter, found himself among seventy other hopefuls auditioning for an announcing job at CBS. Not only did Edwards land the job, he quickly became the number-one announcer in radio. During one time, his voice could be heard over forty-five shows a week, including soap operas and even Byron's *What My Name?* "I was running from studio to studio with seconds to spare between programs," he recalls. "It was no way to live. I thought that if I could develop my own program, sell something to the networks that was mine, I could get out from under a little." Edwards tried a couple of abortive ideas for radio dramas on Proctor and Gamble, the sponsor of the serials he announced. Then he had another, totally different idea, based upon a game he had played as a child, "Heavy, heavy, hangs over thy head." Ralph Edwards' future show, *Truth or Consequences,* would become one of the most successful programs in the history of broadcasting and make Edwards one of its wealthiest men.

Initially, Edwards conceived his program as a serious quiz. But before long, when it swiftly became clear that the contestants wanted to pay the consequences, Edwards quickly metamorphosed the quiz questions into jokes impossible to answer correctly: "Three water glasses are on a shelf. Two are filled with champagne. What famous king does that remind you of?" Answer: "Philip the Third." When couples did not know the answer to the question in the required time ("Shhh! No snitching in the audience"), they would hear from "Beulah the Buzzer," whereupon, their good sportsmanship would then be tested if not by fire, then certainly by a good deal of water and whipped cream. "Aren't we devils?" Edwards would ask.

Had *Truth or Consequences* been content to play little measly practical jokes, its novelty might soon have worn off. The show's staying power, however, was due equally to its capacity to be angelic. One night in 1941, for example, Edwards singled out of the audience an out-of-work secretary, and during the course of the show, transformed her into a "princess," complete with new dress, a mink coat, new shoes, a new hairdo, glamorous make-up, and a handsome "prince," an officer in the National Guard assigned to escort her from the NBC studios to a ball at the Armory. Before allowing her to step out into the night, Edwards announced, "Unlike the real Cinderella, the clothes you are wearing will not turn to rags at the stroke of midnight. The dress, mink coat, and everything else belongs to you. Furthermore, if you will appear at the address on the card now being given to you, a job will be waiting Monday morning." With this famous "Cinderella stunt," Ralph Edwards had unwittingly, prophetically, tapped one of the most important elements of all good game shows, the chance to have your dream come true.

But New York in 1940 was not the only place for budding radio producers to gravitate. In Chicago that year, a young man named Louis G. Cowan had already begun to pull the strings that fifteen years later would lead him to buy *Take It or Leave It* from Milton Biow, escalate its sixty-four-dollar stakes into $64,000, and catapult himself into the presidency of CBS. But Cowan was a man dogged by a painful, even tragic, irony. Blessed with a sharply felt social conscience, over the years, he would make some fifty serious radio and television documentaries on democracy, racial harmony, and the importance of education. They would flop. But when it came to glib little quizzes, he ruefully had to concede, he had the Midas touch. Born into money, the tall man with the lulling voice excelled academically, then rapidly displayed an even greater flair for communications. Graduating from the University of Chicago with a degree in philosophy, Cowan's first job was for the public relations firm that handled the Kay Kyser show. He found the time as well to volunteer his pubic relations acumen to the Salvation Army, Hull House, and the Methodist Episcopal Church.

Cowan's first quiz show was *Quiz Kids,* an immediate hit that featured exceptional children answering exceptionally difficult questions. Cowan co-owned the show with ex-*Time* magazine correspondent John Llewellyn. It would run for fourteen years in all, on both radio and TV. Cowan's wife, Polly, dreamed up the name one night at dinner. The show, rooted in Cowan's idealism, was meant to stimulate American children to do well in school. During one segment, the Quiz Kids, wearing academic caps and gowns, paid their respects to "the teacher who helped me the most," and called special attention to the low pay teachers received. Do-good sentiments aside, Cowan fully understood that to stay on the air, a show had to be entertaining. Quizmaster Joe Kelly was chosen with care to play the quintessential "adult," easily baffled but respectful, warm, and friendly. Questions on *Quiz Kids* were difficult: "I want you to tell me what I would be carrying home if I brought an antimacassar, a dinghy, a sarong, and an apteryx," was the first question asked on the première show. Still, to guarantee ratings and keep sponsor Alka-Seltzer happy, Cowan and Llewellyn took precautions. Even though the children were the mental prodigies of their generation, the Quiz Kids were coached before the show to make sure they did well. Such precautions would become a hallmark of all future Lou Cowan productions.

Men like Byron, Biow, Edwards, and Cowan could not have entered radio at a more opportune time. For with the coming of war in 1941, the proliferation of quiz shows abruptly ceased. Throughout the war, until V-J Day in August of 1945, the federal government would control the nation's airwaves, and quiz shows, freely using open microphones as they did, fell under especially tight jurisdiction. All telephone jackpot games, already subjects for possible Federal prosecution, vanished. And so did all television broadcasting, with the exception of the Du Mont network's. Producers and announcers went off to war, including Louis Cowan, who was picked by Elmo Roper to head the New York Office of War Information, an organization that after the war would become Radio Free Europe.

Whatever quizzes and games did remain during the war years patriotically altered their formats, even bending the questions a bit when the contestant was a serviceman or woman. Quizzes called *Yankee Doodle Quiz* and *Thanks to the Yanks* came into being. On *Singo,* a show in which contestants wove three song titles into a story, each contestant had to include the name of a serviceman or woman with whom he would divide his four-dollar prize. On *Beat the Band,* if a question did indeed beat the band, its members had to "throw a pack of cigarettes on the old bass drum for the men in the service overseas." On *Blind Date,* servicemen won an evening on the town. There was even a wartime movie featuring a quiz show's generosity to a serviceman; named after the quiz and even featuring emcee Phil Baker, in *Take It or Leave It,* a young serviceman got to marry his girl after he answered the sixty-four-dollar question.

No show, however, did more for the American war effort than *Truth or Consequences.* Every week throughout the war, the show dreamed up stunts that enlisted its listeners into patriotic service. On one occasion, it had listeners each mail a penny to the mother of a Marine fighting overseas who was then required to buy war bonds with the contributions. Three hundred thirty-thousand pennies poured in, which the show turned over to the government's copper drive. Before the war was over, *Truth or Consequences* would be responsible for selling half a billion dollars in war bonds. Another stunt mobilized school children to collect waste paper; the resulting tons singlehandedly ended the country's wartime paper shortage. But the most famous of all of its wartime stunts was the *Truth or Consequences* Victory Book Campaign, staged to provide needed recreational reading for servicemen. Seventeen thousand books arrived in the mail at the home of one contestant, sent by listeners for him to hunt through in his

Quiz Kid little Naomi Cooks.

search for the one in which the show had hidden a hundred dollars and the text of Winston Churchill's "blood, toil, tears and sweat" speech.

Though the airwaves were restricted during the war, there was none-theless room for a few new quizzes. Nineteen forty-two, for example, saw the debut of *It Pays to Be Ignorant*. First heard in June 1942 on New York's local station WOR, this fully scripted comedy program parodied the quiz show as three panelists, George Shelton, Lulu McConnell, and Harry McNaughton repeatedly exasperated quizmaster Tom Howard with their dogged failure to come to grips with such obvious questions as "What color is a white horse?" and "Which player on a baseball team wears the catcher's mask?" *It Pays to Be Ignorant* moved to network radio and was first heard over CBS, later NBC, and then had a short stay on early television. *Quick as a Flash,* the first show to use bells, buzzers, and flashing lights, also bowed during the war, as did *Grand Slam, Quizzer Baseball,* and *Detect and Collect.* But for all practical purposes, on the East Coast anyway, the great quiz show avalanche had stilled.

Out in Los Angeles, on the other hand, things had never been better, at least for one creative young advertising man named John Guedel. A man with a penchant for persuasive letter writing and a charming capacity never to take "no" for an answer, Guedel had already made a modest mark writing scripts for Laurel and Hardy, and he had invented the singing commercial. Then, as luck would have it, while others pined for a show to call their own, one day, thanks to one of his advertising accounts, the Wilshire Oil Company, a show just fell into Guedel's lap. The show was a local traffic quiz called *Pull Over, Neighbor.* Guedel tossed out the driver's manual questions and substituted a few parlor games cribbed from a library book. Though it was weak in format, *Pull Over, Neighbor* had strong ratings because it was fortuitously scheduled between *Information, Please* and the NBC Sunday-night run of comedy blockbuster shows, *Fibber McGee and Molly, Bob Hope,* and *The Red Skelton Show.* Still, Guedel was smart enough to see that with the right personality hosting it, his show could grow beyond such silliness as having contestants try to sing with a mouthful of ice cubes. Guedel's second piece of wartime good fortune happened in 1942, when he met an extraordinarily likable young radio interviewer named Art Linkletter, who was then doing a show from a hotel lobby in San Francisco. Together with Art Baker, the original emcee of *Pull Over, Neighbor,* they made an audition record, changing the original name of their show to the catchier *People Are Funny.*

That all four radio networks turned it down did not deter Guedel (such things never did). When he read in *Variety* that the government had given a program called *Captain Flagg and Sergeant Quirt* one week in which to leave the air because it threatened public morale, (showing as it did officers socializing with enlisted men,) Guedel sent the pilot record and a telegram to the show's advertising agency. "I have the answer to your problem," he wrote. The desperate sponsors agreed. *People Are Funny* went on the air the same week and remained for the next nineteen years.

Nor was this Guedel's only wartime coup. Two years later, he sold a second show called *House Party* to an otherwise reluctant sponsor. "Turn it down?" he railed. "You can use my show to sell women new appliances 'for every room in the house.'" General Electric instantly saw the merit in the idea, and the new Guedel-Linkletter bonanza, shrewdly re-named General Electric *House Party,* remained on the air for the next twenty-six years. Three years after that, Guedel would score yet another time with a radio show starring Groucho Marx called *You Bet Your Life*. More about all three anon.

But Guedel's wartime success proved exceptional. Up in San Francisco opportunities in radio were so bad for a young radio announcer named Mark Goodson that in 1941, he pulled up stakes and headed for New York City, where it would take him the next five years to sell his first show. Luckily for the future of game shows, however, Mark Goodson had that special motivation to succeed that often drives those who start out in life poor. Goodson's father had held a progression of jobs: he had been a some-time masseur, the owner of a chicken ranch in Haywood, California, and the proprietor of a health food store. All had failed. It had been the Goodson family's goal that young Mark make good as a lawyer, and to that end he had graduated Phi Beta Kappa in economics from the University of California at Berkeley. The lure however of the Berkeley campus radio station, where the tall shadow of Ralph Edwards still lingered, proved stronger. In college, Goodson had his own show, a modest quiz called *Pop the Question,* which consisted of contestants throwing darts at colored balloons on a board. Wearing a dinner jacket, he broadcasted the show from the basement of San Francisco's TeleNews Theater. When Mark Goodson came East, resourcefully, he had looked up Ralph Edwards, who had done what he could, setting up interviews with Walter Wade of Wade Advertising and John McMillen at the Compton Agency.

More receptive than they, however, to Mark Goodson's quiz show proposals was a junior copywriter named William Todman who was working for Milton Biow. Bill Todman was Goodson's complete opposite. Raised on New York's Park Avenue, Todman came from a family as wealthy as Goodson's was poor. He had attended private schools and taken pre-med courses at Johns Hopkins University. His hobbies were a rich man's: hunting, fishing, and riding, and, some have hinted, an enormous capacity for whiskey. Fond of solid-gold accessories (he carried a gold pen, a gold lighter, and a gold stopwatch), Todman also dabbled at writing and had seen his stories published in *Redbook*. He would soon prove to be more than a dilettante, however. For William Todman was a confident, hypnotic salesman as well, impervious to the objections of sponsors and network middlemen. Together, the ambitious newcomer and the fledgling adman reworked the details for a show called *Winner Take All,* the idea for which Goodson had brought with him from California. Even then, Goodson displayed the creative flair, while Todman played the role of devil's advocate and financial logistician. But that had been in 1941, and when *Winner Take All* hadn't sold, the two had gone their separate ways.

Goodson hadn't starved those first five years in New York—he was radio's Answer Man, then the director of soap operas: *Portia Faces Life, Just Plain Bill,* and *Appointment with Life.* He wrote and directed spots on the *Kate Smith Show.* But whenever he'd brought up *Winner Take All* to the executives he met, he would be turned down cold. "You're not a quiz man," the director of *Take It or Leave It* flatly told him. The closest Goodson could get to the world of games in which he eventually would make his fortune came when he hosted the local New York Jack Dempsey sports quiz. Not even *that* had been easy: knowing nothing whatever about sports, Goodson, had had to go out and buy *The Rules of Baseball.*

At last the war was over, and with the airwaves clear again for quizzes, a whole new crop of producers appeared. Indeed, in 1945, some were so hungry if necessary they would even work in television. That was hungry. In 1945, there were fewer than a thousand primitive video receivers in the entire country offering wrestling, telephone bingo, and cooking demonstrations. If you didn't mind working around those, or a kiddie puppet show called *Howdy Doody,* air time was there for the taking. Dennis James (born Demis James Sposa) had been telecasting over the Du Mont network since 1941. By the mid-forties his show, *Okay, Mother,* filled the daytime hours. Minnesota-born Johnny Olson and his wife, Penny, weren't too proud for television either. Their long-running housewife show, *Ladies Be Seated,* broadcast simultaneously on both ABC radio and TV in 1945.

Other newcomers found radio more hospitable. In 1945, a young writer from Pittsburgh named Walt Framer helped shape the fortunes of two of the first big post-war radio quiz shows, *Break the Bank* and *Double or Nothing,* gaining there the experience he'd need two years later to launch his own radio show, the notorious *Strike It Rich.* The following year, a young writer on the *Uncle Don's Children's Show* named Jack Barry and his new partner Dan (born Ehrenreich) Enright, who had worked on *Quiz of Two Cities,* sold their first show, a comedy panel discussion program for

Accordion-playing Phil Baker has a $64 war bond for some lucky sailor on *Take It or Leave It.*

children called *Juvenile Jury*. Two years later, they reversed their formula with a second successful show, a panel for oldsters called *Life Begins at Eighty*. The pair would soon bring their unlikely properties to television, then produce two more generation-linked shows, *Winky Dink and You* and *Wisdom of the Ages* before they launched a series of brilliant but corruption-tainted television quizzes in the mid-fifties, *Dough Re Mi, Tic Tac Dough,* and *Twenty-One*.

Things had improved so much by 1946 that Mark Goodson and Bill Todman finally sold *Winner Take All*, and then quickly, four more locally aired quizzes, *Hit the Jackpot, Spin to Win, Rate Your Mate,* and *Time's A'Wastin'*. It was still only a modest beginning for the two, crammed as they were into a tiny office at CBS stacked high with whatever merchandise they could finagle. Every time they broadcast, Goodson and Todman had to bodily cart the prizes from their cluttered cubicle down to the studio. One time, scurrying to a show, Todman stumbled, sending percolators and toasters flying. Comedy writer Goodman Ace chanced to witness the mishap. "Hey, Todman, you dropped your script," he cracked.

If it was easy for newcomers to stumble, it was even easier for them to be trampled by the sudden revival in interest in the lavish radio jackpot. Now that rationing was over, there were real prizes to give away again, not just cartons of cigarettes and savings bonds. Now there were nylons, refrigerators, ranges, freezers, wristwatches, and shiny new cars. Old jackpot shows like *Pot O' Gold* came out of mothballs to dispense them and were joined by newer shows with names like *Heart's Desire, Hope Chest,* and *Queen for a Day*. Over the next three years, the largesse of some forty of these new "giveaways" would total $150,000 a week.

Critics of the new postwar breed of quiz, and there were many, pointed an accusing finger at Ralph Edwards. Hadn't he started it all with the Cinderella stunt? Well, then, Edwards announced, if he had unwittingly started it, then he would have to end it "once and for all." To show the American public how ridiculously venal it had become, Edwards announced on *Truth or Consequences* that he was staging the giveaway stunt to end all giveaway stunts. Instead of a jackpot, Edwards proclaimed, his stunt would have a "crackpot," which he proceeded to fill with mink coats, automobiles, houses, personal maid service, airplanes. Listeners could win it, he announced, if they could simply phone in each week to tell him the identity of the mystery celebrity he called Mr. Hush. Each week, Mister Hush would read a cryptic clue, and for each week that his identity remained a mystery, three more gigantic prizes were added to the crackpot. To make matters more interesting, during the show when the phone lines were open,

Edwards took special pains to wring every drop of suspense from his obviously frantic callers: "You say Mister Hush is John Wayne?" he'd purr. "You say Mister Hush is John Wayne!". . . No, I'm sorry, Mrs. Jones, John Wayne is not Mister Hush, but thank you for your entry."

Despite Edwards' avowed intentions, few people regarded the Mr. Hush contest as a joke. They began to pour into Los Angeles, where *Truth or Consequences* was broadcast, hoping to catch a glimpse of the mysterious celebrity during the show. The furor over the contest grew so intense that when a navy lieutenant from Fayetteville, Arkansas, finally identified Mr. Hush as Jack Dempsey, rather than abandon the contests as he had originally promised, Edwards felt now compelled to channel the public's energies to more charitable ends. From here on, he announced to participate in the Mrs. (Clara Bow) Hush, Miss (Martha Graham) Hush, Mr. and Mrs. (Moss Hart and Kitty Carlisle) Hush, and Mama and Papa (dancers Velez and Yolanda) Hush contests, listeners had first to submit a twenty-five-word sentence telling "Why we should all support the March of Dimes, the Arthritis Foundation, the American Cancer Society, or the Mental Health Foundation, as well as pledge donations to them. The *Truth or Consequences* contests ran through 1948. In the last of them, before it was finally guessed that Jack Benny was "The Walking Man," the show had raised over $1,639,000 to start the American Heart Association.

The nation's hunger for bigger and bigger jackpots was far from sated. To accommodate it in the summer of 1948, there came yet another, the biggest and overwhelming radio giveaway yet, a show called *Stop the Music. Stop the Music* was emceed by Bert Parks, a man who once described the secret of his success: "I never walk when I can run; I never sit when I can stand; I never talk when I can shout." If the prizes in the *Truth or Consequences*' "crackpot" had been staggering, those offered by *Stop the Music* far eclipsed them: a two-week uranium-prospecting tour, a furnished four-room bungalow, a Hollywood screen test, and more—all to the lucky caller who could supply the correct title to the mystery tune hummed by vocalists Kay Armen and Dick Brown. The ratings of *Stop the Music* soared by the end of summer to kill the once-popular longtime comedy classic of radio, the *Fred Allen Show*. "If I were king for one day," said Allen, "I would make every program a giveaway show; when the studios were filled with the people who encourage these atrocities, I would lock the door. With all the morons of America trapped, the rest of the population could go about its business."

Stop the Music was the property of Louis G. Cowan, his first major program since before the war. But he had not conceived it, in fact, at first, he wasn't even interested. Back from his post at the Office of War Information, Cowan was more interested in loftier matters, in making his documentaries, working on the Henry Wallace presidential campaign, in getting black people jobs in broadcasting. Rather, *Stop the Music* had come to Cowan unsolicited in the form of a pilot record based upon an already unsuccessful CBS show bandleader Harry Salter had briefly aired the year before. Salter still liked the concept—a jackpot based on popular music. So did a young man named Howard Connell, who'd further shared the idea with Mark Goodson. Well versed in the difficulties outsiders face in gaining network attention, Goodson had brought the property to Cowan, who grudgingly recognized a hit. "I'll buy it," he'd said to Goodson. "I'll produce it. But only if you do it my way." Cowan then made a very advantageous financial arrangement for himself. Mark Goodson would direct the show and his wife, Bluma, who, Cowan noted, had a knack for such things, would be responsible for acquiring the show's merchandise.

Stop the Music became a post-war phenomenon. It ran over ABC for an unprecedented hour. Its sponsorship was innovative as well: for the first time advertisers bought time in quarter-hour segments. But its success, though intense, was brief, for *Stop the Music*—and all the jackpots—represented not the beginning but an end. Television, it was becoming clear by now was here to stay and no further efforts at bribing audiences into listening could change that.

Certainly *Stop the Music* marked a turning point for Goodson, who hadn't liked the experience of working on it. Even today, his lip curls at the artificial, now illegal, steps Cowan took to boost his ratings. Each week, to fire up listener interest, the show would plant the answers to that week's mystery tune in Walter Winchell's column. Guest celebrities, seemingly participating spontaneously, were paid fees to appear, their casual chitchat carefully scripted. And during a broadcast, when the telephone calls came pouring in, *Stop the Music* would screen them first, then deliberately stack them in a dramatic order: five, ten incorrect answers first, to build listener suspense before Bert Parks was allowed to shout the correct answer to a white-knuckled, rapt America.

Even if one's own show were a mishmash like *Winner Take All,* it was still better than this alternative. Goodson acted now to legally cement his partnership with William Todman, and never again worked for anyone else. Together they would head into the uncharted waters of television.

Television would be different, and anyone who tried it would have a lot to learn. Radio allowed for loopholes; what was unseen could be left unfinished to be filled in by the listener's imagination. Too, radio was a medium of anticipation, of awaiting the inevitable: the crash in Fibber McGee's closet, Jack Benny's pregnant pauses, the jingle of Dr. I.Q.'s silver dollars, the gales of laughter on *Truth or Consequences,* the cash register and that rooster on *Information, Please.* Television would be the opposite, its parameters narrowly defined by what the eye took in. To work, a TV game would have to be made very, very simple, to fit inside the screen. It would have to function without a single loose end. Only then could *its* particular brand of imaginativeness work; for if radio dealt in the inevitable, TV dealt in the surprise. Within that miniature world would have to be unguessable variables, a multiplicity of thicknesses and textures, conflicts, and dilemmas so agonizing and suspenseful that the viewer would spontaneously assist in their solution. Over the next thirty years, more than seven hundred games would try—games whose titles posed questions to the viewer and familiarly called him "you," that slapped him on the back with homey maxims and clichés, that promised him companionship, action, and fun, that, above all, coaxed him over and over to participate. Forty of them would succeed, one fourth of them the games of Goodson-Todman.

The Best TV Games
of the Forties

In the beginning, there was chaos . . . and a lot of empty air time to fill. Anybody with a half-baked idea did game shows. Mercifully, most of them came and went after just one airing. Still, they weren't *all* dreadful. There was *Auction-aire,* an early prototype for *The Price Is Right* and *Blind Date* with Arlene Francis, a show that twenty years later Chuck Barris would camp up and rename *The Dating Game.* Pretty soon radio producers began to hedge their bets by simulcasting shows in both media. Louis G. Cowan did with *Quiz Kids, Stop the Music,* and *What's My Name?* It was sobering to see how many of radio's biggest hits failed. Then there were *these* early games that took to TV like ducks to water.

1. Winner Take All

It was the forerunner of the modern television game show. Embarrassingly primitive by today's standards, requiring as it did two contestants to vie for merchandise prizes by answering questions based on songs and sketches they had just witnessed, its creator Mark Goodson freely acknowledged, "We made our first mistakes on the show, ones that everyone makes who first gets into television. We tried too hard to dramatize, to make the game 'visual.' We had questions about pictures; we paraded models and dogs around the stage. We had yet to learn that what's interesting on television is not appearance but *content*."

Goodson-Todman got all their mistakes out of the way on this, their television debut. Bud Collyer's overseeing the fun.

Nonetheless, *Winner Take All* would permanently influence the structure of all future TV games. It was the first contest to employ a "lock-out device": whichever contestant buzzed in first automatically shut the other out. That created drama and suspense. *Winner Take All* was also the first game show to create "the champion," a winning contestant viewers could identify with and follow until he was unseated.

Already airing on radio since 1946, along with such now-forgotten Goodson-Todman shows as *Spin to Win* and *Hit the Jackpot, Winner Take All* first came to television over CBS on June 15, 1948, and would run until October 3, 1950, switching from prime time to daytime as its ratings sagged.

Bill Cullen marked his television debut as the host, assisted by Sheila Connolly and the incomparable Dolores "Roxanne" Rosedale. Betty Jones Watson, Jerry Austen, and Howard Malone provided the entertainment. In 1952, the show would enjoy a brief revival on NBC, hosted by New York radio personality Barry Gray.

2. Pantomine Quiz

Charade shows seemed tailor-made for pre-network television. In New York alone, thanks to its large pool of available actors, there was *Act It Out,* emceed by Bill Cullen; *Charade Quiz,* emceed by Bill Slater; *Say It with Acting,* emceed by Bill Berns, Maggie McNellis, and Bud Collyer, which each week pitted the casts of Broadway plays against each other in a charade contest; and *What Happens Now?* featuring such unknown actors as Jack Lemmon and Cloris Leachman.

"You got it!" That's earnest Glenn Gangan struggling to get through to Mercedes McCambridge, Richard New, and Anita Louise while rivals Hans Conried, Frank deVol, and someone's back observe. Note the old clock on the wall.

None would leave a mark but one lone West Coast offering. From the time *Pantomime Quiz* first appeared on network television over CBS in 1949, you knew it was different. For one thing, the actors playing the parlor game were not the down-and-out sort looking for work or those out pushing their latest play. They were big-name Hollywood movie stars, "big-enough-name" in fact to play the game for fun. And they played it hard, creating there right before your eyes the now familiar signals such as "number of syllables," "past tense," "quote," "gag saying," "sounds like," "little word," "stretch out," and "cut down." Soon it seemed as if no challenge, no matter how abstract or strange, could best them.

Pantomime Quiz was played by two teams of three players each, one the home team, the other, the visitors. The object of the game was to convey wordlessly a title or common expression mailed in by a home viewer. Each team member got a turn. At the end of the show, the team with the most points won. Host and owner Mike Stokey officiated. An instant TV success, *Pantomime Quiz* would be the first game show to win an Emmy, in 1949, and for the next eleven years, it would reign as the unchallenged summer replacement champ of television.

Pantomime Quiz did not begin life as one of the first major network programs. It first came to television locally in Los Angeles in the best of "show biz" traditions: when an actress scheduled to star on another show became ill and could not "go on," Los Angeles station KTLA gave "understudy" Stokey, then a drama school graduate from UCLA, thirty-six hours in which to come up with a replacement. Stokey recruited from around town six other drama students, among them Roddy McDowall. The night in 1947 that *Pantomime Quiz* first aired, many movie stars in nearby Hollywood were watching. The next day, Jack Webb, Lucille Ball, Steve Allen, and Danny Thomas called Stokey to ask if they could be included the following week. Hollywood's biggest stars became regular participants, a turn of events that made it most palatable for CBS to pick up the show for national viewing two years later.

Other early stars on *Pantomime Quiz* included Hans Conried, Jackie Coogan, Coleen Gray, Robert Stack, Morey Amsterdam, Una Merkel, Beverly Garland, Vincent Price, Eve Arden, and Joan Davis. Later arrivals to its ranks were Howard Morris, Carol Burnett, Dorothy Hart, Stubby Kaye, Tom Poston, and Milt Kamen.

Pantomine Quiz would air over CBS irregularly throughout the early fifties. It would be seen over ABC in 1955 and again in 1958 and 1959. In its later years, between 1962 and 1963, it again ran over CBS known as *Stump the Stars*. Stokey hosted throughout. Especially fondly remembered on the show: the night Buster Keaton did his deadpan interpretation of "The Face on the Barroom Floor."

Other Act-It-Out Games

Follow the Leader with Vera Vague, seen over CBS during the summer of 1953

Celebrity Charades, emceed by Jay Johnson, syndicated in 1979

It's Your Move, emceed by Jim Perry, seen over ABC during the fall of 1967

The Rube Goldberg Show, seen locally in New York over WPIX-TV in 1948

Who Knows? with Chet Huntley and panel, seen over ABC in 1952

Your Lucky Clue with Basil Rathbone, seen over CBS during the summer of 1952

3. Break the Bank

To say it owed its great success on early TV to its former life on radio is not to appreciate how many other popular radio quizzes flopped when they tried to make the transition. *Dr. I.Q.* did, and so did *Information, Please, Quick as a Flash,* and *Truth or Consequences,* while other shows like *Stop the Music* and *Quiz Kids* were only marginally successful.

Some of the reason for *Break the Bank*'s TV triumph lay in its host Bert Parks, still riding the crest of his huge summer of 1948 radio hit, *Stop the Music* when *Break the Bank* first came to television that fall. It was lucky that Marshall McLuhan had not yet announced that TV was a cool medium, for cool Bert Parks most definitely was not. It was a freneticism that would eventually come to grate on audiences, but now, while television was still a novelty, the sight of Parks's slicked-down hair and his large, mobile face, his brash friendliness and his loud, boundless energy, drew large numbers of viewers.

Even without Bert Parks, however, *Break the Bank* would have been a hit, structured as it was to build maximum suspense with a huge jackpot awaiting its winners. *Break the Bank* was played by a team of two contestants who had, before the show, selected one of its eight categories. Couples then had to answer correctly eight questions worth five dollars each to reach "the gateway to the bank," as the jackpot was known. To in-

Bert Parks, emcee of the quiz that's survived everything.

Here it is again in the seventies, chock-full of your favorite celebs.

crease the tension, contestants could miss a question without being disqualified, but if they missed two in a row, they were automatically eliminated and the money they had accumulated was taken away and added to
"the bank." Losers left the show with a consolation prize of five dollars.
Answering all eight questions correctly, however, netted a couple five
hundred dollars. Now, if they could answer one final, much more difficult
question from their designated category, they could "break the bank" and
win the entire, often very handsome jackpot.

Even becoming a contestant on *Break the Bank* was suspenseful. Because of its popularity, hopeful contestants waited months for tickets. Before airtime, producer Walt Framer would select fifteen possible couples
from the studio audience. Of these, only five ever made it onto the air.
Once contestants had gotten that close, some, at least, were willing to go to
extreme lengths to insure themselves a berth. One night, a young couple,
obviously very much in love, approached Framer as he surveyed the audi-

ence. "Please pick us," they begged. "We need the money desperately to buy furniture so we can get married. Holding hands, gazing into each other's eyes, the young lovers were so irresistible that Framer gave them the nod. Together on the show, they won four thousand dollars. Then, money safely in hand, they confessed: they had only just met that night outside the studio. To others, getting on the show was as easy as pie. One night a little girl slipped away from her mother and ran up on stage. When her embarrassed mother pursued her, Bert Parks spontaneously invited the woman to participate and she won a $13,000 jackpot.

Break the Bank first aired in 1945 over the Mutual network. Its original emcee was John Reed King, who was later succeeded by Johnny Olson. Writers for the show were Joseph Kane, who would later edit a large compendium of trivia called *Famous First Facts,* Jack Rubin, also the show's director, and Walt Framer. The show's orchestra was directed by Peter Van Sleeden. *Break the Bank* made its television debut over ABC on October 22, 1948, and ran on ABC until September 23, 1949. NBC then acquired the show in October of that year, airing it through 1953. Clayton "Bud" Collyer hosted a daytime version. Janice Gilbert was the show's assistant, and Win Elliott the announcer.

Between 1954 and 1957, during the era of the big money quizzes, the show, now known as *Break the $250,000 Bank* and again hosted by Bert Parks, returned to the air. In deference to its high stakes, contestants were permitted to bring along an expert for help with the jackpot question.

In 1976, Jack Barry would buy the name "Break the Bank" from Framer and build a whole new show around it. In its new format, two contestants, one male, one female, competed to win three sets of adjacent boxes by determining which of eight celebrities seated at a gridded table was bluffing, which giving a truthful answer to a general knowledge question. In the end game, the winning contestant could break the bank if he or she avoided the one jinxed celebrity. Tom Kennedy hosted the new daytime version of *Break the Bank* which was seen on ABC. Barry himself hosted the syndicated version of the game.

QUIZ

See if you can "break the bank" with these questions actually asked on the original show: I warn you: they're pretty obscure.

1. For $5,620: What famous six-footer played Lincoln in Robert Sherwood's *Abe Lincoln in Illinois,* produced in 1938?

ANSWER: Raymond Massey.

2. For $6,350: What bestseller became a favorite text for temperance lectures?

ANSWER: *Ten Nights in a Barroom.*

3. For $7,500: What journalist wrote *The Gorgeous Hussy* and *The Harvey Girls?*

ANSWER: Samuel Hopkins Adams.

4. For $8,870: Name the B-50 that first flew nonstop around the world.

ANSWER: *Lucky Lady II.*

5. For $9,020: What hit play of 1933 became the film *Summer Holiday?*

ANSWER: *Ah, Wilderness.*

---

4. Twenty Questions

"Animal, vegetable, or mineral?" On this high-brow game of the late forties and early fifties, the panel of four had twenty questions in which to find out. Home viewers submitted subjects which could be, well, abstruse. *Was King Arthur's round table animal, vegetable, or what? What about the key to the observation tower of the Empire State Building?* If a viewer's suggestion was used on the air, he or she received an outfitted travel kit and a twenty-five-dollar bond. A special feature of the show called upon panelists to identify a celebrity mystery voice.

Twenty Questions was owned by Fred Van Deventer and his wife, Flo Rinard, a nice, brainy Indiana couple relocated in Princeton, New Jersey, where they published pamphlets for the Educational Testing Service and for the Gallup Poll. The Van Deventers were also the stars of *Twenty Questions* and its best players. Also seated on the panel was Herb Polesie, a writer and producer for Bing Crosby, Frank Sinatra, Al Jolson, and Bert Lahr. A veteran panelist, Polesie also appeared on early TV's *Charade Quiz.* *Twenty Questions'* fourth panelist was youngster Johnny McPhee. In 1954, when Johnny was a no-longer-so-young Princeton sophomore, he retired to take his junior year abroad and make room for fourteen-year-old Dick Harrison. Bill Slater moderated the show; Jay Jackson succeeded him.

More memorable to many than the show's often nit-picking questions were its sexy live commercials. Charlotte Manson was the show's Ronson girl, and Roxanne, the very animal Miss Mennen.

Twenty Questions was first heard over ABC radio in 1946. It came to early television in 1949 simulcasting over ABC in both media for a time. During the next six years, it aired on three different stations—over ABC, Du Mont, local New York Station WOR-TV, and back to ABC in its last year and a half. *Twenty Questions* finally left the air in 1954.

The Best of the Fifties

They called the fifties television's golden age. The quizzes and games of the period certainly bear that out. Just imagine, they were all so good they aired in prime time. Toward the end, though, the "golden age" turned tarnished.

5. What's My Line?

Somehow, one foot in the door with *Winner Take All* just didn't seem enough, not with television still crying out for programs. Mark Goodson and Bill Todman's new show was dreamed up by a young man named Bob Bach who had worked on their musical radio show, *Spin to Win*. Bach's new idea stemmed from his favorite barroom pastime: trying to guess the occupations of his fellow patrons in the bar based solely on their exterior appearances. "The idea has possibilities," his bosses told him, but first they threw out his title, "Occupation, Please." Then they set to work on an innovative format that for the first time made the contestant the puzzle. Out on stage would step an ordinary-looking person, who would then proceed to write his extraordinary occupation for the studio and home audience on a large blackboard placed out of viewing range of *What's My Line?*'s four-member celebrity panel. The contestant would then take a seat beside moderator John Daly. "Mr. Smith is salaried," Daly would say, his only clue before turning matters over to his panel one at a time. Each panelist could continue questioning the contestant until he elicited a no. Each "no" answer earned the contestant five dollars. Ten "no's" earned him the show's top prize of fifty dollars and the victorious right to reveal to the defeated panel his elusive line of work. During *What's My Line?*'s most popular segment, the panel put on sequinned blindfolds and attempted to guess the identity of a famous mystery guest.

Figuring out the rules for *What's My Line?* was easy. Selling it was harder. When Mark Goodson and Bill Todman first presented *What's My Line?* to CBS program executive Charles Underhill, he flatly turned it down. Though CBS eventually reconsidered, the early shows were "dull as dishwater," according to Mark Goodson himself. The problem lay with the program's first "cast." Two were perfect from the start: John Daly as the dignified, ear-tugging moderator, and Arlene Francis as the gracious sophisticate; but the others on the original shows, Harold Hoffman, the former governor of New Jersey; Dr. Richard Hoffman, a psychiatrist; and author Louis Untermeyer, left much to be desired.

Not until 1951 would *What's My Line?*'s magic really start to happen. That was the year its two other famous players joined: determined and intense newspaper columnist Dorothy Kilgallen and avuncular, punning publisher Bennett Cerf. Even then, the panel's second seat from the left long remained a problem. When comedy writer Hal Block proved too overbearing, he was replaced by Fred Allen, who promptly died, then by Steve Allen, who left. After that, the vacancy was filled by invitation—and not always happily, either; one famous guest panelist would never be asked

Sign in, please! John Daly introduces Miss X to Arlene Francis, Arthur Godfrey, Dorothy Kilgallen, and Bennett Cerf.

back after he was discovered fielding answers from a hand-signaling friend in the audience.

Such setbacks aside, soon the ratings were soaring. Out each week the four panelists would stride, suavely attired in evening gowns and tuxedos, looking very "Manhattan," to shake hands with Daly and engage in brittle banter, before addressing themselves to the awaiting challenge. On their first few shows together as a team, their intuition seemed so uncanny, it swiftly drew unwarranted charges of coaching. But the panel soon learned the art of asking questions in a dramatically logical sequence that shared their line of reasoning with the audience. More than the others, Kilgallen clearly played for keeps, even bursting into tears one night after the show because she hadn't solved anyone's occupation in three whole weeks.

Once *What's My Line?*'s panel-related troubles had been solved, that left only the problem of finding willing mystery guests. Phil Rizzuto was the first to "sign in, please." Until the show caught on, scaring up others proved tougher. "No's" came from Dean Rusk, the Duchess of Windsor, Greta Garbo, Mrs. Woodrow Wilson, and John F. Kennedy. Still, enough of the famous did consent to appear, including Carl Sandburg, Sister Kenny, Admiral Halsey, Earl Warren (a shoo-in for the show; Daly was married to his eldest daughter), Frank Lloyd Wright, and Marian Anderson.

The task of finding the non-celebrity contestants fell to Frances Trocaine and Ann Kaminsky. Every week, they received twenty-five hundred letters, some from as far away as Saudi Arabia. The show developed a policy of saying "no" to all occupations dealing with death, mental illness, laxatives, and breasts. Other rejects: "the king of the hoboes ("He looked the part"), and a striptease dancer ("Too provocative"). Despite such screening, a few dubious people did manage to make it onto the air: the show's elephant trainer was arrested by the FBI after the program; he was wanted for crossing the state line in a stolen car. Another contestant tricked the producers into believing that his "line" was thief; it wasn't.

What's My Line? would air on network television for seventeen years, from February 1950 until September 1967, longer than any other network show except Ed Sullivan's *Toast of the Town,* becoming for millions a Sunday-night-at-10:30 P.M.-tradition. It would win three Emmys, in 1952, 1953, and again in 1957. It would outlive two of its members, Bennett Cerf and Dorothy Kilgallen. The surviving panel learned the fate of the show over breakfast, when CBS leaked the story of the cancellation to the New York *Times.* The most loyal of its viewers were now over fifty, CBS would claim, demographics which were undesirable to advertisers.

Between 1968 and 1974, a syndicated version of *What's My Line?* returned to the air, hosted first by Wally Bruner, then by Larry Blyden. Panelists on the syndicated version of the game included Arlene Francis, Soupy Sales, Jack Cassidy, Kaye Ballard, Anita Gillette, Gene Rayburn, Alan Alda, Nancy Dussault, Joanna Barnes. Bert Convy, and many others. A British version of *What's My Line?* is still on the air, hosted by Eamonn Andrews.

Great Moments on *What's My Line?*

The night Arthur Godfrey almost forgot. Godfrey had just showered and stretched out on his sofa to watch TV when the announcer said, "Stay tuned to *What's My Line?*" "Oh, my God," said Godfrey, jumping up and reaching for his clothes. "I'm tonight's mystery guest!" He arrived just in time to make the show.

The night no one guessed Bob Hope. It soon became obvious to the panel that the mystery guest was a comedian, but the real joke was on Hope when the quartet blithely named everybody *but* him. Hope was furious until it became clear that the otherwise astute panel was doing it all in fun.

The time Samuel Goldwyn ratted. "See you later this week," Goldwyn casually told Kilgallen. "I'm the mystery guest." "What a dope I am," he then told Bennett Cerf. "I told Dorothy I'm the mystery guest." That Sunday, half the panel had to excuse themselves, leaving the task of guessing the sheepish Goldwyn to the others.

The night they guessed Frances the Talking Mule. The show's staff had carefully wrapped her hoofs in burlap. But when the wind shifted, the secret was out.

No one guessed Roz Russell when she appeared with laryngitis.

Jury Garland proved difficult. Easy to guess—but difficult.

Remember the show's last mystery guest? It was John Daly himself, moving back and forth between two seats to answer the panel's questions.

Wait, there's one last story. Were you watching the night the mystery guest was *such* a mystery the panel never bothered to put on blindfolds? *Nobody* recognized the governor of Georgia, Jimmy Carter, in 1974, just one year before he ran for President.

Did I mention the show's very first "line"? She was a hatcheck girl.

6. Beat the Clock

When people think of a Goodson-Todman game as epitomizing good taste, it's clear they've forgotten this one. *Beat the Clock* was the show that promised married couples a Sylvania television if they would appear in public wearing rubber suits and shower caps, roll about the floor wrapped around one another, squirt each other with water and whipped cream, fling crockery at each other (couples broke some twelve thousand plates the first six years the show was on the air), and stagger around the stage blind-folded balancing eggs on spoons.

Then there was that clock: huge menacing, positively existential, its every amplified tick sent the frustrated contestants into frenzies. Each week a single designated couple had to confront first the "one-hundred-dollar clock" and then "the two-hundred-dollar clock." If they proved successful in those stunts, the couple then got the chance to perform a particularly fiendish bonus stunt worth up to thirty-two hundred dollars.

The stunts for *Beat the Clock* were dreamed up by the show's producers, Frank Wayne and Bob Howard, *and* none other than Neil "Doc" Simon and his brother Danny. Each week they would concoct twenty ideas which they would then narrow down to six. The show paid stand-ins to pre-test

I think she's aiming at the paper cup behind him. Bud Collyer and tyke observe.

and rehearse them all to prove they could be accomplished. Bud Collyer, wearing a checkered suit, emceed. He was assisted by the statuesque Dolores "Roxanne" Rosedale, whose job was to snap a picture of each couple with a Sylvania Blue Dot flashbulb at the very height of their humiliation. Somehow Roxanne always managed to stay just out of range of the whipped cream and the contestants' wild thrashing about, but not of rumors that she made Collyer jealous.

Beat the Clock began on radio as *Time's a' Wastin'* in 1948. It made its television debut over CBS television on March 23, 1950, and ran for ten years until September 1958. Its best-remembered time slot on CBS was Saturday nights at 7:30 P.M. Thereafter, ABC carried the game until January 1961, during the afternoon. A syndicated version of *Beat the Clock,* hosted by Gene Woods and featuring guest celebrities instead of Roxanne, aired in local markets throughout the early seventies.

Stunts from *Beat the Clock* to Try at Your Next Party

1. Mouth the Marshmallows. Equipment needed: two fishing poles and lines, and two marshmallows. During the stunt a couple, seated on stools six to eight feet apart had to get marshmallows at the end of the fishing pole into each other's mouths within forty seconds without using their hands or bodies.
2. Setting the Table. This stunt required the couple to unfold a bridge table without spilling any water in four cups sitting in their saucers. Time limit: thirty seconds.
3. Dig for Marshmallows. In this one, the husband knelt over a table with a spoon in his mouth. His assignment: to dig three marshmallows out of a two-quart bowl of Jell-O in front of him within thirty-five seconds without dropping any.
4. Spring the Mousetrap. The husband, holding a fishing pole with a frankfurter at the end, had forty seconds in which to spring six out of nine mousetraps placed on the floor. His wife got to release the frankfurter and urge him on.
5. Egg Carry. This time the husband had forty seconds in which to carry two eggs, one at a time, on a spatula across a finish line ten feet away. His wife followed with a net.
6. Long Underwear Balloons. Finally, the husband, aided by his wife, had forty-five seconds in which to stuff twelve balloons down the front of a suit of long underwear without breaking any.

Practice, practice, practice, and who knows? Maybe *next* time will be *your* time to beat the clock!

Other Stunt Games

People have proved willing to make fools of themselves on other stunt shows than *Beat the Clock*. To wit:

Anything You Can Do, emceed by Gene Wood. Seen over ABC in 1971.

Almost Anything Goes, emceed by Charlie Jones and Regis Philbin. Seen over ABC in 1975.

County Fair with Win Elliott and Jack Bailey in its radio version. This show came to TV with Bert Parks over NBC during the summer of 1959.

Dollar a Second, emceed by Jan Murray. Seen first over Du Mont between 1953 and 1954, later over ABC between 1954 and 1956.

One in a Million, emceed by Danny O'Neill and seen over ABC in 1967.

Reach for a Star, emceed by Bill Mazer and seen over ABC in 1967.

Take the Break, emceed by Don Russell and seen over CBS in 1951 and 1952.

7. You Bet Your Life

Not only was it one of the most successful game shows ever, it was one of the most successful television programs, **period**. For eleven years, *You Bet Your Life* with Groucho Marx and his shy announcer, George Fenneman, consistently earned ratings high enough to place it in the Top Ten. The quiz was secondary, of course. People tuned in year after year to watch "The one . . . the *only* . . . GROUCHO!" the graying man with the mustache, cigar, rumpled suit, and the wooden duck.

Few people remember that until the debut of *You Bet Your Life* on radio in 1947, Groucho Marx was considered "washed up." His last movie, *The Big Store,* had been in 1941. His four previous attempts at having his own radio comedy show had fallen flat. A chance encounter with *People Are Funny/House Party* producer John Guedel during a Walgreen Drugs radio special dramatically changed Marx's luck. Guedel was watching from the wings when Marx and Bob Hope threw away their prepared routine and began to ad-lib with far funnier material. When Groucho came backstage, Guedel approached him. "They're wasting you on radio," he enthused.

"Hiring you to read a script is like using a Cadillac to deliver coal. I have a good idea for a quiz show and you'd be perfect."

"Anything," said Marx.

Selling Marx on being a quizmaster proved a lot easier than selling the networks on Marx. When all four turned the pilot down, Guedel, never one to give up on a good idea even in the face of rejection, resourcefully tried another tack. When he read in *Variety* that the Elgin Compact Company was planning to sign Phil Baker for a new quiz show, Guedel called and offered them Groucho instead. Elgin, unaware that Marx was considered a "has been," excitedly bought the show. *You Bet Your Life* went on the air two weeks later, first as a radio quiz, moving to television on October 5, 1950. Baker fired his press agent.

Groucho Marx appeared on *You Bet Your Life* as himself, without his painted-on movie mustache and without his funny walk. Seated behind his podium, puffing his cigar, mildly bemused by all he was hearing, he conducted the famous interviews that preceded and overshadowed the quiz. Groucho took on everyone, from beauty queens to small-town mayors to the mighty General Omar Bradley, gently deflating them all. *You Bet Your Life* always teamed a male contestant with a woman—and in deference to Groucho the younger and prettier she was, the better. Each show, Groucho met two, sometimes three, such pairs of contestants, who competed in a quiz for the right to answer a final two thousand-dollar question. In later years, a wheel of fortune determined the size of the final stakes, which ran as high as ten thousand dollars. To qualify for this round, contestants had to correctly answer four questions of increasing difficulty worth between ten and one hundred dollars from a pre-selected category. Following each question, the couple could confer before giving their agreed-upon answer. Missing two questions in a row disqualified a couple. Questions on *You Bet Your Life* were difficult, but the only one anyone ever remembers is "Who's buried in Grant's tomb?" The question was Groucho's way of make certain even losers left with something: fifty dollars each.

One of the most popular features on *You Bet Your Life* was "the secret word." At the beginning of the show, a wooden duck with glasses, bushy eyebrows, a mustache, and cigar would drop down to be introduced, bearing in his beak a small sign on which was printed "a common word, something you see around you every day." In the course of the preliminary interview or during the quiz itself, if one of the contestants happened to utter the word, the duck would reappear amid enormous fanfare, and the couple would divide one hundred dollars. The original idea for the secret word came from Guedel's *People Are Funny*. Host Art Linkletter used to give contestants one hundred dollars if an alarm clock sounded while he was talking to them. In an inspired moment the producer of both shows, Bernie

The one, the only . . . in a contemplative mood.

Smith, changed the alarm clock into the duck that looked just like Groucho. Sometimes, to Marx's delight, model Marilyn Burtis carried the secret word and descended on a trapeze.

Providing humor and suspense was so important to the staff of the show that even though it was rarely divulged, *You Bet Your Life* was a fully scripted show. Obviously, it wasn't that he couldn't ad-lib, Groucho would explain later; he could like no one else. Rather it was that he felt funnier when nothing was left to chance. Nothing was. Every week a staff of twelve people would scour the country looking for contestants with personalities, occupations, and circumstances lending themselves to good quips for Groucho. Then the show's team of comedy writers subjected prospective contestants to in-depth interviews, milking their every response for joke material. Each contestant was informed as to which of his remarks were apt to draw a humorous rejoinder from Groucho. Marx himself was guided, joke by joke, by cue cards projected overhead on a bowling screen. Often, when it appeared that he was coyly gazing heavenward during a big laugh, he was really only reading his next ad-lib.

In a day when all of television was live, *You Bet Your Life* was filmed. Each week, eight 35-mm cameras collected an hour and a half of film which the show would edit down to a half hour of Marx's best moments. "We feel an obligation to the folks who watch at home every week to make the show as professional as possible," Bernie Smith would explain.

Long before most shows, *You Bet Your Life* also made use of a laugh track. One censored episode on the show provided a laugh so huge it was used frequently not only on *You Bet Your Life,* but on dozens of NBC shows for years to come: "I was rooming with a three-hundred pound fellow," said one contestant, confiding his most embarrassing moment to Groucho, "and the bedroom caught fire. In my panic, I put on the big fellow's trousers and shoes. I was coming down the ladder when a shoe came loose. I tried to retrieve it and I dropped the trousers. There was a crowd of five hundred people below, and they could all see my predicament."

Still, despite all the pre-show manipulations, *You Bet Your Life* succeeded where Marx's many imitators failed. Because he was the one, the only. And if his lines were prepared in advance, no one could deliver them as well. See for yourself. The show's still running in syndication. And when you do, tell 'em Groucho sent you.

For more about John Guedel, see pages 112–113.
For more about *You Bet Your's Life*'s more memorable contestants, see pages 16–17.

Rumors of My Death . . .

In 1950, the broadcasting industry formally acknowledged that they had been premature in announcing the demise of Groucho Marx's career. Thanks to *You Bet Your Life,* Marx won an Emmy that year for being television's "Most Outstanding Personality."

QUIZ

NO one ever remembers the questions on *You Bet Your Life.* Well, I do. Try your hand at these.

1. Who was our only bachelor President?
   ANSWER: James Buchanan.

2. What is the name of the town in Ontario, Canada, where the Dionne quintuplets were born?
   ANSWER: Calendar.

3. What is the French word for potato?
   ANSWER: *Pomme de terre.*

4. What river separates Manchuria from Korea?
   ANSWER: Yalu.

5. Who was the ringleader of the mutiny on the *Bounty?*
   ANSWER: Fletcher Christian.

6. What were the first words sent over the telegraph by its inventor, Samuel Morse?
   ANSWER: What hath God wrought?

7. These are the four largest places in what state? Milford, Elsmere, Newark, and Dover.
   ANSWER: Delaware.

8. What plants do silkworms feed on?
   ANSWER: Mulberry.

9. Who jumped off the Brooklyn Bridge in 1888?
   ANSWER: Steve Brodie.

10. What is the name of California's only volcanic peak?
    ANSWER: Mount Lassen.

Other Comedy Games

Groucho made it look so easy that scores of comedians tried to copy him. Over the years there were such joke games as:

Can You Top This? emceed by Dennis James and Ward Wilson and seen over ABC between 1950 and 1951.

Gags to Riches, emceed by Joey Adams which aired locally over New York's WATV-TV in 1958.

Laughs for Sale, emceed by Hal March over ABC in 1963.

Stop Me if You've Heard This One, emceed by Morey Amsterdam and seen over NBC in 1949.

Tag the Gag, emceed by Hal Block and seen over NBC in 1951.

What's the Joke? emceed by Paul Killian and seen over ABC in 1955.

There have been cartoon games like:

Draw Me a Laugh with Walter Hurley, seen over ABC in 1949.

Draw to Win with Henry Morgan, seen over CBS in 1952.

Droodles with Roger Price, seen over NBC in 1954.

Laugh Line with Dick Van Dyke, seen over NBC in 1959.

Many comedians would also try—and fail—to match him as hosts. There would be:

Fred Allen's *Judge For Yourself,* seen over NBC in 1953.

Edgar Bergen and Charlie McCarthy's *Do You Trust Your Wife?* (see pages 176–179).

Jackie Gleason's *You're in the Picture* (see page 294).

The only comedy quiz to approach decent ratings was *Two for the Money,* featuring Hoosier humorist Herb Shriner. In 1956 Shriner tired of the job. His replacements, Sam Levenson and Dr. Mason Gross failed to keep the laughs coming, and the show, which had been on the air since 1952, departed. To prove just how elusive a winning format can be,

Groucho Marx's own effort at duplicating his previous triumph with *You Bet Your Life* never rated. His follow—up effort was *Tell It to Groucho,* seen over CBS in 1962.

Also singing the spin-off blues would be *You Bet Your Life*'s announcer. George Fenneman's stabs at hosting were in 1958 with ABC's *Anybody Can Play* and again in 1961 with CBS's *Your Surprise Package.* Neither drew even a smile.

8. I've Got a Secret

It was created by Allan Sherman, the portly, multitalented genius who would later write the hit record, *My Son, the Folksinger.* It was owned by Goodson-Todman. *I've Got a Secret* faltered dangerously at first; in fact, the original version of the game was canceled by CBS after thirteen weeks. Given another chance, kinks ironed out, it returned to the air and ran for fifteen years, from June 19, 1952, to April 3, 1967.

Goodson-Todman bought the idea for *I've Got a Secret* from Sherman and his friend Howard Merrill, two comedy writers down on their luck. Then they treated them shabbily; for in signing the contract Bill Todman offered them, Sherman and Merrill discovered that they had handed over all the rights to their idea including rebroadcast, world-wide subsidiary rights, motion-picture rights, dramatic, musical, toy-, and souvenir-manufacturing rights. In exchange, they each received a flat fee of $100. Should the show be canceled, the contract read, the undersigned would become eligible for a royalty of $62.50 a week. Todman then hired Sherman to be associate producer of the show at a weekly salary of $125.

Before it ever aired it took *I've Got a Secret* eight months to find a sponsor, three months more to translate the show into a viable format, and three months after that of playing the game over and over in all-night sessions. Even then, the first shows were a disaster. That *I've Got a Secret* awarded only one hundred dollars in prize money was not the problem. Dressing the host as a judge, the panel as a jury, was. *I've Got a Secret*'s original panel of Orson Bean, Louise Allbritton, Laura Z. Hobson, and Melville Cooper lasted just two weeks. Its original secrets were all insipid: Boris Karloff confessed that he was afraid of mice; Monty Woolley said that he slept with his beard under the covers. When that failed to get a laugh, he informed the audience that he had just lied. "I was told to say that by the producers," he told America. At least the public had heard of *them;* most of the early contentants were Sherman's friends, the only people who would consent to appear.

Things began to improve as soon as the show stopped trying so hard. Garry Moore was the perfect host, casual and offbeat. And the choice of Henry Morgan as panelist was a stroke of genius; his steadfast refusal to take anything about the game seriously helped separate this show in the minds of the viewers from *What's My Line?* which it originally had resembled. As the show relaxed, secrets became zanier: sequestered elephants and army regiments appeared; George Gobel emerged from hiding in a broom closet. Two squirrels emerged from a contestant's pocket prematurely. Eddie Fisher emerged wearing his secret in the form of a twenty-dollar tie. As success bred success, Sherman found himself working around the clock, often sleeping on the office couch. He would book Sir Edmund Hillary on his return from first climbing Mount Everest, and John Glenn the day after he broke the record for flying from Los Angeles to New York in three hours and twenty-three minutes. Before long, *I've Got a Secret*'s ratings passed those of *What's My Line?*

Though the show was thriving, Goodson and Todman refused to share the wealth. They made Sherman a full producer but did not give him a raise, and it took him three years to get a secretary. With some bitterness, Sherman, in his autobiography *A Gift of Laughter* would describe Mark Goodson and Bill Todman as petty despots in a barony now equipped with a gray flannel men's room with gold fixtures, monogrammed towels, and seven kinds of cologne. He would depict Goodson seated behind a desk that had once belonged to Napoleon, dictating blizzards of memos, and brandishing a foot-and-a-half-long letter opener. At least, Sherman claimed, Goodson could make himself understood; Todman spoke an advertising man's double-talk Sherman labeled "Todmanese"; looking for a new host once, Todman would turn to Sherman and say, "Who do you know who does warmth?" Sherman would also be in Todman's office the day he ordered a custom-made Lincoln directly from Henry Ford himself.

Slowly Sherman would be squeezed out, his chaotic, undisciplined imagination no longer fitting in with the Goodson-Todman increasing propensity for memos and meetings, order and organization. In 1955, he was replaced by new producer, Chester Feldman, who would mesh so well he is still working there, long after the demise of *I've Got a Secret.*

As the show settled into middle age, other regular panelists came aboard to join Henry Morgan: Steve ("Is it bigger than a breadbox?") Allen and his wife, Jayne Meadows. Betsy Palmer became a favorite panelist on the show when she consistently proved incapable of guessing even the most obvious of secrets: when a man came on with two carrots in his ear, Palmer missed.

In the sixties, *I've Got a Secret* continued to have its unforgettable moments: the man whose secret was that he'd collected seven miles of string; the man who could blow up inner tubes—and almost killed himself on the

That's Bill Cullen, Jayne Meadows, Henry Morgan, and Betsy Palmer with their heads together, and Garry Moore on the receiving end. Mark Goodson himself looks on approvingly. He should. This show and others made him millions.

show proving it. Ernest Borgnine appeared with the secret that while posing as a cabdriver, he had driven Jayne Meadows to work without her knowing it. Paul Newman went Borgnine one better. His secret: that while posing as a vendor, he had sold Henry Morgan a hot dog at Ebbets Field. Morgan didn't recognize him, but the fans did. Newman ended up having to sell them twenty-five dollars' worth of hot dogs before he could get away.

Host Garry Moore presided over the secrets for most of the show's run, often finding he'd taken on more than he'd bargained for. On one show, Moore wrestled an alligator; on another, a nine-year-old girl hit a golf ball off his nose. A burglarproof jewelry case blew up, injuring his thumb. He let "archery expert" Johnny Carson shoot an arrow at him. Only once did Moore draw the line: when he refused to put his head in a lion's mouth. Toward the end of the show's run, Steve Allen hosted.

Recognize whose secret is that she plays the flute? It's Bess Myerson.

Viewers continued to tune in week after week, year after year, to watch a private club of sophisticates "cut up" on live TV. As they grew older, so did the show and its stars. Younger viewers did not come aboard. In 1967, CBS decided that *I've Got a Secret* was no longer demographically viable. Canceled the same year as *What's My Line?* two of TV's oldest, best-loved games passed from the scene. *I've Got a Secret* began a run in syndication in 1972, hosted by Steve Allen.

9. Masquerade Party

This long-running panel game of the fifties had an interesting twist: celebrities appeared in heavy drag, and I *do* mean heavy. Each week, a parade of mystery guests staggered out beneath the hot studio lights got up in costumes obviously borrowed from the wardrobe rooms of Hollywood's period movies, their faces buried under layer upon layer of grotesquely painted latex facial make-up. They then confronted a panel of their peers whose mission it was, through questions, to unmask them. Panelists were aided by the costumes themselves which were meant to communicate a clue to the mystery guest's identity. One night, for example, Mickey Mantle wore a long cloak, or mantle. When the moment of revelation was at hand, the celebrity's make-up was obviously excruciating to de-adhere. But the stars always acted as if it were nothing. Usually, anyway. There was the night the panel immediately identified "Keystone Kop" Gloria Swanson (the clue her costume imparted: she'd begun her career in a Mack Sennett movie). Livid at the ease with which she had been detected, especially since the disguise had taken her two hours to achieve, Swanson stormed out of the studio. To prevent future tantrums, *Masquerade Party* subsequently altered its rules. Thereafter, even if a panelist did guess the identity of the star, he or she was instructed to forestall the announcement for at least one minute.

The show, which ran on all three networks at one time or another, usually as a summer replacement for other shows, first came to the air in 1952. *Masquerade Party* had a succession of hosts: Bud Collyer, Eddie Bracken, Bert Parks, Robert Q. Lewis, and Douglas Edwards. But the emcee most associated with *Masquerade Party* was Peter Donald, the son of Scotch vaudevillians who had played Ajax Cassidy, the choleric Irishman in Allen's Alley, on the Fred Allen radio show. A young lady, known only as Renee served as the game's timekeeper. Memorable panelists were Bobby

Sherwood, Betsy Palmer, Johnny Johnson, Ilka Chase, Sam Levenson, Audrey Bowman, Faye Emerson, Phil Silvers, Ogden Nash, Dagmar, and the ex-Mrs. Mike Wallace, Buff Cobb.

In 1974, *Masquerade Party* returned to the air with a "face lift" to its format. Mystery celebrities no longer donated money to charity for stumping the panel, as had been the show's earlier custom. They played instead for merchandise won on behalf of lucky members of the studio audience. Richard Dawson hosted this syndicated version of the game, which was owned by Hatos-Hall.

Kathryn Grayson's in the get-up beside Robert Q. Lewis. Recognize the panel? Pat Carroll, Johnny Johnston, Jinx Falkenburg, and Jonathan Winters. Johnston's taking a special interest. Ms. Grayson's his wife.

QUIZ

Before each show, panelists on *Masquerade Party* were told by producer Herb Wolf what costumes they would be seeing that night. How many of these could *you* have figured out? Don't groan.

A Spanish cavalier wearing a long cape?
   Mickey Mantle.
William Tell?
   Lee Bowman.
A Chinese empress?
   Audrey Meadows. Everyone knows she was born in China.
Pirate Jean Laffitte?
   Faye Emerson. Born in Louisiana, just like Jean.
The Duke of Kent?
   Bert Parks, at the time spokesman for a certain cigarette with a Micronite filter.

---

10. Name That Tune

Name That Tune, the first successful TV music game, dates back twenty-five years to 1953. Harry Salter's new game stood head and shoulders above *Stop the Music*. His famous radio and TV predecessor reduced *its* contestants to phantom voices at the end of a phone. *Name That Tune's* contestants were equally hard to see, but that was only because they were literally required to run for their money. They wore sneakers, the better to ring the ship's bell at the other end of the stage and identify the easy little tune Salter's orchestra played. The tunes were *always* easy, but somehow the rattled contestants always seemed to miss. That was part of *Name That Tune's* genius, for as all producers know, home viewers love to feel superior to contestants. Sometimes the tunes were sung, in which case Vicki Mills was the vocalist who always abruptly got cut off when a contestant reached the finish line. To give the show some semblance of difficulty, *Name That Tune* also sported a highly popular novelty feature: words to some of the songs were sung in obscure foreign languages: Afghan, Icelandic, and prophetically, Vietnamese. At the end of each show, the panting contestant who had amassed the greatest number of points now had sixty seconds in which to identify a "golden medley" of ten more song titles. The winnings in this portion of the show could total up to $1,520 in cash, although in 1956, in response to the bigger prizes of the day, the stakes escalated to $25,000.

Name That Tune was first seen over NBC on Monday nights during the summer of 1953, and its original host was AL "Red" Benson. Bill

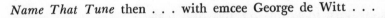

Name That Tune then . . . with emcee George de Witt . . .

. . . and now, with Tom Kennedy.

Cullen hosted the game throughout 1954. Then, in the fall of 1954, when the show switched over to CBS, George de Witt became its best-remembered emcee. De Witt remained on the program until it left the air in 1960.

In 1970, Ralph Edwards acquired the rights to the long dormant show. *The New Name That Tune,* hosted by Tom Kennedy, with Tommy Oliver and his orchestra, boasted a greatly modernized format full of all new mini-games. Contestants now vied to unscramble song titles from a magnetic board, to pluck dollar bills from a "money tree," to spin a "melody roulette" wheel of fortune, and play a game called "bid a note," in which contestants challenged each other to identify a title in the fewest number of syllables:

"I can name that tune in five notes."

"Four."

"Three."

"All right. Name that tune!"

The New Name That Tune preserved the "golden medley" end game but offered merchandise prizes. This daytime version of the new game aired over NBC between 1973 and 1974.

A syndicated nighttime version of *Name That Tune,* also hosted by Tom Kennedy, has been on television since 1975. In this version, however, contestants who successfully identify all ten songs in the "golden medley" earn the right to try to identify a $100,000 "mystery tune" from an isolation booth. Their answers are instantly recorded and played back before Kennedy dramatically reveals whether the contestant had indeed won. The $100,000 *Name That Tune* featured vocalist Kathy Lee Johnson. In 1978, its format was updated once again adding two rock bands and some disco dancers, and a more dramatic elimination competition to determine the winner. As a result of network regulation, contestants won their money $10,000 at a time spread over a ten-year period.

Memorable Moments on *Name That Tune*

Nineteen fifty-eight. A star is born. A young boy named Eddie Hodges appeared on *Name That Tune,* and took time out from the quiz to entertain the viewers with a few gospel tunes. Broadway was listening, and Hodges won more than the game when the director of *The Music Man* tapped him to star in the show. Anybody remember Hodges' even more famous partner that day? He was future astronaut John Glenn.

Name That Tune frequently boasted celebrity guests from the sports world whom the show misguidedly enjoyed furnishing with embarrassingly bad jokes. Anybody remember the following eminently forgettable sallies:

Heavyweight-boxing champion Joe Louis appeared one night only to be "stumped" by the strains of "Mister Sandman."

"Who puts you to sleep?" hinted George de Witt, presumably trying to help the slugger out.

"Rocky Marciano?" hazarded the Brown Bomber.

Another time Willie Mays and Leo Durocher appeared to be similarly set up. When they were unable to recognize a song called "Sympathy," host De Witt hinted, "It's something an umpire needs beginning with "s."

Said Leo the Lip, "A seeing-eye dog?"

Sometimes a brush with *Name That Tune* could cause you to *lose* your celebrity. That was the case in 1956 when the last five minutes of the show were summarily pre-empted by a political message purchased by Adlai Stevenson during his presidential campaign against Dwight D. Eisenhower. So many viewers protested that Stevenson had to issue a public apology.

Other Music Games

Games with music, date, of course, back beyond *Stop the Music* to the many radio games and quizzes of the forties. *These* have aired on TV:

Dough Re Mi, emceed by Gene Rayburn and seen over NBC between 1958 and 1960.

Hold That Note, emceed by Bert Parks and seen over NBC in 1957.

Music Bingo, with Johnny Gilbert, seen both over NBC and ABC between 1958 and 1960.

Musical Chairs I, emceed by Bill Leyden, seen over NBC in 1965.

Musical Chairs II, emceed by Adam Wade and seen over CBS in 1975.

Sing It Again, with Dan Seymour and seen over CBS in 1950.

Sit or Miss, still another game with a musical chairs theme, seen over ABC in 1950.

Songs for Sale, emceed by Jan Murray, Steve Allen. Seen during the summer in 1950, 1951 over CBS.

What's This Song? emceed by Wink Martindale and seen over NBC between 1964 and 1965.

Words and Music, emceed by Wink Martindale and seen over NBC between 1970 and 1971.

Yours for a Song with Bert Parks and seen over ABC between 1961 and 1963.

11. Strike It Rich

It was the most notorious show on television, once referred to by New York *Times* critic Jack Gould as "an instance of commercial television gone berserk." *Strike It Rich* was the quiz show for the lame, the halt, and the downright pitiful, asking participants as it did to mail in letters telling their sob stories and detailing why they urgently needed help. The show then chose the most deserving candidates and put them on camera, where an often tearful Warren Hull coaxed them to tell America their stories. Contestants were given a chance to earn the artificial limbs, arthritis treatments, and hearing aids by answering five easy questions. When many could not pass this test, the charity—and tears—really flowed. At the close of each show, *Strike It Rich* opened up its Heart Line to give viewers across America the opportunity to phone in whatever cash, clothing, merchandise, or jobs they had at their disposal. Celebrity guests, known as "Helping Hands," frequently appeared to answer questions for contestants.

In 1954, *Strike It Rich* became the object of controversy when the New York City Department of Welfare ruled that the show was in reality a welfare agency, and that without an operating license from the city to solicit funds, it would have to leave the air.

The charge left producer Walt Framer indignant. The show never gave anybody more than five hundred dollars, he said, which automatically screened out the truly desperate. In fact, Framer pointed out, before ever bringing his show to television, he had actually reduced *that* amount; the radio version of *Strike It Rich* had given away eight hundred dollars to the neediest. Despite the uproar, *Strike It Rich* weathered the storm. Welfare Commissioner Henry L. McCarthy dropped his complaint when Framer acquiesced to two of his demands. The show was now required to warn its audience not to come to New York unless specifically invited to do so by *Strike It Rich.* It also agreed to investigate the background of each contestant.

Strike It Rich, which began on radio in 1948, moved to daytime television sponsored by Palmolive Soap, over CBS in May 1951, spent several summers airing simultaneously in prime time, and ran for six and a half years to the beginning of 1958. On one occasion, Monty Hall substituted for Warren Hull. *Strike It Rich* aired in syndication in 1973, hosted by Tom Kelly.

Heart Line! Warren Hull's got help for these two deserving folks on *Strike It Rich.*

12. The Big Payoff

Ever wish, you self-sacrificing wife and mother you, that someone, let's just say that man in your life, would notice what a swell person you are, tally up all the good deeds you've done in your day, and take it upon himself to tell the world? In the fifties, *The Big Payoff* fulfilled this housewifely fantasy in spades, *and* in mink, modeled by Bess Myerson, former Miss America and later New York City Commissioner of Consumer Affairs. At the show's climactic moment, she'd stand with her back to the audience, wheel to face the camera, and caress the coat that could be *yours*. To see *that* once was to have the picture etched forever in one's mind; to see it daily was *never* boring.

Only women could be contestants on *The Big Payoff*. Only men could vouch for their deservingness. The show selected its contestants on the basis of heart-rending letters written in to the show by husbands, fathers, sons, any male close enough to the lady to attest to her saintly character. But a male's mere praise was not enough. While the chosen lady sat off to the side, her hands damply clutched in anxious anticipation, her champion, like any knight in shining armor, had first to subject himself to a test. In this case, that consisted of answering a series of three questions and submitting to the show's musical song-and-dance numbers. Answering the three questions correctly earned six hundred dollars in merchandise and entitled the male to tilt for "the big payoff" itself: the mink and a trip to anywhere in the world. Though the payoff questions were often difficult, on the whole the show was generous. By the end of *The Big Payoff*'s first two years, it had given away some two million dollars' worth of prizes.

Owned by Walt Framer, telecast from the New Amsterdam Roof Theater on West 42nd Street in Manhattan, *The Big Payoff* came to television over CBS and soon moved to NBC where it aired for eight years at 3 P.M., from June 1952 until 1960. In the early fifties, it made occasional prime-time appearances on Sunday night during the summer. The show's original emcee was Bert Parks, but the host who made *The Big Payoff* famous was Randy Merriman. He was later succeeded by Mort Lawrence and then by Robert Paige. Later models who succeeded Bess Myerson were Betty Ann (Sandy) Grau, Denise Lor, and Dori Anne Grey.

Bess Myerson again, in mink with Randy Merriman.

QUIZ

Questions on *The Big Payoff* could be hard. These were missed. How well would *you* have done?

1. We're looking for the largest island of Denmark, site of Copenhagen and Elsinore.
2. We're looking for the writer of these frequently quoted lines: "She's no chicken, she's on the wrong side of thirty if she's a day."
3. We're looking for that famous Connecticut Yankee, U. S. Secretary of the Navy between 1861 and 1869. Noted for his incorruptibility and efficiency, he built the powerful Union fleet.
4. He was the famous English statesman-orator who fought British policy in the American colonies, favored the French Revolution, and supported Irish home rule. His toast, "Our sovereign: the people," upset the British Government.
5. Who first said: "The time of my departure is at hand, I have fought a good fight, I have finished my course, I have kept the faith."?
6. Who said: "For of all sad words of tongue or pen, the saddest are these: 'It might have been!' "?
7. We're looking for a famous queen, married to two brothers, the daughter of Ferdinand and Isabella and the mother of Mary I.
8. Who was the author of *The Task* a poem in six books, from which came "Variety's the very spice of life, that gives it all its favor."?
9. He was the composer from Connecticut who wrote the opera *Rip Van Winkle* and was most famous for the love song, "Oh Promise Me."
10. It was the famous prison in the French Revolution. This former royal residence in Paris became the seat of the Court of Justice in the fourteenth century. Marie Antoinette spent her last days there.
11. The pen name of Cecily Fairchild Andrews, Irish-born political writer and novelist who wrote *The Thinking Reed* and a famous report of the political treason trials of the day.

ANSWERS:

1. Zealand
2. Swift
3. Gideon Welles
4. Charles James Fox
5. Paul
6. John Greenleaf Whittier
7. Katharine of Aragon
8. Cowper
9. Reginald de Koven
10. The Conciergerie
11. Rebecca West

----

13. This Is Your Life

It defied categorization, but you couldn't ignore it. In 1953, it split an Emmy with *What's My Line?* as the "Best Quiz or Audience Participation Show" of the year. In 1954, it shared its Emmy with no one. *This Is Your Life* was a surprise party, only you didn't laugh, you cried. All America certainly did, when every Wednesday night, an impishly grinning Ralph Edwards, clutching a thick album full of dusty photos and souvenirs, would amble up to an unsuspecting celebrity whose friends had lured him or her to the El Capitan Theater in Hollywood. "Excuse me," he'd say, innocently enough, "but aren't you . . ."

"Why yes," the celebrity would say, confusedly trying to understand why TV cameras had begun to roll into place, why his or her friends had begun to wink and grin and nudge each other. "Then," Edwards would boom, firmly clamping his hand to his victim's elbow, "if you're who you say you are, This Is Your Life!" The show was live and the resulting portrait of total shock was pure "television." Then, as the music of the studio orchestra swelled, Edwards would guide his still-stunned prey down the aisle of the filled El Capitan auditorium, up on stage, and into a badly needed chair. Much more was to follow. For this ultimate of all his "consequences," Edwards had carefully selected a subject with a life melodramatically full of ups and downs. For the next half hour, no "up," no "down," would be left unexplored as Edwards proceeded to fill his subject's ears with mystery voices, his tear-brimmed eyes with photos salvaged from the days of his youth, or, in the event that some friend or relative had proved unable to attend, with a lachrymose, film-clipped tribute. "Do you remember whose voice that is?" Edwards would ask. The cameras stood ready to catch the first flickering of recognition, then every kiss and hug of the reunion, as the celebrity was faced in person with a long-forgotten relative or friend. After the evening was over, Edwards would present the exhausted subject with a copy of the album and a gold bracelet from Marchal Jewelers full of charms commemorating the major events of the subject's life. A gift which launched the chain-bracelet fad in the fifties.

Though celebrities like Lillian Roth, Eddie Cantor, BeBe Daniels, Martha Raye, Lily Pons, and dozens of other stars are the show's best remembered subjects, *This Is Your Life* often singled out ordinary folk whose lives exemplified a sympathetic or inspiring theme: the GI just back from Korea, the treasured teacher, boss, friend, relative, or clergyman.

The Edwards staff took great pains both to keep its subjects in the dark and their identities from leaking to the press. Friends and relatives were carefully screened and sworn to secrecy, key missing persons tracked down

It's Ralph Edwards, a still-stunned Lily Pons, and a bevy of her relatives from the white-gloved, cultured-pearl set.

from afar, plane schedules co-ordinated. If by some remote chance, the subject chanced to find out in advance the show's intention to do their life (Ann Sheridan and Joe Louis did), all plans were immediately scotched. When a subject's heart was known to be weak (like Eddie Cantor's) or life especially embarrassing (like Lillian Roth's before her victory over alcoholism), the show informed its subjects beforehand. And should a subject prove ungracious, or even bellicose when Edwards sprang his trap, an emergency standby kinescope of a previous show always stood by in readiness.

This Is Your Life was wildly popular and was frequently parodied. Ralph Edwards himself was especially vulnerable to teasing, and on one occasion, he declared himself to be not nearly so good a sport as his subjects. "What would you do if your staff pulled a fast one one night and surprised *you?*" he once was asked.

"I'd fire each and every one of them," he replied.

This Is Your Life first aired over NBC radio in 1948, moving to NBC television in October 1952. It ran until 1960. During its last two years, the show devoted itself entirely to non-celebrity subjects.

In the early seventies, *This Is Your Life* returned to air briefly in syndication, hosted once again by Edwards. Subjects this time included the likes of Johnny Cash, *Hee Haw*'s Roy Clark, and David Cassidy.

Other Tearjerk Games

Chance of a Lifetime, with John Reed King, Dick Collier, Russell Arms, and Dennis James seen irregularly over ABC between 1950 and 1952.

End of the Rainbow, with Art Baker, seen over NBC in 1958.

The Girl in My Life, with Fred Holliday, seen over ABC in 1974.

Have a Heart, with John Reed King, seen over Du Mont in 1955.

It Could Be You with Bill Leyden, seen over NBC in 1956.

The Neighbors, with Regis Philbin, seen over ABC in 1976.

Place the Face, with Jack Smith, Jack Paar, and Bill Cullen, seen over NBC between 1953 and 1955.

This Could Be You, with Bill Gwynn, seen over ABC in 1951–52.

Turn To a Friend, with Dennis James, seen over ABC in 1953–54.

Your Big Moment with Melvyn Douglas, seen over Du Mont in 1952–53.

And for the ladies with looks, there was the chance to cry through mascara on these beauty-contest games:

Dream Girl of '67, emceed by Dick Stewart, Paul Petersen, and Wink Martindale, seen over ABC in 1967.

Glamour Girl, emceed by Harry Babbitt, seen over NBC in 1953.

Video Venus, with Herb Sheldon, seen over ABC in 1951.

And more recently, *The $1.98 Beauty Show* with Rip Taylor.

14. Truth or Consequences

Truth or Consequences was a decade old when it first came to television over NBC in 1950. The year of its TV debut, it had won an Emmy, seen the town of Hot Springs, New Mexico, officially change its name to "Truth or Consequences," in its honor . . . and had flopped. Owner-host Ralph Edwards had tried to steer the show through early TV's troubled waters, first in prime time, then daytime, innovating where he could. *Truth or Consequences,* for example, had been the first show on television to use three cameras. Edwards had tried such ratings-boosting stunts on the show as promising a young woman $100,000 if she could break out of a hypnotist's trance; she couldn't. He'd staged more jackpots; he'd invited celebrities on. They'd failed to rally the show. More than for any other reason, *Truth or Consequences* lagged because Edwards was just too busy with his new hit, *This Is Your Life,* to devote his full attention to it. By the end of 1950, it had left the air.

But only temporarily. *Truth or Consequences* would return in 1954, hosted this time by *Queen for a Day*'s Jack Bailey. Still the ratings lagged. Again *Truth or Consequences* departed, then limped back in 1955 to be canceled yet again.

Reprieve for the show came in 1956 when on his car radio one night, Ralph Edwards chanced to hear the voice of Bob Barker, then an unknown disc jockey from Springfield, Missouri, by way of the Rosebud Indian Reservation in Mission, South Dakota. Edwards called Barker in the next day to audition, then signed him to host his languishing brainchild. Their relationship would last the next eighteen years.

Thanks to Barker, at last the floundering show began to flourish. Fresh and friendly where Bailey had seemed slick and jaded, Barker fully appreciated that no matter how funny the stunts on *Truth or Consequences,* without the full, spontaneous participation of the audience, there would be no show. Now, before every telecast, the show's entire staff plunged in to create in them an anything-can-happen atmosphere. Every day before airing, the audience got to meet the members of the "loyal" staff chained together in striped prison garb. Next they witnessed the shooting of an "audience member." "Now maybe *you'll* stay in *your* seat during a broadcast," they were told by a gun-toting member of the crew. Another *Truth or Consequences* staffer, bandaged from head to toe, would be borne in on a stretcher, claiming to be a contestant from the day before. Just before airtime, lest anyone in the audience still be tense, two burly males were required to come on stage and struggle into corsets. *Truth or Consequences* was back all right. Every day you never knew. Today, you might see mem-

Ralph's got their street clothes, but then again, they've got his bathing suits and shower caps.

bers of the audience drummed into zany skits known as "Barker's follies," paraded about in silly costumes ("If you're going to be a baker, you've got to look like a baker,"), or touchingly reunited with a long-separated loved one.

If anything could happen on *Truth or Consequences,* one time, back in 1958, things got more out of hand than usual. As part of a Robinson Crusoe stunt, the show had marooned two contestants for a week on an island off the coast of Southern California. They fared better than their rescuer who had to be fished out of the Pacific when his helicopter capsized on his way to picking them up. All ended well, however. That Saturday night, safely back in civilization, the contestants appeared on the show and won nine thousand dollars. The episode made headlines around the world.

Never a surprise on the show: its famous consolation prize, a bottle of Jungle Gardenia perfume by Tuvache.

15. People Are Funny
16. House Party

He was born in Moose Jaw, Saskatchewan, in 1912, to some folks named Kelly who abandoned him. Thirty years later, and for the next twenty-eight years after that, he would be adopted by every family in America. He was beloved for his capacity to turn a studio full of strangers into a cozy living room, and then to engage them all in hilarious double-, and sometimes triple-, crosses which somehow always seemed to involve prolonged wild-goose chases across Los Angeles. He made the Jolly Green Giant into a household word. He proved that kids say the darndest things. He was the first, and one of the best, game show hosts there ever was.

His name was Art Linkletter. Although he did indeed prove to be a natural host, it took young Linkletter awhile to find himself. He worked as a busboy in Chicago, a harvest hand in North Dakota, a meatpacker in Minneapolis, a forester in Washington, a stevedore in New Orleans, a clerk on Wall Street, a seaman in Buenos Aires, all before enrolling in college at San Diego State. There, he captained the basketball team and set the school record in swimming for the fifty-yard free style. Finally, in 1935, Linkletter found his vocation—doing man-in-the-street interviews. His Whitmanesque adolescence had stood him in good stead; Art Linkletter excelled in sizing up people from all walks of life and instantly winning their confidence. Then his baby face would slacken in feigned amazement over experiences more unbelievable than his own that he'd gotten them to reveal.

Producer John Guedel swiftly sensed that Linkletter's gift could be turned to gold. Meeting Linkletter in 1942, Guedel at once saw in the young announcer the chance to parley his local Los Angeles program, *Pull Over, Neighbor,* into something much bigger. However, Guedel first had to replace the show's current host, the more pedestrian Art Baker. The affair turned ugly when Baker groundlessly threatened to sue over his ouster. The matter was settled out of court and Baker later went on to host his own hit, *You Asked for It.* Guedel and Linkletter then became partners and the co-owners of two of the hottest properties in broadcasting, NBC's radio hit *People Are Funny* and, in 1944, its CBS daytime radio cousin, General Electric's *House Party.*

For the following ten years both shows were radio hits with ratings so high that neither Guedel nor Linkletter showed the least inclination to experiment with TV, preferring instead to watch archrival *Truth or Con-*

sequences try and fail. Guedel's phenomenally successful third show, *You Bet Your Life,* was the first to take the TV plunge in 1950. That same year, Linkletter gingerly took his TV screen test with the short-lived *Life with Linkletter,* following that appearance a year later with a fifteen-minute

Mr. and Mrs. C. D. Ozanick have an eavesdropper, Sonny Tufts. Art Linkletter orchestrates the fun on *People Are Funny.*

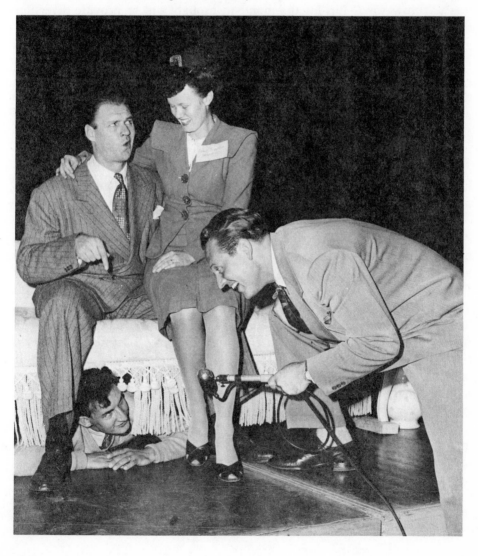

show called *Art Linkletter and the Kids*. Finally, in 1952, *House Party* would bow on daytime television over CBS, where it remained for the next eighteen years, winning an Emmy as Best Daytime Show in 1954. *People Are Funny* would arrive on NBC in the fall of 1954 as part of a $3 million, two-year deal, airing during prime time on Sunday nights for the next seven years.

Neither show was, truly speaking, a game show as we use the term today. Rather, both provided the matrix from which dozens of game show concepts sprang. "Here's a box and here's a box," Art Linkletter might say, descending into his audience and dragging a retired school principal up on stage. "Which one contains the prize?" To Linkletter and Guedel, the stunt was a "throwaway," fun for the moment, brought out to provide diversion between celebrity guests and kiddie interviews. Nevertheless, this "throwaway" guessing game contained the main ingredient of the original *Treasure Hunt, Let's Make a Deal,* and many of the pricing games on *The New Price Is Right*. Or, Linkletter might ask a grandmother in the audience to try to guess, say, a young husband's occupation; here, the kernel of *What's My Line?* Still another time, he might have a young housewife try to anticipate, through ESP, the next word out of her seatmate's mouth; here, the core of *Match Game* and *Password*. Blithely, and long before *The Dating Game, People Are Funny* conducted "marriage roundups," with its Univac computer. Other times, it might program its computer to unscramble anagrams with the audience, an idea that might easily have "spun off" into still another full-fledged game.

If Guedel and Linkletter didn't ordinarily value the little stunts played on their shows, on one occasion in 1956, they did. That year Chicago television columnist Harriet Van Horne, chancing to watch one *People Are Funny* game called "Detecto" accused Guedel and Linkletter of plagarism. "You stole the idea from *To Tell the Truth*," Van Horne would accuse in her column. Her readers knew better and they wrote in by the thousands to correct her. *"People Are Funny* has been playing "Detecto" for at least ten years," they chided, "long before *To Tell the Truth* was ever dreamed of." Van Horne apologized. Still, Guedel and Linkletter would muse, perhaps she had a point, and in 1959 they sued Goodson-Todman, the producers of *To Tell the Truth*. The case never came to trial, for NBC, which was at the time televising both *People Are Funny* and Goodson-Todman's popular *The Price Is Right,* arrived at an out-of-court sum large enough to mollify its plaintiffs: $3 million. When it comes to fun and games on television it seems, *everybody's* got their price.

17. To Tell The Truth

The idea for *To Tell the Truth* had been in circulation long before *People Are Funny* played "Detecto." If you want to get pedantic, you can officially trace it back to ancient Greece to the famous logic problem of Epimenides, "All Cretans are liars." Or to state it simply: bluffing's fun. Already *Masquerade Party* had proved that anyone can escape detection behind a disguise, just as Goodson-Todman's own *What's My Line?* had shown that anyone can dissemble when one's opponents are blindfolded. What was so revolutionary and (John Guedel and Art Linkletter to the contrary) original, about *To Tell the Truth* was that rarely before had anyone, except Cretans and criminals, attempted the trick barefaced. Indeed, when first confronted with the idea for *To Tell the Truth,* not even Mark Goodson and Bill Todman believed it could possibly work.

But then, Mark Goodson and Bill Todman had been pessimistic about life in general of late. Not since *Winner Take All* and *Beat the Clock* in 1949, *What's My Line?* in 1950, and *I've Got a Secret* in 1952, had anything new they'd tried resulted in a hit. Even such marginal early fifties shows of theirs as *The Name's the Same* and *It's News to Me* had copied their own now stale formula. *The Web,* their exploratory plunge into television drama, had bombed. Things looked so bleak that one day in 1955, Mark Goodson, emerging from a staff meeting, was heard to lament, "Doesn't *anybody* around here have any new ideas?"

"I've got a whole pocket full of them," spoke up a short, stocky young man seated in the reception area, "and I'm your next appointment." The man was Bob Stewart, an ex-adman from Philadelphia and one of the most skilled craftsmen ever to work with TV games. Thankfully for the future of G-T, Mark Goodson would have the sense to hire him. Bob Stewart, it seemed, had a perfectly dandy bluff game in mind (he also had *The Original Price Is Right* and *Password* in his pocket that day, but that's another story), and he was confident, above Mark Goodson's doubts, that he could make it work. The solution to playing *To Tell the Truth,* Stewart knew, lay in exhaustive briefing. Having rounded up two plausible-looking imposters to appear with a truth-teller, all three of them offering the same implausible story, Stewart and his staff would have to be willing, year in, year out, to spend several hours before each show with each team, force-feeding them every conceivable fact about the person they'd be impersonating, coaching them on every related subject about which they would have to be knowledgeable. The procedure would be very much like cramming for an exam—though the information would fade fast, it would still be

To tell the **TRUTH**

Tom Poston, Peggy Cass, Orson Bean, and Kitty Carlisle sniff out the Oriental imposters as Bud Collyer referees.

fresh when the contestants needed it to face a panel of laymen with only superficial knowledge of the subject. To survive even the most penetrating of questions, Stewart would suggest that his imposters hold onto some familiar facts. "Use your own birthplace," he would advise. "Keep in mind the names of friends and relatives." To further hone them for their ordeal, Stewart would first have his impersonators take part in a dress rehearsal in front of a stand-in panel whose job it was to try to trip them up. Still, the hardest panelist Stewart's first three teams would ever have to face was the still-skeptical Mark Goodson. Goodson would confront team after trial team Bob Stewart brought before him. Each would fool him. Goodson was delighted. "Can you do the same thing every day?" he asked. He already knew the answer.

Once the impregnable foundation of *To Tell the Truth* had been laid, solving the game's other kinks seemed minor. Finding the right name involved some trial and error. A faltering early version of the game, then called *Nothing But the Truth* and played in a courtroom setting, would air briefly over CBS in the summer of 1956, hosted by newscaster John Cameron Swayze. By the fall, its catchier name was in residence and so was a more homespun host, *Beat the Clock* veteran Bud Collyer.

Taking charge of tracking down players would become the task of a full-time staff of six: Gil Fates, Geraldine Toohey, Willie Stein, Joyce Weiss, Roger Kielty, and Jack O'Neill. To them fell the challenge of lining up future contestants, photographing and filing them, then briefing and grilling them and briefing them again. Before long New Yorkers became accustomed to being approached by this crew in elevators, on the street, at parties, and in one instance, to having a license number jotted down at a toll booth, if they had a mien that might allow them to pass for a wrestler, belly dancer, snake charmer, chimney sweep, or log rolling champion. Before long, America was chanting, "Will the real (fill in your favorite) please stand up."

Matching wits with the extraordinary contestants on *To Tell The Truth* were a sharp-witted celebrity panel of four that might often as not over the next twenty years consist of Polly Bergen, Don Ameche, Kitty Carlisle, Tom Poston, Ralph Bellamy, Hy Gardner, a demoted John Cameron Swayze, Orson Bean, Peggy Cass, Hildy Parks, Dick Van Dyke, Bill Cullen, Soupy Sales, Nipsey Russell, and sometimes even the old convert himself, Mark Goodson. Panelists each got one minute in which to grill contestants, at the end of which they had to choose the real from the ringer. Contestants received fifty dollars for each panelists wrong guess. In the event that the contestants fooled the entire panel, they divided five hundred dollars. Throughout all, Bob Stewart's original briefing technique weathered even the most penetrating of attacks. Usually, anyway. Occasionally, even the most superbly briefed contestants cracked. There was the "psychologist," for example who slipped on "Dr. Fraud," and the "Siamese" liar who didn't know the meaning of his own name in his native language.

To Tell the Truth would air both in prime time and in daytime over CBS until 1969. It would air in syndication until 1979, hosted by Garry Moore and later by Joe Garagiola. Though it is no longer in production, Mark Goodson still refers to *To Tell the Truth* as "the most golden game show idea of all." He ought to know.

Other Bluff Games

Bluff games have always been a big favorite over at Goodson-Todman. There was:

The Better Sex, with Bill Anderson and Sarah Purcell in 1977 over ABC.

Call My Bluff, with Bill Leyden over NBC in 1965.

It's News to Me, with John Daly and Jack Paar, the *first* bluff game, seen over CBS between 1951 and 1955.

Play Your Hunch, with Merv Griffin and Robert Q. Lewis, seen both over CBS and NBC between 1958 and 1963.

and *Snap Judgment,* with Ed McMahon and Gene Rayburn, seen over NBC between 1967 and 1969.

Other folks' bluff games have included:

Back the Fact, with Joey Adams and Al Kelly, seen over ABC in 1953.

The New Break the Bank (see page 127–130) .

Hollywood Squares (see page 243–249) .

Hot Seat, emceed by Jim Peck and seen over ABC in 1976.

The Liar's Club, emceed by Rod Serling and Bill Armstrong, syndicated throughout the seventies.

18. Queen for a Day

Not a quiz, and not even close to being a game, nonetheless, this supremely popular show epitomizes the Cinderella fantasy at the core of the best games. Besides, it's just too outrageous to overlook.

Like *Strike It Rich, Queen for a Day* existed for the sole purpose of wringing tears from its sympathetic viewers; like *The Big Payoff,* its beneficiaries were always women. Resemblances, however, stopped here. If nothing else, *Queen for a Day* was what you'd have to call original. Every day before the show, emcee Jack Bailey would sally forth into the studio audience and return to the stage with the five most deserving women he could find. Then,

That's Jack Bailey in drag, crowned by Darlene Coats (left) and Marilyn Burtis. Marilyn got around. She was also the "secret word" girl on *You Bet Your Life* when the duck couldn't make it.

his finger dramatically aimed straight at the camera, he would bellow the words that set thirteen million home viewers aquiver: "WOULD YOU LIKE TO BE QUEEN FOR A DAY??" The five hopeful women would be brought on stage and regaled with an almost endless parade of beautiful models bearing all the things it might be possible to win: furs, televisions, trips, and appliances, appliances, appliances. Indeed, there was so much loot on this show, it took forty-five minutes every day to reveal it all. During the show, the five would tell their stories. Whoever could convince the audience that *she* was indeed the most deserving (votes were determined by that most democratic of ballots, the applause meter) , was selected Queen, and draped in a sable-trimmed red velvet robe and a jeweled crown. And more: whatever she had requested was granted. If it was a bed, she got her bed *and* the sheets, the pillows, the blankets, the spread, and of course, a whole new bedroom including lamps, chaise, bureau, and carpeting to go with it.

To the losers, very little. A dozen pairs of stockings, a toaster, a percolator. And to liars, nothing at all. Every potential Queen had to sign a release stipulating that if she were found to have faked her miseries, she would collect nothing. It happened more than once. Naturally, no matter how worthy or needy a contestant might seem, if she could not articulately plead her case, she stood a poor chance of winning the audience. Finally, the show had a (tacit) catch: if a contestant's wishes were not merchandise-related, she did not stand a chance of even being selected as a contestant. After all, the show derived no manufacturer's freebies from tending to a woman's medical or legal problems.

Queen for a Day began on radio in 1945 and then aired locally in Los Angeles over KTSL-TV in 1950. It did not air nationally until 1955, when it was seen on ABC at 4:30 P.M. from July of that year through September 1960, dividing its time between Los Angeles and New York. NBC picked up the show and carried it until 1964, and Jack Bailey remained the emcee until the show's demise, ably assisted by Jeanne Cagney (Jimmy's sister) . A syndicated version of *Queen for a Day* aired briefly in 1970.

19. Who Do You Trust?

By now practically everybody knows Johnny Carson and Ed McMahon hosted this zany quiz with its offbeat contestants. But do you remember its first incarnation, when it was called *Do You Trust Your Wife?* and served as a comedy vehicle for ventriloquist-host Edgar Bergen and his three "assistants," Charlie McCarthy, Mortimer Snerd, and Effie Klinger? That version of the show ran on Tuesday nights after *The $64,000 Question.* It pitted two teams of husband and wife against each other then gave them little slates. Fast writing counted; whichever team could scrawl down the answer first scored. So did a little ESP. Each team had to decide, before a question was asked, which of them would try to answer. The stakes on *Do You Trust Your Wife?* were especially gratifying: $100 a week for life. One couple, named Gude—a $6,000 a year pipefitter and his South American wife—had grossed $120,000 when the original show left the air.

When *Do You Trust Your Wife?* returned in September 1957, the undefeated Gudes returned, the first contestants. *They* were the same; but everything else about the show had changed. Gone now were the high stakes. In their place comedy questions and off-beat contestants. With Carson as its flip, irreverent host, the show soon developed a huge cult following. Since it was now televised at 3:30 in the afternoon, teen-agers especially used to rush home from school to watch it every day. So evidently did the NBC brass. In 1960, they tapped Carson for the *Tonight Show* to replace another ex-game show host, Jack Paar. The rest is history.

"What few people realize about *Who Do You Trust?*" says former staffer Stu Billett, "was that it was a completely scripted show. Like *You Bet Your Life,* the people would come in before the show with their stories. The show's writers would listen to them and write jokes.

"Johnny got a reputation as the ad-lib king of television. Well, Johnny, not because he wasn't funny, was not an ad-libber. I mean, if there were thirty seconds at the end of the show, Johnny would just say good-by and walk off and leave us with thirty seconds of organ music. He did everything off the cue cards. If he did a demo—if some girl came on to do a Weider Body demonstration, and Johnny had to stand on his head to do it—the cue cards went upside down. The 'takes' " (a show business expression meaning to "react for the audience")—we had 'takes' written in red. Everything. When he went to the *Tonight Show,* for the first six months he was a nervous wreck. He was just sweating. Because there were no more cue cards.

"Then, on *Who Do You Trust?,* we couldn't book any celebrities. Groucho would have anybody on—celebrities, non-celebrities, opera singers—he could field anybody that came on. Johnny didn't like anybody who came on too strong. And so we couldn't book celebrities. So we booked kooky people . . . really way-out people. We got into all kinds of stories.

"The show was on at three thirty live every day," Billett continued. "Kids used to run home from school to watch it. . . . After we'd taped, on the

Edgar Bergen emceed the first version of *Who Do You Trust?* with "friends" Charles McCarthy and Mortimer Snerd.

way back from the studio, all the bartenders used to yell out to us, 'Hey, where'd you get that crazy guy?' That sort of instant feedback's gone from the business today with everything taped. It was marvelous."

When Carson went to *The Tonight Show*, he and Ed McMahon were replaced by Woody Woodbury and Del Sharbutt. *Who Do You Trust?* ran until December 1963.

20. Treasure Hunt

Treasure Hunt was as "ship-shape" a quiz as you'd ever hope to see. Unless seeing contestants answering questions from a fake pirate ship made you sea sick. It turned Arthur Godfrey green, that's for sure. At its height, *Treasure Hunt* attracted an unprecedented 52 share, more than half the audience, and more than enough to make its redheaded rival walk the plank.

But *Treasure Hunt* survived on more than its set bedecked with rigging, masts, and portholes. It was a shipshape game as well full of innovative drama. First, two contestants tried to answer four questions selected by their opponents from a category board, each worth $50. The winner of the first round then qualified to go on a "treasure hunt." Assisted by one of several of the show's Pirate Girls, Pat White, Marian Stafford, or Gretta Thyssen, a contestant got to choose from one of thirty numbered pirate chests arrayed on the stage. Each one contained a different prize, a gift certificate or humorous booby prize. One contained a check for $10,000. To make things interesting, there was a catch. Before a chest was opened, host Jan Murray presented a contestant with an alternative: rather than risk the booby prize, he or she could play it safe by choosing instead an envelope that guaranteed him anywhere between $500 and $3,000 in cash. Another popular feature of the game invited home viewers to mail in their hunches. Postcards were stored in a big cask on stage. In its prime-time version, *Treasure Hunt* offered a $100,000 jackpot.

Popular comedian Jan Murray owned the show. Nor was it his first. Murray, whose roots lay in vaudeville and nightclubs, first came to game shows on radio in 1948 with *Songs for Sale*. His first TV quiz, *Go Lucky*, a version of the parlor game "coffee pot," aired during the summer of 1951, to be followed in the fifties by *Meet Your Match, Blind Date,* and *Dollar a Second.* Two other Jan Murray games, *Charge Account* and *Chain Reaction* would come in the sixties. None, however, would approach the success of *Treasure Hunt.* The game aired over ABC between 1956 and 1957, then

Treasure Hunt pictures are hard to find; here's host Jan Murray and fifties-endowed assistant from the later *Charge Account*.

moved to a position of even greater visibility over NBC where it aired both in daytime and in prime time until 1960.

Popular hit though it was, *Treasure Hunt* left the air under a cloud. Although Murray's own honesty was never questioned, the quiz show investigations turned up evidence that members of his staff had solicited bribes from contestants in exchange for a berth on the show. Though the jury handed down suspended sentences, "to spare NBC further embarrassment"—as the official press release then put it—Murray asked that the show be canceled.

Still, you can't keep a good show down. In 1974, Chuck Barris bought the rights to *Treasure Hunt* and returned it to the air in an utterly astonishing, unrecognizable reincarnation. For more about *The New Treasure Hunt,* see pages 260–263.

21. The Price Is Right

Back in 1956, games were either elitist quizzes dispensing astronomical sums to eggheads, or brittle parlor games played by a panel of celebrities. Then out of nowhere burst *The Price Is Right,* the first game on television that literally *anyone* could play. By rewarding shrewd bidding on small grocery items as well as on lavish showcases, it made a virtue of being a thrifty, knowledgeable shopper. Everyone in the audience became a vociferous consumer expert.

Today we take such democracy for granted in games; but in 1956, no one took *The Price Is Right* for granted. To intellectuals, its frenzied pack of housewives clamorously coaching each other to bid Higher! Lower! Freeze! in an effort to win a washer-dryer represented America at its crass, materialistic worst. Pollyannas of the day like psychologist Allan Fromme daringly hazarded a good word, suggesting that no one on *The Price Is Right* was ever made to feel inferior, as they often did on all those hard quizzes. In *TV Guide* he commended the show's joy, its fun, its absence of greed. Whether you loved or hated it (there was no middle ground) *The Price Is Right* rocked the country and during its heyday could be seen in full color both in daytime and prime time over NBC.

If today you were to watch the original version, you would be bored to tears. On that version, as today, four contestants vied in an auction to estimate as accurately as possible the retail price of a piece of merchandise, without going over that price. But contestants could make *three* bids, each of which had to be at least fifty dollars higher than the previous bid. At any stage of the auction, a contestant could "freeze." As in today's game, the two best bidders of the day won the right to bid on one of two showcases. But unlike today, the best bidder on the showcase showdown earned the right to return the following day and continue as champion until he or she was unseated. Boyish and bow-tied Bill Cullen presided over the hysteria.

A special feature of the original show called for the home audience to bid by mail on deluxe special showcases. The first time the mail-in game was played, three and a half million viewers responded. Goodson-Todman, the show's packager, had to hire the Radioland Mail Service to tally the vote. Thereafter, the number of postcards received by the show leveled off to a mere million a week. Some home viewers went to desperate lengths to win. At least thirty-eight-year-old Brooklyn viewer Gerard Mignone certainly did: he tried to give the show's mailroom staff a two-thousand-dollar bribe to let his postcard win. He displayed even more poor sportsmanship

How much *was* a range in 1958? Bill Cullen knows but isn't telling till all the bids are in.

when he refused to surrender to the police. In the resulting chase, Mignone was shot and injured while trying to escape.

The Price Is Right was created and produced by Bob Stewart. Innovative and exciting though it was, *The Price Is Right* was not the first auction game ever to air on television. Back in television's earliest days, in 1949, there had been a highly popular prototype called *Auctionaire,* emceed by Jack Gregson and Charlotte "Rebel" Randall, in which contestants bid on canned goods labels (from Libby) and tried to identify a "mystery chant" delivered in "auctionese" by Gregson. That static game failed quickly. Stewart's entry succeeded because it added an exciting subliminal dimension: though *The Price Is Right* looked like an auction game, it actually worked more like the casino game of blackjack wherein the player risks losing the game if he exceeds a limit—twenty-one at the blackjack table, the retail price of the coveted prize on *The Price Is Right.*

Like all Goodson-Todman shows, *The Price Is Right* survived the scandals unscathed. Make that barely scathed; most people have forgotten that *The Price Is Right*'s name surfaced during the congressional hearings. Several contestants alleged that prior to airtime, the show furnished them with a list of ceiling prices over which not to bid. When Goodson-Todman announced that the practice had been abandoned the previous year, *The Price Is Right* left the headlines and survived to run its nine-year course over NBC from September 1954 to September 1961, and over ABC for another two years until 1963. It would be born again an entirely new show in 1974, but without Bob Stewart. When *The Price Is Right* was canceled, its entire staff was fired, and Stewart and Goodson-Todman parted ways, Stewart to become a successful independent packager and the father of *The $20,000 Pyramid.*

For more about *The New Price Is Right,* see pages 276–283.
For more about Bob Stewart, see pages 171–173, and 258–259.

Great Moments on the Original *Price Is Right*

The original *Price Is Right* was known for its lavish prizes (remember the time they gave away a five-piece band, twelve jars of caviar and a case of champagne, a sixteen-foot ferris wheel, and a chauffeur-driven 1928 Rolls-Royce?) Better still, you never could be sure when you might win one of these *bonus* prizes:

1. To go with a piano: Ivory. The show had a $4,000 elephant flown in from Kenya. The contestant, a Texan, kept it.
2. To go with a barbecue pit: a mile of hotdogs and a six-foot jar of mustard; to another contestant, a live Angus steer.
3. To go with a color TV: a live peacock to serve as a color guide.
4. To go with a complete home soda fountain: a home gym and barbells —to work off all those extra calories.
5. To go with a raccoon coat worth $29.95: a sable worth $23,000.
6. To go with a pair of Afghan hounds: walking equipment; fifty pairs of shoes, two hundred fifty pairs of stockings, and a portable hydrant.
7. To go with bathing suits for the whole family: a portable beach house.
8. To go with a swimming pool: a wishing well. The contestant wished for a four-door car. Her wish was granted.
9. To go with 100 shares of Union Pacific railroad stock: a safe and a chihuahua to guard it.
10. To go with another color TV: a part in *Jefferson Drum,* one of Goodson-Todman's abortive efforts at branching out into drama. Oh well, you can't win 'em all.

Other Pricing Games

The Price Is Right and *Auctionaire* weren't the only games with an auction or shopping theme. Remember any of these?

Bid 'n' Buy, with Bert Parks, seen during the summer of 1958 over CBS.

Sale of the Century, with Jack Kelly and Joe Garagiola, seen over NBC in 1969–73.

Say When, emceed by Art James, seen over NBC in 1961.

Spending Spree, with Al Hamel. Syndicated during the late 'sixties.

Temptation, emceed by Art James. Seen over ABC between 1967–1968.

TV Auction, with Sid Stone. Seen over ABC during the summer of 1954.

TV Auction Club, with Johnny Olson, seen locally in New York over WOR-TV in 1952.

What Am I Bid? seen locally in New York over WOR-TV in the summer of 1950.

What's Your Bid? with John Reed King, Robert Alda and Leonard Rosen. Seen over ABC in 1953.

22. G.E. College Bowl

This totally selfless little quiz far outlasted the more infamous games of huge personal aggrandizement. The undergraduate contestants in the Emmy-winning (in 1962–63) *G.E. College Bowl* won nothing for themselves. All glory and a $1,500 check went to their alma maters, with the General Electric Corporation endowing the winning schools with a matching grant scholarship fund worth up to $19,500. The schools of losing teams received $500.

G.E. *College Bowl* was structured like a sporting event. Each week the show's production crew traveled to the "home court" of the challenging team, whose vociferous rooting sections could always be heard in the background. Each team had a coach and five members, each specializing in a

Allen Ludden's making the girls of Sweet Briar feel right at home before their *G.E. College Bowl* match with Colorado State.

different area of knowledge. A team gained control of a question by first correctly answering a "toss up" question The team then attempted to answer one of the wide-ranging, multipart questions that were often accompanied by maps, charts, reproductions of works of art, and snippets of classical music or famous speeches. Any member of the team could buzz in, but he had to be right or the questions passed to the other team. Answering correctly then entitled a team to try for a more difficult "bonus" question. Competition was keen and lesser-known schools often topped academic giants. (Sometimes, if one team member proved to be more quick-witted than his or her teammates, marriage proposals resulted, mailed in by appreciative viewers.) Between "halves" each participating team was permitted to show a short public relations film extolling the virtues of its school, a maneuver that frequently resulted in boosting that school's alumni donations. The questions for *G.E. College Bowl* were written by a housewife from Darien, Connecticut, named Nancy Fobes.

College Bowl Cribbers

College Bowl spawned a couple of imitators. Remember *Alumni Fun,* hosted by John K. M. McCaffery and seen over ABC in 1963? New Yorkers will also remember *It's Academic,* hosted by Art James and played by local high school students over NBC in 1963 and for several years thereafter.

G.E. *College Bowl* had its roots in radio, where it had played over NBC since 1953. It aired on television for the first time in January 1956, and ran on Sundays at 5:30 over CBS until 1966. A Moses-Reid-Cleary Production, the show was first developed and hosted by a quiet, likable, bespectacled young chap named Allen Ludden. Later, in 1961, when Ludden left *College Bowl* to host *Password,* his job was filled by Robert Earle, an Ithaca College professor. Earle, reading of the hosting vacancy in *TV Guide,* auditioned and won the job by erasing Ludden from an old videotape of the show, splicing a tape of himself in his place, and mailing it to the producers.

QUIZ

Put on your cap and gown. Here are some questions from *College Bowl.*

1. For ten points: quote the two famous lines which precede: "If a clod be washed away by the sea, Europe is the less."
2. A common chemical process involves the combination of oxygen with a compound of sesquisulphide of phosphorous, chlorate of potash, and a small piece of wood. For twenty points, what is the process?
3. "Cut and Shoot" and "Puttencove Promise" were two odd-sounding names that came up in some big sports stories last year (1958). For ten points apiece, what or who are they?
4. Each of these geography questions is worth ten points.
   (a) What two European capitals begin with the letter "P"; (b) What three European capitals begin with "M"; (c) What six European capitals begin with "B"?
5. Lunik is one of ten planets orbiting the sun. For thirty points name nine others.

ANSWERS:

1. "No man is an island entire of itself; every man is a piece of the continent, a part of the main."
2. Lighting and burning a wooden match.
3. Cut and Shoot was the Texas home town of Roy Harris, who fought Floyd Patterson, Puttencove Promise was the poodle that won "Best in Show" at the Westminster Dog Show.
4. a) Prague and Paris
   b) Moscow, Madrid, and Monte Carlo
   c) Belgrade, Brussels, Bucharest, Budapest, Bonn and Bern.
5. Mercury, Venus, Mars, Earth, Jupiter, Saturn, Uranus, Neptune, Pluto.

If you thought those were hard, cheer up. The students missed them all.

For more about Allen Ludden and *Password,* see pages 221–226.

The Scandal Shows

"If a sponsor wants to give away loot, it's his own business how he does it."
—Bud Granoff, producer of ABC's *Treasure Hunt*.

23. The $64,000 Question

24. The $64,000 Challenge

25. Twenty-One

Three of the best games ever were also the crookedest. First they became a national obsession, drawing ratings not equaled again until *Roots*. When at last unmasked, they would betray the nation's confidence to a degree not duplicated until Watergate. Game shows that can do that, we cannot ignore.

And so, the story of the rise and fall of the big-money quizzes . . . and you are there!

The Rise . . .

January 1955: Louis G. Cowan, the forty-five-year-old TV packager and father of the long-time radio hits *Quiz Kids* and *Stop the Music,* is sitting at home in his Park Avenue study one morning when he dreams up a quiz show that will showcase the common man with uncommon knowledge. The figure $64,000 pops into Cowan's head, a quantum leap from the $64 question once offered on the radio quiz *Take It or Leave It.* Experiencing a decided euphoria, he quickly heads downtown to his office to share the good news with his staff.

There are a few preliminary kinks to iron out before the new show can air six months later. The right to use $64,000 in the show's title will have to be purchased from Milton Biow, the producer of *Take It or Leave It.* And a sponsor is needed—a job that falls to Cowan staffer Steve Carlin. Carlin first approaches cosmetic queen Helena Rubinstein, who turns it down. She doesn't own a television and is completely unaware of its advertising potential. Chrysler also demurs, fearing that the sponsorship of a big-money quiz will foment labor unrest in its ranks. Another "no" comes from the Lewyt Vacuum Cleaner Company: too glamorous for their image. Carlin then approaches his friend Walter Craig at Norman, Craig, and Kummel advertising agency. Does Craig think he can deliver one of his plum accounts as a sponsor? Can he get to Charles Revson of Revlon? Craig can and does. No one knows it at the time, but having Revlon as a sponsor will later spell trouble. Charles Revson is a fanatical perfectionist.

If he is going to invest his millions in a venture that will bear his name, he will want guarantees; he will want control.

In the meantime, Louis G. Cowan has been quietly negotiating a way to leave the packaging business. Repeatedly embarrassed by his golden touch with quiz shows, he still seeks to do something more socially redeeming. In the spring, months before this new show will air, Cowan approaches Frank Stanton of CBS asking about a possible berth in program development at the network.

Still, when *The $64,000 Question* sells, Cowan is enthusiastically involved with working out details. One more time, it seems that he cannot resist a quiz. Cowan picks Hal March to be the show's emcee. He wants a fresh face for this show,—an actor, someone who will be poised under the pressure of giving away so much money on live television. Harry Fleischman will run the office, Steve Carlin produce the show. Joe Kates will work on the soon-to-be-famous musical theme and the show's sets and graphics. In preparation for his anticipated exit, Cowan renames his company. No longer Louis G. Cowan Productions, it will become known as Entertainment Productions, Incorporated, shortened to E.P.I.

Later Louis G. Cowan will maintain that he never intended for *The $64,000 Question* to be dishonest. The isolation booth—Charlie Andrews' idea—was not for showmanship, Cowan will insist. It was actually meant to guard against the contestants' inadvertantly overhearing an answer blurted out in the audience. Allowing the contestants to use an adviser once they have reached the $64,000 level was meant only for fairness to them.

"I also thought we should disclose at the beginning of the show," Cowan later contends, "that contestants had been preselected and that they had previously played a run-through game before the show for camera placement." Later, when the scandal breaks, Cowan by now the president of CBS, will profess to be as shocked as the general public by the charges leveled against the people to whom he had turned over his early-morning brainstorm.

One wonders though. All other Louis G. Cowan games had practiced a little sleight of hand, a little manipulation—none of which were, strictly speaking, illegal—then.

June 5, 1955: Tuesday night at 10 P.M. It is *The $64,000 Question*'s première performance. America has seen quiz shows before, but certainly nothing like this. What other quiz has offered an IBM sorter that riffles through questions with an undulating motion before it selects the proper one? What other quiz has had a bank officer seated behind an official-looking desk flanked by two uniformed guards? What other quiz has encased con-

It's Gino and Hal.

testants in a glass-enclosed cage resembling the elevator in a French provincial hotel? What other quiz has ever offered $64,000?

Into this rarefied environment steps a Staten Island policeman named Redmond O'Hanlon. He is *The $64,000 Question*'s first contestant. He is an expert on Shakespeare. He has been chosen from eight thousand applicants. Before he is through, he will win $16,000 for knowing the date and printers of Shakespeare's first folio. "You're right! You're absolutely right!" Hal March will shout, scarcely able to contain himself. O'Hanlon achieves overnight fame. He is invited to go on the lecture circuit. He receives an offer to write a book on Shakespeare's puns. And this for winning only $16,000. More madness lies ahead.

The show's format is guaranteed to drive Americans into a frenzy. Reaching $64,000 takes eleven steps correctly answering the first four questions brings contestants to the $512 level, known as "the first plateau." Questions at this level are selected by the IBM sorter. From there on in, however, the questions are kept in a New York Manufacturer's Trust Bank vault guarded by a nice balding little man named Ben Feit, who is an officer at the bank. "All questions come from the locked vaults of Manufacturer's Trust," he tells America. "Manufacturer's Trust guarantees that only authorized members of the bank have the keys and combination of the vault. And except for the producer, no one has seen these questions. Not Mr. March. Not even myself."

Answering the $1,000, $2,000 and $4,000 questions correctly brings contestants to the second plateau. Any misses beyond this level guarantees a contestant a Cadillac convertible. At the $8,000 and $16,000 levels, contestants enter the isolation booth ("You have thirty seconds to consider your answer. Think carefully.") While thinking, contestants are serenaded by high-pitched, high-tension "think" music whose tempo underscores the passing of the seconds. At the $32,000 level, contestants are given a week to go home and decide whether they want to continue to the final question. They are provided with three reference books. Once a contestant reaches the $64,000 question, he or she is permitted to bring along an expert. Never before has the format of a quiz contained such drama, such suspense.

Each week, the American people tune in, their breath bated. The summer of 1955, on Tuesday nights, the nation's crime rate drops. So do movie, baseball, and bingo attendance, water consumption, and long-distance calls. Two things rise: *The $64,000 Question*'s ratings and Revlon's profits. One particularly tense evening, 55 million people are watching. The show receives a 57.1 Trendex rating and 84.8 share. In the first six months the show is on the air, Revlon's sales increase 54 per cent. The shelves of America's drugstores are stripped bare of Living Lipstick. The following year, sales will triple.

Whodunit?

Quiz shows so captured the imagination of the American people that they became the subject of other forms of TV entertainment. On June 18, 1958, a play aired on *Kraft Theater* called *Now Will You Try for Murder* by Harry Olesker. According to *TV Guide* that week: "One of the biggest money winners in TV quiz history is murdered on the day he is to try for a record sum. An investigation reveals that a number of people connected with the show had a motive: the top executive, the director, the producer, and the producer's lovely assistant."

On the payroll at EPI are five people whose full-time job it is to sort through the 15,000 to 20,000 letters that pour in every week from hopeful contestants. Of these, those 500 people who seem the most promising are sent a mimeographed form soliciting additional information. Of those responding, the most likely are interviewed. On *The $64,000 Question,* "most likely" means one thing. It means you are the "common man" with uncommon knowledge; the "little guy" about whom you'd never suspect such knowledge.

Before America steps Catherine Kreitzer, a grandmother who works as a typist in a supply depot in Pennsylvania. Her specialty is the Bible. She wins $32,000 for knowing eight of the twelve apostles. Her fame also wins her an appearance on the *Ed Sullivan Show,* where she reads from the Scriptures. After her appearance, she receives dozens of requests through the mail for cash handouts, totaling nearly $150,000.

In the early weeks, Gloria Lockerman, a black twelve-year old from Baltimore who lives with her grandparents, also appears to win $32,000 in spelling.

And there's Gino Prato, the five-foot-four-inch cobbler from the Bronx whose specialty is grand opera. Probably no contestant in the history of television is as beloved as this man. Americans dote on every detail of his life. They know that Prato is an Italian immigrant who has made a successful business resoling shoes; his family life is happy; he plays three instruments—the guitar, the accordion, and the mandolin (badly, he confesses). He owns three hundred opera records, and frequently waits in line for two hours to get standing-room tickets for New York's Metropolitan

This is a posed shot of one of *The $64,000 Challenge*'s more harmless dress rehearsals; see the positioning marks on the floor and the beat-up desk?

Opera. As he ascends the plateaus on the show, Prato acquires sophistication and a sense of showmanship. He waves, blows kisses to the camera. He is totally charming. He successfully answers the four-part $32,000 question about the opera which launched Toscanini (the answers: *Aida*, Brazil, Cairo, Christmas Eve). Will he now go on for the $64,000 question? America will have to wait until the following Tuesday to find out.

The following week, Prato appears in the sweltering studio to announce his decision. Reading his answer in Italian, he tells the audience that his father, who is still in Italy, has made the decision for him. He translates, "Stop where you are. That's enough this way. Regards, Papa." Says Prato, "Because all my life, I take my Daddy's advice, I take it—the money." In the furor, no one seems to notice that Prato is never asked about any but Italian operas.

America has been softened up enough. The moment, so carefully orchestrated, is at hand. It is time that someone actually win the $64,000. The man to do it is a young crew-cut Marine captain named Richard McCutchen whose specialty is cooking. "Identify five dishes and two wines on the now famous menu of a royal banquet given in 1939 by King George VI for French President Albert Lebrun." "Consommé quenelles," says McCutchen, "Filet de truite saumonée, petits pois à la française, sauce maltaise; Corbeille, Château Yquem, Madeira Sercial," from his isolation booth. Charles Revson himself presents him with the check for $64,000.

If Americans have been receiving an education in the arcane aspects of opera and gourmet cooking, they are also receiving an education of another sort. Until *The $64,000 Question* no one has quite realized how much the Internal Revenue Service collects. Now everyone in America becomes a tax expert. Win $8,000 on the show, and the government takes $2,000. Win $16,000, and the bite is $4,640; $32,000, and it's $11,910. Of the $64,000 Captain McCutchen has won, he must return almost half, $31,150, to the government!

Late Fall 1955: To no one's surprise, Louis G. Cowan achieves the post to which he has aspired. He becomes a vice-president at CBS. Now that he is gone, his successors at EPI are anxious to show what they can do on their own. While *The $64,000 Question* amasses its huge ratings, they now mount a second big-money quiz with even higher stakes. It is *The $100,000 Big Surprise,* and it first airs on October 5. Despite the size of its jackpot, *The Big Surprise* never catches on. The format is a mishmash, as one critic puts it, "a hopeless melange of machinery," that includes an electronic brain and a typewriter that works by itself.

The show's emcee also falls under criticism. He is Jack Barry, who with his partner, Dan Enright, is also an independent producer. Together they own such shows as *Juvenile Jury, Life Begins at Eighty,* and *Winky Dink and You.* Though Barry has a proven television personality, someone says of him on the *Big Surprise,* "He has as much warmth as a head waiter someone forgot to tip." Before too long, he is summarily fired. Barry's replacement: an ambitious, dark-haired fellow named Mike Wallace.

He does not save *The Big Surprise*. The night a New York police sergeant wins $100,000, the ratings are only 15.3 compared to the 50's and 60's ratings *The $64,000 Question* is receiving. Plagued by too much well-meaning interference from producer, packager, network, two sponsors, and two advertising agencies, *The Big Surprise* is soon canceled.

Spring 1956: Undaunted by its failure, EPI decides to return to the tried and true of *The $64,000 Question*. On April 8, 1956, a Sunday evening, America watches the first telecast of *The $64,000 Challenge*, which pits champions from *The $64,000 Question* against new contestants who seem to be mostly celebrities. On the first program from twin isolation booths Vincent Price challenges Edward G. Robinson on art.

Even with a proven successful format going for it, *The $64,000 Challenge* needs some adjustments. The show's original host, Sonny Fox, is a disaster. He fluffs his lines repeatedly and seems unable to maintain the necessary objectivity. He is quickly replaced by Ralph Storey, the man to whom EPI had originally offered the hostship of *The $64,000 Question*. Storey now reveals why he had turned it down: "Too short-term," he'd feared. Storey swiftly stabilizes the show. By July, *The $64,000 Question* and *The $64,000 Challenge* are the number-one and number-two rated shows on television.

If astronomical sums of money is what the public wants, then that's what they'll get—so, at least, reckon the networks. A rash of imitations crowd the airways the summer of 1956: *High Finance, Giant Step, Can Do, Brains and Brawn*. Mediocre in concept, they prove that large prizes are not enough. Audiences cannot be bought. There must be both drama and suspense.

What if, though, there could be a quiz that pitted two people against each other—not show-biz types like on *The $64,000 Challenge*—but in a true gladiatorial struggle? What if these two did battle not for a mere $64,000 but for an *unlimited* amount of money. Wouldn't *that* get big ratings?

Fall 1956: NBC certainly hopes so. The big quizzes on CBS have driven from the air one of their most prestigious shows, the *Edward R. Murrow Show*. Now they pin their hopes on a new quiz called *Twenty-One*.

Twenty-One comes to television on Wednesday evening, September 12, 1956. The show is owned by Jack Barry and Dan Enright, and Barry is its host. Its sponsor is Pharmaceuticals, Inc., the manufacturers of Geritol and Serutan ("that's nature's spelled backwards"). The game's format is loosely based on the rules of blackjack, with many complex twists. Contestants, in their twin isolation booths, answer questions worth between one and eleven

Not *another* tie score? The show is *Twenty-One*.

points, with eleven-point questions being the more difficult. The first contestant to score twenty-one without missing any answers along the way earns the right to return indefinitely until someone defeats him.

At first *Twenty-One*'s ratings are desultory. The show seems to lack the pomp and spectacle, and above all, the *personality* of *The $64,000 Question*, where viewers still very much want to see Mabel Morris, the welfare client with high blood pressure, quit at the $32,000 level on the advice of her doctor. They like hearing that mailman-poet Roscoe Wright donated the $16,000 he won to his church for a new organ. They love it when opera contestant Michael della Rocca goes for the $64,000 question and uses Gino Prato as his expert. They meet the portly twin Egan Brothers who answer questions on all subjects and together win $32,000, and flamboyant jockey Billy Pearson, the art expert, who wins $64,000. And where else can the public see Randolph Churchill, Winston's son, miss a question on British history in the very first round, missing the derivation of the word "boycott?" These are memorable moments, infinitely more dramatic than anything *Twenty-One* has been able to muster in all its months on the air.

Spring, 1957: Then, suddenly, in the spring of 1957, *Twenty-One* hits its stride. Out of the wings, before the cameras, walks a boyishly handsome young assistant professor at New York's Columbia University. He is Charles Van Doren, the scion of a distinguished literary family. Van Doren faces Herbert Stempel, a smug, supercilious champion who has won $48,000. Stempel is bright, but not very likable. The audience finds itself pulling for this thin, modest, well-bred challenger. The night Charles Van Doren defeats Herbert Stempel, there is elation in the hearts of America. In the weeks that follow, he routs all challengers. And his winnings keep mounting: $104,500; now he's won $17,500 more. *Time* magazine puts his picture on its cover. Hollywood calls with a film offer. The ratings of *I Love Lucy*, CBS's formidable offering in the same time slot, begin to slip. At last Van Doren's championship seems in jeopardy. A brilliant and determined contender named Vivienne Nearing comes forward to challenge him. They battle to a tie; in the next round Van Doren holds his own. But it is obvious that he is struggling. He perspires in his isolation booth, stammers, pats his forehead, skips parts of some questions and returns to them later. But Nearing is just too formidable; finally, after winning $129,000, Charles Van Doren, the young man all America has taken to its heart, goes down to defeat.

Unlike so many quiz show contestants, Charles Van Doren is not forgotten. His ease and grace and gentlemanliness have left an indelible mark. He becomes a frequent guest on the *Steve Allen Show*, a summer guest host on the *Today Show*. He is just too likable, too special, too important an icon to the American dream of success to fade from view.

Even without Van Doren, *Twenty-One* continues to hold its own in the ratings war. Vivienne Nearing, after several ties, falls to Hank Bloomgarden, who wins $98,500 before falling to James Snodgrass. He in turn falls to dairy farmer Herbert Craig. Elated with *Twenty-One*'s turnaround, NBC offers Barry-Enright Producers $2.2 million for *Twenty-One*. By owning the show themselves, the network will be able to guarantee their hit will continue to clobber *I Love Lucy*.

Twenty-One's new success is not lost on EPI. The ratings of its two juggernauts have been flagging, and so on the day following Charles Van Doren's defeat, and as a new year breaks, *The $64,000 Question* announces that it will quadruple its stakes. A contestant will no longer have to stop at the $64,000 level, or make an appearance on *The $64,000 Challenge*.

Thats my boy! Charlie and Jack Barry.

After winning $64,000, he or she can answer up to six questions worth $32,000 each, and then *still* appear on *The $64,000 Challenge* to win more.

Equal to the task is ten-year-old Robert Strom from the Bronx. Strom has already appeared for twenty-six weeks on EPI's revived *Quiz Kids* show, and he's already won a college scholarship on *Giant Step*. Now he becomes the first contestant to win over $64,000. Choosing his questions from the field of mathematics, he wins $192,000, and finally goes on to win $224,000.

No sooner does *The $64,000 Question* make its adjustment than *Twenty-One* counters with a super-contestant of its own. She is Elfrida Von Nardroff, a thirty-two-year-old, forthrightly attractive, short-haired personnel consultant from Brooklyn Heights. If she wins, she says, she will return to school and earn her doctorate. Von Nardroff is on *Twenty-One* for sixteen weeks. Her category is history, and her final winnings are $220,500.

Where will it all end? The public is beginning to show signs of boredom. The formulas are wearing thin: *The $64,000 Question,* with its psychologists like Dr. Joyce Brothers who are experts in boxing; its grandmothers like seventy-year-old Mert Powers who are experts in baseball; *Twenty-One,* with its ties and rematches. And always there is the rumor of the quintessential quiz, the one that will award a million dollars. Then what? some cynics wonder, will someone then come along with a *two-million-dollar* show? Only the Groucho Marx show, *You Bet Your Life,* seems to have things in perspective. When informed of the escalating competition between Barry-Enright and EPI, Marx announces that he is upping the stakes on *You Bet Your Life* for saying the secret word from $100 to $101.

Trapped in its own ascending spiral, EPI doesn't get the joke. All they know is that they need a contestant who will win more than Elfrida. They find him in Teddy Nadler, a sixty-dollar-a-week St. Louis army depot laborer, who knows *everything.* From his prodigious memory spring the whole of Caesar's Gallic Wars; all of *Macbeth,* word for word; ten thousand battles; two thousand kings; three thousand generals; two thousand assassinations. Ask him anything and the facts spill from his lips. Before he finally draws a blank on *The $64,000 Challenge* in August 1958, he will win $264,000, the largest amount to be won on a quiz show before or since.

The Fall . . .

Though the public has not been aware of it, even as Von Nardroff and Nadler rake in their winnings, trouble has been brewing in quiz-show land for the past year and a half. Immediately following his loss to Charles Van Doren early in 1957, Herbert Stempel has cried foul. "I was told by the producers of *Twenty-One* purposely to lose to Van Doren," he attests, "and I can prove it."

Stempel approaches New York's newspapers. It's a juicy story, all right, but when questioned, *Twenty-One* producer Dan Enright flatly denies the allegation. The papers, fearing libel if they proceed, decline to print Stempel's accusations.

There have been other rumblings, rumors really, about how these shows with their huge stakes are "controlled" by their producers. In April 1957, a contestant named Dale Logue sues *The $100,000 Big Surprise* for $103,000, claiming rigging.

The matter is quietly settled out of court. In August of 1957, *Look* magazine breaks the first story about behind-the-scenes string-pulling on quiz shows. *The $64,000 Challenge* is partially controlled, *Look* reveals. *Twenty-One* and *Tic Tac Dough* are controlled. *Two for the Money* is not controlled. *Treasure Hunt* is controlled. *Name That Tune* is not controlled. *Strike It Rich* is partially controlled. So is *You Bet Your Life*. And so is a quiz called *High-Low*. This story and others are not very specific, and they fail to make waves.

May 1958: The first hard evidence of rigging comes not from the big quizzes but from a peripheral NBC game called *Dotto,* which requires contestants to guess famous caricatures by filling in the dots. Waiting backstage, standby contestant twenty-four-year-old Edward Hilgemeier, Jr., chances to witness *Dotto's* current champion, Marie Winn, a twenty-one-year-old Radcliffe graduate, studying a notebook. When she goes before the cameras, Hilgemeier leafs through it. To his amazement, the book contains the answers to the questions that Miss Winn is answering right that minute. Hilgemeier informs the losing contestant and together they

Jack Narz rallies contestants on *Dotto,* but the fix was in.

demand financial recompense. *Dotto*'s producers comply. Still, Hilgemeier believes, the story is too hot to keep under wraps. He calls the New York *Post,* informs the FCC and the New York City District Attorney's office. When *Dotto* is abruptly canceled, the *Post* prints Hilgemeier's story.

The resulting impact on the public serves to give focus to the rumors so long circulating about *The $64,000 Question, The $64,000 Challenge,* and *Twenty-One.* Quiz show ratings abruptly plummet. And finally, in August 1958, the New York *Journal-American* prints Herbert Stempel's story.

What Stempel has to say makes lurid reading. He reports that producer Dan Enright has said to him, "Look, kid, play ball with me and you'll win $25,000." He reports that he had been instructed to get a "white wall marine style" haircut and to wear a worn-out suit—all to look like a penniless GI. Stempel reports that he was coached how to grimace and stammer, that all of his questions were fed to him before each show, that he received an $18,500 advance from Enright.

"Wholly untrue," protests *Twenty-One*'s co-producer Jack Barry. "At no time has any contestant ever been given advance information about any questions." *Twenty-One* does more than demur. They sue Herbert Stempel for libel and infer that he may not be mentally competent.

Still, others come forward. More contestants from *Dotto,* and now from *The $64,000 Challenge* begin to volunteer information about how they have been coached.

August 1958: New York City District Attorney Frank Hogan responds to the public's mounting demands for hard information about the quiz shows by opening a grand jury. It will sit nine months and hear 150 witnesses. At first, the grand jury will hear lies and cover-ups. Hogan will later estimate that 100 of the 150 people from whom he has collected testimony have not told him the truth. "I find these charges very hard to believe!" an indignant Elfrida Von Nardoff will huff at the time. Four years later, she and twenty-two other contestants will plead guilty to a charge of perjury. When Hogan asks Dan Enright to produce his show's controversial pre-test, he is told that it has inadvertently been destroyed.

One contestant who does not lie is *Twenty-One*'s James Snodgrass. Snodgrass, who has won only $4,000 on the quiz, becomes the first person to validate Herbert Stempel's claims, testifying that he was given answers in advance, then told to lose to Hank Bloomgarden. Snodgrass testifies to the grand jury when he had at first protested about having to lose so soon, the show's staffer Albert Z. Freedman had come to him in tears. "I'll lose my job," Freedman had sobbed. "The show will go over budget." Dramatically, Snodgrass produces for the grand jury three sealed registered letters which he had mailed to himself before one of his appearances on the show. The letters contain not only the questions and answers that were asked on that show, but a list of histrionic instructions detailing how he was to behave. Then, in case the grand jury doubts the allegations, Bloomgarden himself appears before them, and confirms the testimony they have just been hearing.

Shades of Watergate

There were never any burglaries committed; there were no "plumbers." Still, the parallels between the Watergate coverup and the lengths to which certain members of the television industry were willing to go to keep the public from knowledge of the fraud are remarkable. "When Watergate happened, it was just like déjà-vu," says a producer very much on the scene then who still prefers to remain anonymous. "I found myself able to predict correctly Nixon's every move, one by one. It was just uncanny."

The waves produced by Snodgrass and Bloomgarden rock NBC. "We had no idea," they say, pledging to begin an immediate probe into the internal affairs of their packagers. To devote their full time to "disproving the unfounded charges against the integrity of our programs," Jack Barry and Dan Enright resign. Albert Freedman does not escape so easily. He is indicted on two counts of perjury and led away in handcuffs.

The $64,000 Challenge contestant The Reverend Charles E. "Stony" Jackson also gives the grand jury an earful. He details how *The $64,000 Challenge* had "screened" him in advance with information that enabled him to win. The week of Jackson's testimony, P. Lorillard Tobacco drops *The $64,000 Challenge*. By October, both *Twenty-One* and *The $64,000 Question,* though the latter had not yet been directly implicated, will be gone.

Still, there is no law on the books making it illegal to rig a quiz show, and it looks at first as if the matter will die with no indictments forthcoming when the grand jury disbands late in May 1959. The official record is sealed from public eyes, impounded by Judge Mitchell D. Schweitzer.

Michael O'Rourke of *Tic Tac Dough* accepts congratulations and dabs his brow. Those isolation booths were unventilated on purpose, so as to create that suspenseful-looking perspiration; $132,800 ain't hay.

Fall 1959: It is the grand jury foreman, Louis M. Hacker who finally breaks the silence. "The public should have access to these facts," he declares. Many of the quizzes he knows to be rigged, including Barry-Enright property *Tic Tac Dough,* are still on the air. Hacker further reports that NBC has been attempting to suppress the report. NBC quickly issues a denial. "We welcome its distribution," the network says.

Hacker is about to get his wish and more, for the United States Congress has entered the picture. Oren Harris, a Democrat from Arkansas in the House of Representatives, calls the House Legislative Oversight Committee to probe first the big-money quizzes, and later, the use of "payola" on radio and TV. Unlike the grand jury hearing, this inquiry will not be held behind closed doors. The press is welcome to attend, and the covers of *Time* and *Newsweek* are waiting.

Surely Charles Van Doren can quiet all the furor. Has he not steadfastly maintained his innocence throughout all the clamor? Since his appearance on *Twenty-One* almost two years before, Van Doren has continued to be a living, breathing emblem of America's most mythic success story, an example incarnate that knowledge is golden. He now possesses his doctorate and teaches English at Columbia University. He has married. With his winnings he has purchased a sports car and a townhouse in Manhattan's Greenwich Village. Best of all, he has just accepted a fifty-thousand-dollar-a-year job as anchor and companion to Dave Garroway on NBC's *Today Show.*

Now, however, seriously disquieting tremors are beginning to shake the base of Van Doren's enviable new life. Stempel's story is filling the front pages. Snodgrass has produced still another registered letter. Those who lied to the grand jury now find themselves reversing their stories. Even Dan Enright, who for months has been denying everything is now saying that the quizzes have been rigged for years: standard operating procedure. In the committee's second week, band leader Xavier Cugat confesses that he was coached on *The $64,000 Challenge.* "Of course I got help," he shrugs. "I didn't want to make a fool of myself." Child star Patty Duke also takes the stand. Her appearance on *The $64,000 Challenge,* she testifies, was pre-arranged by her agent John Ross for a $1,000 fee paid to the show's celebrity booker, Shirley Bernstein (conductor Leonard Bernstein's sister) out of her $32,000 winnings.

Quizzlings

As the scandals broke, wags of the day had a field day. *Variety* termed the turncoat contestants "quizzlings" after Vidkun Quisling, World War II traitor who betrayed Norway to the Nazis.

Quipped Bob Hope, "Successful contestants are being brought back for one more question: 'How do you plead?' "

Some reacted more piously. Said David Susskind: "Quiz shows like *Dotto* are monuments of mediocrity, stupidity, and dullness. I'd like to see them driven off the air." For remarks on Susskind's own game show, *Supermarket Sweep,* see page 292.

As the testimony continues to pour forth, CBS cancels its remaining big-money quizzes: *Top Dollar, The Big Payoff,* and *Name That Tune.* NBC is keeping its quiz shows but acknowledges that the public may have been deceived. Prudently, they suggest that Van Doren take a leave of absence from *Today,* until everything returns to normal.

"Normal" will not return. On October 9, the Harris committee issues a subpoena for Charles Van Doren to appear. But they will have to find him first. As Van Doren's moment of truth approaches, he panics and flees to the family's retreat in Connecticut. It will not be until November 2 that a cornered Charles Van Doren faces America. Pale and intense, he confesses at last, "I was deeply involved in a deception." Reading from a prepared statement, Van Doren now reveals that when he was a standby contestant *Twenty-One* producer Albert Freedman came to him. Co-operate with us in unseating the unpopular, ratings-damaging Stempel, Freedman had begged. You will be performing a great service to the intellectual life of the country, to teachers and to education in general by increasing public respect for the life of the mind.

Van Doren reveals how he next met with Dan Enright in his office. "He instructed me how to answer the questions," Van Doren confesses, "to pause before certain answers, to skip certain parts and return to them, to hesitate and build up suspense, and so forth." The aim, Van Doren testifies, was to be as entertaining as possible. Enright then instructed Van Doren to tie Stempel three times before defeating him. Later, when Van Doren was to fall to Vivienne Nearing, the scenario was to be the same. Van Doren also reveals that he regularly received, in advance, the questions and answers, sometimes entire show scripts, as well as large advances of money from Freedman.

At the close of his statement, Van Doren acknowledges that he has lied not only to the New York grand jury, but also to NBC and his lawyer. His account has meshed with Stempel's now in every detail.

When Van Doren is finished, the nation sits stunned and betrayed. It can speak of nothing else for days. On *The Today Show,* Dave Garroway breaks down and cries. Even President Dwight D. Eisenhower is moved to speak of it. Addressing the country, he compares the revelation to the "Black Sox" scandal in baseball back in 1917. "What a terrible thing to do to the American public," he declares.

The committee has heard an earful, but it is not quite through. If there has been rigging, it wants to know why. The producer of *The $64,000 Question,* Mert Koplin, supplies some insight. "We had to," he testifies. Revlon, the sponsor, wanted high ratings. To achieve them, the cosmetics company insisted upon control over the contestants. Koplin estimates that between 60 and 70 per cent of the winners on his two shows received some form of "help," often without their knowledge, but just as often with it. For instance, the questions kept in the bank vault were frequently substituted at the last minute for those more tailored to a contestant's abilities. The committee learns that Revlon's Martin Revson, brother of sponsor Charles, instructed EPI whom to ax if a contestant was not deemed likable enough. Angry reprimands resulted if a decision was not followed to the letter. Dr. Joyce Brothers, the country now learns, had been marked for eradication because she was considered dull. Brothers survived the questions meant to do her in; her expertise in boxing was genuine.

Whoops!

You could control 'em, you could rig 'em, but you could never guard against the biggest nemesis of all, that television then was live.

> Were *you* watching the night Hal March put the contestant in the isolation booth and then forgot to ask the $32,000 question?
> The night he inadvertently revealed the $16,000 baseball answer?
> The night he scratched the record for the jazz question?

One night, it wasn't so funny. Home viewers suddenly found themselves looking at the rafters of the studio instead of the stage. The cameraman had just been stabbed by a man who'd walked in off the street.

If Brothers was not coached, then what of the others? Convincing denials come from Gino Prato and Teddy Nadler. Said jockey Billy Pearson, "I studied like hell for a question on Chinese art, but they never asked it." Others, emerge more blemished. Before the revelations have been completed, Captain Richard McCutchen, the first man to win $64,000, will relinquish his commission in the U.S. Marines, tainted by his involvement in the scandals. Twenty-two more face formal charges of perjury that will take four chastening years to come to trial.

One man never appears before the committee. He is Louis G. Cowan, now president of CBS. Throughout, he has insisted upon his ignorance. "I asked them," he will say of Koplin and Carlin at EPI, "whether there

Not *Tic Tac Dough,* too? Say it isn't so.

was anything to these stories, and they assured me there was not. I was just as shocked by that Van Doren boy as the next person. I've known his parents for years." Cowan himself never appears before the committee because of illness. He has been confined to the hospital with phlebitis. Others will hint the illness is contrived, that Cowan has paid someone $150,000 not to have to appear. If so, he is only buying time. His golden quiz, his magnificent quantum leap, will finally do him in, as *Twenty-One* has done in Van Doren. Cowan is forced to resign from the presidency of CBS never to work in television again.

At CBS all public records pertaining to his presidency are sealed. If one searches today in the files at CBS, it is as if Louis G. Cowan and his quiz shows never ever existed. Cowan is not the only network casualty. Everyone connected with a quiz show is axed and temporarily blacklisted. By the time the Oversight Committee hearings come to an end, all the giveaway shows are gone from prime time television. In their places are Westerns, whose networks, sponsors, and advertising agencies, went right on looking for the next hit—as the ratings war for viewers and profits continued on unabated.

YOU GOTTA START SOMEWHERE. . . .

Forget those big questions. To answer them, you had to be coached. How would you fare on these "$64 questions, taken word for word from *The $64,000 Question?*

1. Stradivarius was one of the three great masters of violin making whose instruments have never been surpassed in tone and craftsmanship. What was Stradivarius' first name and the name of the town where he was born?
    ANSWER: Antonio; Cremona. The question went to Jack Benny; the subject was The Violin. Benny stopped at $64.

2. Jack Dempsey was one of the most popular heavyweight champs we've ever had. What was his nickname?
    ANSWER: The Manassa Mauler. Joyce Brothers answered that one on her way to winning $64,000. Her subject was Boxing.

3. If you save your pennies, the entire world is readily accessible. In which city would you see the following famous landmark: Waterloo Station?
    ANSWER: London. That was answered by Mrs. Helene Caskin. Her category was Famous Landmarks of the World. Her total winnings: $512.

4. Many great writers were often known by pen names or affectionate nicknames. Let's see how familiar you are with some pseudonyms. Who was Boz?
    ANSWER: Charles Dickens. Answered by Mrs. Celladore T. P. Crockett, the expert in English literature. Mrs. Crockett won a Cadillac.

5. The nicknames given to men who have sought the office of President of the United States give a colorful clue to their personalities. For $64, what unsuccessful candidate was known as the Happy Warrior?

ANSWER: Al Smith. Politics was the subject; George Dempster the contestant. He stopped at $32,000.

6. In the past seven years, man has conquered the highest mountains. For $64, what mountain was conquered by Maurice Herzog on June 3, 1950?

ANSWER: Annapurna. Answered by Lord Malcolm Douglas-Hamilton, expert on Men and Mountains. His lordship won a Cadillac.

7. When one of the American colonies was established, it was patterned after the English system of nobility with hereditary titles and vast ownership of land passing from father to son. Which colony?

ANSWER: The Carolinas. Dr. Alexander Sas-Jaworsky, who chose American History as his subject, went on to win $128,000. ..

8. Who said, "Am I my brother's keeper?"

ANSWER: Cain. Mrs. Catherine Kreitzer knew that one. Her subject was Bible. Her total: $32,000.

9. What was the name of the kind old hen who lived in the house with the ugly duckling?

ANSWER: Chick-a-Biddie-Short-Shank; also known as Chickie Low Legs. Children's Stories was Boris Karloff's bailiwick. He won $16,000.

10. I'll name a popular food; you tell me what the main ingredient is. For instance, junket is made of milk. For $64, what is Welsh Rabbit?

ANSWER: Cheese. Answered by Captain Richard McCuthen, the first contestant to win $64,000. His subject was Food and Cooking.

11. Science has increased the life expectancy for us all, but which group, male or female can expect to live longer?

ANSWER: Female. Answered by Dr. Ashley Montagu, the popular anthropologist who appeared on the show to push one of his many new books. Montagu won $32,000 on the subject Male and Female. Recently Montagu became a popular name on game shows *again*. The writers on *The Better Sex* frequently dipped into his books for questions.

12. I'll give you the name of a character in one of Shakespeare's plays. You give me the name of his wife or sweetheart. Romeo?

ANSWER: Juliet. That was asked of Redmon O'Hanlon, the first contestant on the show. His expertise in Shakespeare netted him $16,000.

13. I will name some famous horse races. You tell me the name of the tracks where they are run. The Kentucky Derby?

ANSWER: Churchill Downs. Asked of Mrs. Ida M. Sherburne, expert on the Sport of Kings. She also won $16,000.

14. Many show tunes have become America's most popular songs. I'll name

a song; you tell me the production from which it came. "Younger Than Springtime"?

ANSWER: *South Pacific.* Asked of Nancy Wilson on the subject of Popular Music. She missed.

15. I'll give you the name of a man in an opera. You give me his sweetheart or wife. Don José?

ANSWER: Carmen. That was asked of Gino Prato on his climb to $32,000 in the subject of Opera.

16. Which is larger in area: Greenland or Borneo?

ANSWER: Greenland. Asked of Alfred Einfrank in Geography. Einfrank missed on the $64,000 question.

17. I'll describe a famous work of art; you tell me its creator. A man and a woman in a farm setting entitled "American Gothic"?

ANSWER: Grant Wood. Asked of Billy Pearson, jockey, playboy, and expert in Great Art and Artists. Pearson eventually won $64,000.

18. I'll name a musician famous in his field of jazz; you tell me his musical instrument: Count Basie?

ANSWER: Piano. Jazz was The Reverend Alvin Kershaw's bag; $32,000 his take.

19. The symphonic suite has become a musical entity in the hands of composers. Name the composers of the following popular symphonic suite: The Grand Canyon Suite?

ANSWER: Ferde Grofé. That was asked of Don McArdle on Classical Music. He missed at the $2,000 level and took home $512.

20. If you managed to wade through all this trivia of yesteryear, here's one final four part bonus question. Who was responsible for writing these overblown, pretentious, and highhanded questions in the first place?

ANSWER: Dr. Bergen Evans.

What famous Big Ten University was he associated with?

ANSWER: Northwestern. He taught English Literature there.

How'd he get a job in quiz shows?

ANSWER: He knew Louis G. Cowan from the old days back in Chicago.

Now name four other quiz shows with which he was associated in the fifties.

ANSWER: *It's About Time; Top Dollar; The Last Word;* and *Down You Go.*

_____

Now, the most important question of all. It's been twenty years since the scandals. Time to ask . . .

. . . Where Are They Now?

Gino Prato. Directly after his appearance on *The $64,000 Question* the little shoemaker took a $10,000 a year job with the American Biltrite Rubber Company, as good-will ambassador. He sold his shop, traveled, and gained twenty-seven pounds. After the scandals, Biltrite quietly revoked the job. Prato took it stoically; he was tired of traveling, he said. He opened a new shoe shop in the Bronx, worked long hours, did good business, lost weight. And remained essentially the same warm, charming family man he always was. Prato died in 1968.

Charles Van Doren. He leads a quiet, almost hermitlike life in Chicago. His house has a high wall around it; he owns a guard dog. He does not give interviews. For several years after the scandals, Van Doren made his living writing articles and books under a pseudonym; publishers were unwilling to print anything that bore his name. Then in 1961, an old family friend, Mortimer Adler, hired him as an editor on the Institute for Philosophical Research, an arm of *The Encyclopaedia Britannica* company in Chicago. Van Doren writes and edits for both to this day. At fifty-two, Charles Van Doren is still trying to forget.

Teddy Nadler. When last heard from, Nadler, the biggest winner of all, was living in St. Louis, down and out and bitter. The hardest pill for him to swallow is his inability to hold a job. For a while he sold television sets, but quit, accusing his employer of exploiting him. Others refused to hire him; they thought he was joking when he said he needed a job—he with all his money. He flunked a test necessary to become a thirteen-dollar-a-day census taker. Later years brought prostate and hernia surgery. Bitterly he still rails at the world about how much he knows and how little good it does him. "There's nobody better than me," he says from his cramped four-room apartment. "I'm the greatest. I'm the eighth wonder of the world."

Billy Pearson. The five-foot-two-inch art expert, jockey, playboy spent his $174,000 winnings years ago on wine, women, and gambling. But he still makes a handsome living from his gallery of primitive art in San Francisco, and he spends every cent he makes. He has an expensive home filled with costly art objects; he drives a late-model sports car. Married four times, he hobnobs with movie stars. Once a prodigious drinker, he now confines himself to champagne and Coors beer. He worries and wants for nothing: when this is gone, he says, "I'll get more from somewhere. I always have. I was always lucky. Man, have I been lucky."

Dr. Joyce Brothers. A celebrity in her own right, Brothers believes she would have achieved her station in life without the quiz shows. Twenty-seven years old at the time she won the $134,000, Brothers, with her Ph.D. in psychology, knew nothing about boxing. But she boned up on it to fit the show's format and because there are relatively few statistics pertaining to the sport to memorize. Half of her money went to taxes, some went into the bank. The rest enabled her M.D. husband to set up a Park Avenue practice earlier than he might have been able to on his own. Untouched by the scandals, Brothers continues to make her frequent talk-show appearances, write her articles, and stay very much in the public eye as according to one, "a sort of cross between Ann Landers and Sigmund Freud."

Captain Richard McCutchen cuts the cake with his saber as Billy Pearson, Dr. Joyce Brothers, an unidentified contestant, and Hal March prepare to dive in.

Albert Freedman. The producer and righthand man to Dan Enright, the man who fed Van Doren the answers, Freedman until very recently lived in self-imposed exile outside the United States. Shortly after his indictment for perjury, he moved to Mexico City. From there, in the midst of the scandals, he wrote an open letter to the New York *Times,* likening the rigging of the quiz shows to ghost-writing a speech. "No one was hurt by it," he maintained. "The quiz shows were far more uplifting than most of the violence that appears on television." It is a position he still maintains today. For some years, Freedman lived in London, associated with *Penthouse* magazine. Now, for the first time in nearly twenty years, Freedman again lives in New York City where he is currently the editor of *Penthouse Forum* magazine.

Dan Enright. For years, neither he nor his less implicated partner, Jack Barry, could find work in television in the United States. Enright moved to Canada where he continued to develop game shows for Screen Gems. There he operated, in effect, a "finishing school" for dozens of young game show producers currently working in American television. It's to him junior-level people always went to continue their apprenticeship when their network shows got canceled and they needed jobs. In the last several years, Enright has returned to the United States. His old partnership with Jack Barry has been revived and together they again package games that are highly successful in the syndication market. Enright refuses to talk about his past.

Steve Carlin. The producer of *The $64,000 Question* and *The $64,000 Challenge* is back in business with his syndicated show, *The $128,000 Question.* The format's the same as its forebearer; the stakes are just doubled. And of course, *this* time around, it's completely on the up-and-up. Is *that* why the show's so boring? Or is it because we've all grown up?

Louis G. Cowan. Deceased at the age sixty-five. On November 16, 1976, Cowan and his wife Polly were killed by a fire that swept their Park Avenue penthouse apartment. Permanently retired from television, Cowan continued to lead a rich and active life. He served on the boards of several magazines, and colleges including *Partisan Review* and Brandeis University. He helped found the National Book Awards. He served on the faculty and conducted seminars at Columbia's College of Journalism, where he was much revered. Was he involved in the rigging of *The $64,000 Question?* He denied it to his dying day.

The Best of the Sixties

Then a funny thing happened. Scattered to the wind, besmirched and maligned, the shows still refused to die. The networks hadn't axed them all, for five Goodson-Todman games survived. Cautiously, the networks scheduled a few more games during the day, produced by a new crop of packagers: Bob Quigley and Merrill Heatter, Monty Hall and Stefan Hatos, Chuck Barris, Merv Griffin, Ralph Andrews, Ron Greenburg, Randall Fishman and Ed Freer, who came along to fill the vacuum left by the exiled. The networks issued a blizzard of press releases about the new shows first, of course, touting their strict new regulations and the security measures attending them. Rigging, they let it be known, was now a felony punishable by five years in jail and a $50,000 fine. Prizes were de-emphasized and the nature of the questions changed. In fact, you never even heard the word "quiz" any more. And you know something? The new shows were actually better than they'd ever been before, freer, crazier, and more creative, as contestants gave the password, asked the correct question, dressed up in silly costumes, hung out their marital wash . . . and would you believe celebrities scrambling into a giant tic-tac-toe board?

26. Concentration

Actually, this show was born in 1958—not quite the sixties—and not particularly auspiciously either, with scandal breaking all around it. *Concentration* survived for two reasons. Even before the widespread rigging was revealed, Barry-Enright, the company that had created *Concentration,* no longer owned the game. As part of a lucrative pre-scandal arrangement, they had sold its rights to NBC. Network control may make a show honest; it does not, however, guarantee that it will be popular. *Concentration* endured because it was so excellently crafted. Indeed, it was the first truly modern game show, the first proof that a game could be entertaining, suspenseful, involving and challenging without asking a series of boring general-information questions, and without offering contestants numbingly high stakes.

Concentration was named after and based upon the children's card game in which two players alternately uncover two cards at a time from a deck spread out face down until one player gradually collects the greater number of pairs to win the game. On the television version of the game, two contestants played for paired merchandise. Before them stood a large game board containing thirty numbers, each number concealing part of a pictogram, or puzzle, called a rebus. Each successful match entitled a contestant to see two more parts of the puzzle and to temporarily claim the prize described on the face of the two matched squares. However, contestants did not get to keep their prizes unless they solved the puzzle, thereby winning the game.

Concentration was developed at Barry-Enright by Robert Noah, now a producer at Heatter-Quigley. Noah took the childhood game and improved it by including on the board humorous prizes along with luxury merchandise prizes, surprise wild cards, and squares that permitted raids on the opposing contestant's prizes or forfeitures of his own. To further increase the suspense, even though one contestant might, in the course of play, have amassed an entire board full of prizes, he did not get to keep them unless he solved the puzzle. If the opposing contestant could solve the puzzle first, then he won the game, even though he might not have earned any prizes at all. Winning contestants could continue to play until they were unseated or until they won twenty games in a row, at which time they retired undefeated.

Concentration's special effects were wholly innovative. The game board was constructed of multifaced cubes that swung around with a creak and a thud to reveal the rebus. Frequently cubes got stuck in the middle of a

Concentration host Hugh Downs looks as though he's been burning the candle at both ends. He *was*. Co-hosting *The Tonight Show* and a game show could tucker you out, especially in the days before videotape.

swivel, an effect more charming than exasperating. Frequently, the rebuses were more exasperating than charming, calling as they did for a mangling of the English language, as a series of seemingly undecipherable sounds and pictures were linked together by plus signs. One such rebus, reading out to be "I speak from experience," depicted an ice pick, the letter F, a jug of rum, an ax, a glass of beer, the letter E, a hen sitting on a nest of eggs and the letter Z. If the contestant thought that a picture was of something other than what it really was (hatchet for ax, say), then forget the hen, he was a dead duck. Another fascinating element of the game was the contestant's prize board, on which the names of the prizes seemed magically to float into view, or in the event of a raid by his opponent, distressingly float to the other contestant's side.

Hugh Downs was the host most associated with *Concentration,* and in 1968–69 he won an Emmy for his role on the show. In addition to hosting *Concentration,* Downs also appeared on the *Tonight Show* as Jack Paar's announcer. Downs first stepped in when the game's scandal-tarnished original host, Jack Barry, left the show. Other hosts on the network version of *Concentration* were Art James, Bill Mazer, Ed McMahon, and Bob Clayton.

Concentration ran for fifteen years over NBC until it was canceled in 1973. Still, the show remained too good to die and that same year Goodson-Todman purchased its rights for syndication, the only game Goodson-Todman has ever aired that they did not themselves originally develop. In the syndicated version of the game, Goodson-Todman added an end game in which the winning contestant could try for a larger stake, usually a car, by solving two more rebuses in ten seconds. The host of the syndicated version of *Concentration* was Jack Narz.

27. Password

"Thin . . ."
"Skinny?"
"Wood . . ."
"Bamboo?"
Tick tick tick . . .
How *do* you get someone to say "veneer"? In 1962, when *Password,* the rapid-fire, often frustrating, word game of quick deductive reasoning first appeared, the question obsessed America. *Password*'s object: by giving only

Carol Channing and Eli Wallach are hard players. Think Wallach's contestant'll solve it this round?

one-word clues, and without using your hands, to coax your partner to say a designated word before your opponents do. Two teams, each composed of one celebrity and one civilian contestant, took turns in trying to convey the "password." If the first player guessed the word from the first clue given to him by his teammate, his team received ten points. But since the opposing team could listen to that clue, the first team had to decide, based on the difficulty of the word, whether to play or pass the question to their opponents, thereby giving themselves the advantage of eavesdropping. Guessing the password on the second try netted nine points, on the third, eight, and so on. The first team to collect twenty-five points won the round. Then civilian players switched celebrity teammates. The first civilian to win two rounds earned the right to play the Lightning Rod end game for five hundred dollars. Playing at breakneck speed, the civilian tried to guess ten words in sixty seconds from clues given to him by his celebrity partner. Each word was valued at fifty dollars. Whether the civilian champion won this round or not, he or she now faced a new challenger.

Password was the first game to pair celebrities with civilians. It also introduced to game shows an entirely new kind of host. *Password's* emcee was Allen Ludden, a quiet-spoken, bespectacled man with an intellectual bearing and a taste for Ivy League suits. The low-profiled veteran of *G.E. College Bowl* and a number of desk jobs on the sidelines of broadcasting, Ludden took this job over the objections of his teen-aged children, who were dubious about their father's being suddenly thrust into the limelight. But Ludden had hospital bills to pay resulting from the death of his first wife and as the job would triple his salary he took the job. *Password's* viewers also had mixed feelings at first about Ludden in the role of host and there were complaints about his "boy scout" manner. Soon, however, viewers warmed to his earnestness, his friendliness, his shyness, and above all, to his enthusiasm for this amazing game.

And *Password was* amazing. In this game of high-pressure free association, contestants' guards were lowered and Freudian slips abounded.

"Father . . . ?" said one contestant.

"Mean," responded the celebrity.

"Appetite . . . ?" another contestant offered as his clue.

"Sexual," responded his partner, a seminary student.

"Pigeon?" said one.

"Bleep," said Betsy Palmer.

Other successful clues were just plain clever. When Ginger Roger's password was "edge," she tried "razor's" and it worked. For "nation" Tom Poston scored ten points with "indivisible." From punning Bennett Cerf came "Schuster." His password was "salmon."

America was hooked on the game, and so was the *Password* staff. The show's originator, Bob Stewart, producer Frank Wayne, and Allen Ludden found themselves playing it compulsively, backstage, at dinner, in the car with their families. Carol Burnett, Darren McGavin, Zachary Scott, and Abe Burrows especially became addicts. After his appearance, Chuck Connors begged to be invited back. When the *Password* home game came out, the country cleaned out the stores. Between November and December of 1962 alone, *Password* yielded Goodson-Todman $70,000 in royalties. So expert did both civilian and celebrity contestants become at playing *Password* that each year the game began to set aside two tournament weeks to establish the game's best players. Richard Dawson for one, still proudly displays the trophy he won one year.

Redletter Years

1974. Frank Wayne and Howard Felsher of the revived *Password* won an Emmy for producing the Outstanding Game Show of the Year. Two years later, in 1976, Allen Ludden won one for best host on a game show.

That's another crack *Password* player, Elizabeth Montgomery, during the game's second incarnation. Notice how much more distinguished Ludden is looking, how much more chi-chi the set.

Password ran until the fall of 1967, when CBS began canceling all of its game shows, thereby plunging daytime television into its darkest hour: the era of reruns. In 1971, however, sensing that the game had died prematurely, ABC brought *Password* back. Immediately, the game again displayed its capacity for innovation. *Password* thrived in the afternoon, where game shows, were supposed to fail. When ABC moved the show to a morning time slot, its ratings remained just as high. *Password*'s success on ABC motivated CBS and NBC to re-evaluate their programming; perhaps they'd been hasty in canceling game shows in 1969. They retired their reruns of *Gilligan's Island* and, thanks to *Password*, there would be game shows in the seventies.

Early in 1979, an updated version of the game called *Password Plus* returned over NBC, hosted as always by Ludden.

For more about *Password*'s best contestant, see page 16.
For more about the celebrities on *Password,* see pages 48–50.
For more about host Allen Ludden, see pages 184–187.

Other Word Games

Password is just one of many word games that have aired over the years:

Across the Board, emceed by Ted Brown over ABC in 1959 was one. Here are some others:

Baffle, emceed by Dick Enberg and seen over NBC in 1973.

Blankety-Blanks, emceed by Bill Cullen and seen over ABC in 1975.

Chain Letter, emceed by Jan Murray and seen over NBC in 1966.

Cross-Wits, emceed by Jack Clark and seen in syndicated markets since 1975.

Double Cross, emceed by Allyn Edwards and seen locally in New York over WATV-TV in 1959.

Down You Go, emceed by Bergen Evans and seen both over Dumont and ABC between 1951 and 1956.

Fractured Phrases, emceed by Art James and seen over NBC in 1965.

Go Lucky, emceed by Jan Murray, and seen over CBS in 1951.

Jackpot!, emceed by Geoff Edwards and seen over NBC between 1974 and 1975.

Knockout, emceed by Arte Johnson, seen over NBC in 1977.

Now You See It, emceed by Jack Narz and seen over CBS between 1974 and 1975.

Number, Please, emceed by Bud Collyer and seen over ABC in 1961.

Pass the Buck, emceed by Bill Cullen and seen over CBS in 1978.

PDQ, emceed by Dennis James, Bill Cullen, and seen over NBC between 1965 and 1970.

Rhyme and Reason, with Bob Eubanks and Nipsey Russell, seen over ABC in 1975.

Riddle in the Middle, with Bill Goodwin and seen over NBC in 1950.

Shoot for the Stars, emceed by Geoff Edwards and seen over NBC between 1976 and 1977.

Spread the Word, emceed by Bill Nimmo and seen locally in New York over WPIX-TV in 1964.

Stumpers, emceed by Allen Ludden, seen over NBC in 1976.

Top Dollar, emceed by Toby Reed and Bergen Evans, seen over CBS in 1958.

To Say the Least, emceed by Tom Kennedy and seen over NBC in 1977.

TV Crossword Puzzle, seen locally in New York over WPIX-TV in 1952.

TV Crossword Quiz, a syndicated game owned by Aaron S. Bloom.

The $20,000 Pyramid (see pages 255–259).

We Take Your Word, emceed by J. K. M. McCaffery and John Daly, seen over CBS in 1950–51.

Wheel of Fortune, emceed by Chuck Woolery and Susan Stafford, seen over NBC since 1975.

Winning Streak, emceed by Bill Cullen and seen over NBC between 1974 and 1975.

Word for Word, emceed by Merv Griffin and seen over NBC between 1963 and 1964.

You Don't Say, emceed by Tom Kennedy and seen over NBC between 1963 and 1969, over ABC in 1975, and in syndication in 1978.

---

28. Let's Make a Deal

From off camera comes the most unctuous, titilating voice in television, as once more, Jay Stewart launches into one of broadcasting's most spine-tingling spiels: "These people, dressed as they are," he purrs, "come from all over the United States to make deals, here in the marketplace of America. And now (*drum roll*), here is America's top trader, TV's big dealer . . . MONTY HALL!!"

The camera pans a studio full of farmers, carrots, rabbits, and hoboes, all jouncing placards up and down. And to anyone tuning in for the first time, it's at once dead solid certain that they are watching *the* prole game of all time.

Still, if you think greed's its grease, you're wrong. *Let's Make a Deal* would work without prizes and without costumes. It would work with three walnut shells and a pea, for that's exactly what it's based on, the shell game. As such, it will continue working as long as human beings are driven by the curiosity that overrides common sense: to *need* to know what's behind that curtain, beneath that box—to need to know whether their hunches are right.

On the other hand, *Let's Make a Deal wouldn't* work with just any emcee. It has to be Monty (the breezy Manitoban medical school dropout, born Halperin) Hall. Ever since *Let's Make a Deal* debuted back in December 1963, Monty has been the glib, tantalizing catalyst who controls the hysteria he generates. In exchange, he's suffered lacerated ribs, had his neck wrenched, and had the ligaments of his hands cut. He's been beaten over the head with stuffed animals until he's lost his continuity: men and women have wet their pants, pregnant women have broken their water. Many forget their names. And throughout all of it, Hall's seldom missed a taping. When he has, his stand-ins, not possessing his ability to parry and feint, have not fared as well. Once, substitute Bill Leyden, himself no slouch at dealing with euphoria from his years on *It Could Be You*, was knocked all the way down the studio-aisle stairs. What is it about Hall that unleashes such physical energy in his "victims"?

"I'm a con man," Hall acknowledges, "but a friendly con man, and I'm willing to conduct my cons not from the stage, but right out in the audience."

Before him stands a plump woman dressed as a fisherman. She trades away her sign ("I'm angling to make a deal with you," it says) for the chance to be tortured by Monty. Hall, dodging her fishing pole, offers her a choice. Does she want a wallet containing either five dollars or five hundred dollars, or does she want what's in the chest Carol Merrill is holding? She wants the wallet. It contains five hundred dollars. It's a lot of money. But now Jay Stewart has wheeled out onto the trading floor an even bigger box. Who knows what's back there: a new kitchen? a car? appliances? The fisherwoman dances in torment. The audience is in a frenzy. "Keep the money!" "Take the box!"

"Do you want the five hundred or the box?" asks Hall. "What if I give

America's top trader, Jay Stewart, and victims.

you six hundred dollars?" he teases. "Seven hundred dollars?" "Eight hundred dollars?"

Finally, the lure of the unknown is too great. "I came here with nothing," she explains, twisting her hands in delicious agony. "I'll take the box."

Behind it stands a camel. Our fisherwoman has been zonked. Shrugging gamely, she hands the wallet back to Hall and gives him a kiss.

"Isn't she a nice lady?" he says. The audience gives her a hand and then leans breathlessly forward as Hall sniffs out his next victims. They're a married couple dressed as Jack and Jill, and Hall now sets about playing them off against each other, wringing every drop of suspense from their series of dilemmas, their tug of war with the sure thing and the unknown, with security and risk. . . .

. . . It's the end of the half hour and time for the Big Deal of the Day. Hall now approaches the show's two top winners: Jack and Jill, who've amassed thirteen hundred dollars in merchandise, and an overweight young man who's won a silver tea service from Michael C. Fina. Forgetting the struggle getting *that* just took, they trade for one more flirtation with fate. In choosing Door Number 2, Jack and Jill win a year's supply of Chunky chocolate bars and a stereo console valued at less than the merchandise they've traded away. The overweight young man, who's never been farther away than San Diego, wins a trip to Japan. Perhaps tomorrow someone will win the Big Deal, as someone has been doing from the day *Let's Make a Deal* first burst upon America.

In its fourteen-year heyday as a network show, *Let's Make a Deal* broke all records for game show popularity. Whatever its time slot it damaged every competitor it faced. Its first year on the air, it knocked ten points off *Password* and cut deeply into the lead of the redoubtable *As the World Turns*. In a summer evening slot in 1967, it became the only show ever to compete successfully with the *Ed Sullivan Show* and *The FBI*. When contract negotiations broke down with NBC, *Let's Make a Deal* switched to ABC. Within the first six months, NBC suffered a million-dollar loss in daytime advertising revenue. On ABC, *Let's Make a Deal* continued as the hottest show in daytime, steadily holding a thirty share in every time slot. In syndication, its numbers rose to 40, 50, and in some markets, 60 per cent.

Such success could not have been predicted. Monty Hall had been scuffling on the fringes of daytime television for years. Before *Let's Make a Deal,* his credits had been meager: many auditions, no network shows. Hall had announced local New York boxing, wrestling, soccer, and hockey. There had been *Bingo at Home, Monitor,* and an occasional substitute hosting job on *Strike It Rich* and *Twenty-One.* He had hosted the short-lived *Video Village.* Not until Hall left New York for California and teamed up with *It Could Be You* producer Stefan Hatos did his luck begin to change. Their show, *Your First Impressions,* enjoyed a moderate success.

When *Let's Make a Deal* began to evolve it was a composite of two shows each had worked on: one called *The Auctioneer,* which Hall had emceed in Canada; the other a local New York housewife trade-in show called *Ladies Be Seated,* which Hatos produced with Johnny Olson. Now Hatos and Hall began to combine its best features for a national audience. First they conducted extensive run-throughs with whatever charitable groups were willing to have them. The game, with Hall playing carnival barker, worked beyond their expectations with bingo ladies, Lutheran sewing bees, and Weight Watchers in Sherman Oaks. It worked without prizes, without props, without zonks, and without costumes, all of which would spontaneously evolve later.

Convincing the network brass proved tougher. ABC turned it down flat, and even though its run-throughs were sensational, NBC's response was tepid. "Sure, it looks great today," said Jerry Chester, then head of NBC daytime and now an officer at Goodson-Todman, "but what do you do tomorrow?"

Still the idea had generated enough enthusiasm among others at NBC, Robert Aaron and Richard Dunn. The pilot of *Let's Make a Deal* was said to be the best NBC ever made. *Let's Make a Deal* ran on NBC until 1967, switched its affiliation to ABC, and aired until 1976. Still hosted by Hall, it currently airs in syndication taped usually in Los Angeles, sometimes in Las Vegas.

Monty's Secret Fan

Among many, it's just not fashionable to admit you like *Let's Make a Deal*, it's considered so tacky. Here's a testimonial from a *secret* pal: "I had been one of those who had said that a game of pure luck would not succeed, said Mark Goodson back in 1969." Monty is brilliant the way he does it . . . the tension he has built up. He makes those people feel that what they are deciding is decidable on the basis of a judgment they have to make, when indeed it's not. I mean the fact is they could probably do just as well by flipping a coin every time. But he creates tension and there is also that marvelous thing of vicariously sharing the win with someone else. . . ."

29. The Dating Game

Chuck Barris is the first man in America to realize how *desperately* "ordinary" people want to be on television. So he put them on. In fact, Chuck's been putting us *all* on for years.

The Dating Game was Chuck Barris' first show. So bad was it, so repellent, so amazing, so unbelievable, so wonderful, that when it first aired in December 1965, America simply could not take its eyes away. *Where* did he get those people? you wondered. How did he get them to *say* those things? And when is someone going to fix *me* up with *my* dream date and whisk *me* away to the Bahamas?

It was taped in Hollywood, of course, "the dating capital of the world." Onto your screen would step a bachelor, suave, handsome, majoring in pre-law; *all* bachelors seemed to major in pre-law, just as all just loved to ski and backpack and surf. And all were just a little dippy. The bachelor was looking for true love. On *The Dating Game,* he did not have to look far. It sat waiting for him behind a partition. There on stools, perched three young, miniskirted women, who for purposes of identification were dubbed Bachelorette Number One, Bachelorette Number Two, and Bachelorette Number Three. "A little too much make-up," you'd muse at home, "but not bad." That was before a bachelorette oppened her mouth. The game now allotted the bachelor five minutes to screen the candidates for his dream date. This he accomplished by judging their responses to such profound explorations into the human predicament as "We are stranded on a desert island. What are we going to do when the novelty wears off?" For five minutes, the airwaves jiggled with giggles and coy answers given in silken voices: "I can fix it so the novelty *never* wears off!"

"I'll take Bachelorette Number Two," the bachelor would say. "She seems deeper than the other two."

And then, there she was. On *The Dating Game,* the magic moment of meeting, exchanging the first kiss, happened in front of all America. Hand in hand the two young lovers stood to learn of their dream date together— four days' vacation somewhere romantic, complete with chaperone. In a second round a bachelorette grilled three bachelors. And in a final round, a mortal got a crack at a date with one of three celebrities.

There had been, believe it or not, a game like it before. *Blind Date* was hosted by Arlene Francis, and had aired first on radio during World War II and later on television over ABC in 1949. The show gave servicemen the chance to woo young secretaries over the phone, with the winners receiving a Gruen watch and dinner together at the Stork Club. In fact, the owners of *Blind Date* had recognized the resemblance and when *The Dating Game* bowed, they sued. They hadn't a prayer. On *Blind Date,* after all, no one had wanted to know, "How would you control me if I got a little out of control?" or "When you tell me you'll love me forever, for how long do you mean?"

Chuck Barris came to the game show business through the back door, a black sheep made good in spite of himself. Born on Philadelphia's Main Line, he bounced in and out of six colleges before graduating from Drexel.

Then he bounced through a few careers, working first at the United States Steel Corporation, then for a film editor, then for a fight promotor. He was a short-lived NBC management trainee. He sold TelePrompTers. He married CBS president William Paley's niece Lynn Levy (for which, if we are to believe Barris' thinly veiled autobiographical novel, *You and Me, Babe,* she was disinherited). He wrote hit song "Palisades Park." He bummed around Europe for six months. And then he took a job in the ABC Standards and Practices Department, newly formed in the aftermath of the scandals. His job: to keep tabs on the Dick Clark show. From there he headed West as head of ABC's West Coast daytime programming department. The job existed in name only. All of ABC's daytime shows in the early sixties originated from New York. That made quitting easy. Still, the job had planted a seed: there is nothing better than having to judge other people's bad ideas day after day to make you see merit in your own. For Barris' next career, he would become a packager. Living off the royalties of his record, Barris rented a cheap motel room as his office and placed his first calls to the networks. No response. Then he rented a $3,500-a-day bungalow at the Beverly Hills Hotel. Hollywood returned his every call. In November 1965, down to his last seventy-two dollars, Chuck Barris sold *The Dating Game* to ABC.

- -

QUIZ

Many celebrities offered their bodies to *The Dating Game* during its run, including Wilt Chamberlain. Here are a couple of The Stilt's questions:

1. "You know, I'm bigger than the average guy. What are you going to do with all this man?"
2. "I have a question for all of you. #1: When? #2: What? #3: Why?
3. "I have a problem with kissing a girl good night because I have to bend way over. How would you solve that problem for us?"
4. "I date a lot of girls and most of them just one time. What is it about you that's going to make me want to date you more than once?"

- -

In two years' time, the offices of Chuck Barris Productions on Vine Street in Hollywood took up an entire floor in which worked the "Barris

Bandits,'' a staff of girls in miniskirts, and bearded young men in blue jeans, all in their twenties. Their job was to single out all contestants who appeared in the Barris offices displaying a proclivity for saying the embarrassing with equanimity. Finding *that* in a contestant, Barris would say with a smile, was much more important than the game.

Contestants on *The Dating Game,* however, were sometimes apt to find a few strings in Cinderella land. To protect itself from possible lawsuits, Barris Productions required its winners to sign a formidable legal document, in which contestants agreed, while on their dream date, to accede to the presence of a Barris staff chaperone. Ocean swimming and other potentially litigious activities were forbidden. If a couple elected to stay longer than the stipulated three-and-a-half-day period, the parties were required to pay the overage out of their own pockets. On more than one highly publicized occasion, *that* was scarcely the problem when couples realized they detested each other and dream weekends were prematurely nipped in the bud. Still, the complaints were few. Sixty per cent of the couples, *The Dating Game* reported, continued to see each other after their weekend together ended. One contestant named Candy Howard took matters to a conclusion Chuck Barris had to love. Candy not only appeared on the premiere telecast of *The Dating Game,* she was about to appear on Barris' shortlived beauty contest show, *Dream Girl of '67,* when her wedding to the bachelor she'd met on *The Dating Game* interfered. Of course, they appeared on *The Newlywed Game.* Candy was looking forward to an appearance on Barris' *The Family Game,* when it was canceled.

Hosted by Jim Lange, *The Dating Game* was one of the few postscandal shows successfully to air in prime time. It ran in the afternoons over ABC from December 1965 and in prime time on Saturday nights from October 1966 until 1973. It would make millions for both Barris and ABC. *The Dating Game* is still running in syndication.

30. The Newlywed Game

America was still reeling in disbelief over *The Dating Game,* when six months later Chuck Barris flabbergasted the country again with *The Newlywed Game.*

Seated behind sliding desks, out onto a set of silver arching trees, glided four young couples, the ink on their marriage licenses not twelve months dry. There they were, the pert and cloying young wives whose voices all had undertones as grating as a dentist's drill ("Bruce, you *know* my meat loaf is better than your mother's!"), and the callow, flustered husbands with junior white-collar jobs and senior mortgages on their new houses. On national TV they revealed all—sweetly at first, but with increasing snappishness as the show wore on. Host Bob Eubanks' job was to fan the flames of marital discord and a more insidious, snake-in-the-grass emcee there has never been: "He doesn't pay attention to you after you make love? Well, what *does* he do? And you put up with him, do you? Well, let's get him back out here and see what he has to say about that! Don't tell him? Why not? You just told *me*."

Get ready, America, to hear more than you absolutely want to about the wonderful folks behind the latticework.

Bob Eubanks will extract it.

The Newlywed Game was played in three rounds. The first round posed three questions to wives about the personal habits and proclivities of off-stage husbands, worth five points. Wives egged on by Eubanks would write their responses in felt-tip pen on large white cards, which they then placed face down in their laps until they were called upon to reveal them. Then the husbands would return and attempt to match their wives' responses which they held up to the camera. Success resulted in squeals and kisses; misses in pouts. In the second round, questions worth ten points, were now asked of the husbands. At the close of the round, Eubanks asked a 25-point bonus question to determine the winner of the game. The questions on *The Newlywed Game* ranged from the off color ("The first time you made love, what was the loudest sound you heard?") to the banal ("How many drains will your wife say there are in your house?"). The couple with the highest number of points at the close of the show received useful domestic merchandise tailored whenever possible to that couple's predetermined special needs.

Though the Chuck Barris touch could be seen all over *The Newlywed Game,* the idea for the show was not his but that of packagers Nick Nicholson and Roger Muir. Their own children had married within a few months of each other. Shortly thereafter they had all begun to play an informal parlor game, "What color are your new husband's eyes?" and "What is your wife's favorite color?," a test of how well the newlyweds really knew each other. Nicholson and Muir mounted a pilot based on the game and showed it to ABC. It featured an older couple asking the questions of the young couples. Though ABC was interested, they were not completely sold. The network offered the idea to Barris and granted him total freedom to produce it his way. *That* immediately involved throwing out all serious overtones and substituting the elements of embarrassed *faux pas* that came to seem both nostalgic and ludicrous in a sixties obsessed with the sexual revolution and The Pill. Nicholson and Muir received royalties; their names appeared on the show's credits. Later when *The Newlywed Game* aired in syndication, Barris bought them out.

Honk!

Nick Nicholson's other claim to fame: he was *Howdy Doody's* second Clarabelle.

The Newlywed Game bowed over ABC during the summer of 1966, and it was an immediate hit. In large measure, although indirectly, it owed the swiftness of its rise to the war in Vietnam. The day the show debuted, a press conference held by the then Secretary of Defense Robert McNamara pre-empted *Password,* the formidable CBS rival. Droves of hard-bitten game show addicts turned their dials to ABC, and saw *The Newlywed Game.* Mouths open, palms klopped to foreheads, they became instant converts. *The Newlywed Game* enjoyed a successful run over ABC until the end of 1974, and a nighttime version of the game flourished in prime time from January 1967 through August 1971. It is still active in syndication.

Love and Marriage Games

Games shows' preoccupation with love and marriage didn't begin or end with *The Dating Game* and *The Newlywed Game.* Remember any of these?

The Amateur's Guide to Love, hosted by Gene Rayburn and seen over CBS in 1972.

The Anniversary Game, hosted by Al Hamel and seen over ABC in 1969.

Blind Date, hosted by Arlene Francis and seen at times over ABC, NBC, and Du Mont between 1949 and 1953.

Bride and Groom, hosted by John Nelson, and seen over CBS between 1951 and 1954.

Chance for Romance, hosted by John Cameron Swayze and seen over ABC in 1958.

Dream House, hosted by Mike Darrow and seen over ABC between 1968 and 1970.

Feather Your Nest, emceed by Bud Collyer and seen over NBC between 1954 and 1956.

For Love or Money, emceed by Bill Nimmo and seen over CBS in 1958.

It Pays to Be Married, emceed by Bill Goodwin and seen over NBC in 1955.

Honeymoon Race, emceed by Jim McKrell and seen over ABC in 1967 and 1968.

Love Story, seen over CBS in 1955 and 1956.

Manhattan Honeymoon, emceed by Neva Patterson and seen over ABC in 1954.

Matches and Mates, emceed by Art James and seen over ABC in 1967.

Perfect Match, emceed by Dick Enberg and seen over ABC in 1967.

Two in Love, emceed by Bert Parks and seen over CBS in 1954.

Wedding Party, emceed by Al Hamel and seen over ABC in 1968.

31. Jeopardy!

The *shtick* was corny. I give you the correct answer; now *you* give me the correct question. The set was tacky cardboard: the format right out of an elementary game show textbook—three contestants sat behind desks with bells and buzzers. The prizes were chintzy—a small amount of cash (rarely more than fifteen hundred dollars,) an awful encyclopedia, and a home version of the game. Yet *Jeopardy!* was one of the most magic and beloved games ever on television.

Intangibles made it work: the intelligence, diversity, and humor of the fifty-one questions, the dramatic element of the three bonus Daily Double questions hidden on the board, and the intellectual sharpness of the contestants. But the real secret of *Jeopardy!*'s success was its host, portly (230 pounds) and formal Art Fleming. In Fleming seemed preserved the standards and traditions of all western civilization. "Thank you, my friends. Thank you, Don Pardo," he would boom heartily to audience and announcer alike. "And now, my friends, let's play *Jeopardy!*" Fleming had no parallel. He was, off camera as well as on, the perfect gentleman, a deacon in his church, an usher at Julie Nixon and David Eisenhower's wedding, a football star in college, a naval hero during World War II, a man openly moved to tears by ceremonials of chivalry. Fleming's only public lapse was a grammatical one; he was the original announcer on the cigarette commercial which claimed, "Winston tastes good like a cigarette should." On *Jeopardy!*, he cared so deeply whether a contestant played well. "Well *done!*" he would say when one had just run a category or won a Daily Double. "Oh, I'm *so* sorry," he'd say when one didn't. You knew it was genuine.

Jeopardy! was owned by a former game show host himself, Merv Griffin, a man today reportedly one of the richest men in show business, owning in addition to his game shows the syndication rights to his talk show, six radio stations, and the rights to the closed-circuit tote boards in all the Florida race tracks and jai alai *frontons*. Still wealth or success did not come overnight; Griffin would try bandleading, singing, commercials, and movies first, his first big break not coming until Goodson-Todman summoned him back from a Caribbean vacation to audition—successfully—to host their new game *Play Your Hunch*. *Play Your Hunch* would run for five years, from 1958 to 1963 and use Griffin's talents for singing, orchestra leading, and acting as part of the game. Still, like so many before him, the experience of hosting a game had whetted his entrepreneurial instincts to make him want to try owning his own game show property. Griffin would host a

"Thank you, Don Pardo! Thank you, my friends."

few more game shows, ABC's *Keep Talking* in 1959 and NBC's *Word for Word* in 1963, before coming up the following year with the idea that would become *Jeopardy!*

Griffin's idea was not originally the challenging trivia quiz *Jeopardy!* would later become. Rather it was a comic concept, one that Bill Dana had already used on the old Steve Allen television show. Dana would give the correct answer, then ask for the correct question in the form of a joke: "The answer is 9-W. What is the question?"

"Tell me, Mr. Wagner, do you spell your name with a V?"

"Nein, W."

Other Threesomes

As is often the case, the success of one show influences the look and style of others. Though none of *these* imitative shows used "the correct question" in their format, the arrangement of pitting three contestants against each other in a fast-paced, intellectually challenging quiz predominated in the late sixties and early seventies. There was *Split Second,* hosted by Tom Kennedy, which aired over ABC between 1972 and 1975; *Three for the Money,* hosted by Dick Enberg and seen over NBC during 1975; *Three on a Match,* hosted by Bill Cullen, airing over NBC between 1971 and 1974; and *The Who, What, and Where Game,* hosted by Art James, seen over NBC between 1969 and 1974

When NBC bought *Jeopardy!* from Griffin in 1964, the network was expecting comedy. Within a week, however, the show's producer Bob Rubin would realize that *Jeopardy!*'s future as a comedy quiz would be short-lived. The novelty would soon wear off, and besides, the original format was both too nitpicking and too slow. Taking matters into his own hands, Rubin quickly altered the game to the far more challenging "hard quiz" format. Over the years, *Jeopardy!* continued to bear Rubin's touch, its pacing becoming progressively livelier.

In the first round of *Jeopardy!,* contestants could choose from five categories (perhaps this particular day, Famous Quotes, Actors and their Roles, Potent Potables, Sports, and Odds and Ends) , beneath which heading sat a row of five questions valued from ten to fifty dollars. Whichever contestant buzzed in first after it was revealed and Art Fleming read it aloud, controlled the questions and could continue answering until he missed, at which time the two other contestants were given an opportunity to answer it. Thereafter, the "last correct questioner" again selected. A contestant's score was based upon the accumulated value of the questions he answered correctly. If a contestant missed a question, the amount that question was worth was automatically subtracted from his score and had to be rebuilt again. Frequently contestants had minus scores. Hidden somewhere on the board was a "Daily Double Question" that permitted the contestant who located it to wager and add to his score up to fifty dollars if he could successfully answer it. Often Daily Doubles were "audible," and contestants had to correctly identify a song title or the voices of famous people. Sometimes *Jeopardy!* awarded contestants an extra hundred dollars if they could answer all five questions in a category.

In the game's second round, called Double Jeopardy, five new categories (perhaps World Capitals, If They Married . . . , Presidential Losers, Food, and Notorious) appeared on the board. Questions were now worth double the amount they had been in the first round. The Double Jeopardy board also concealed two Daily Double questions.

In *Jeopardy!*'s end game, contestants wagered as much of their money as they dared on one last Final Jeopardy question. Contestants wrote their answers—in the form of a question, of course—on small slates, which, following a suspensefully-timed commercial, Art Fleming held up to the camera, before announcing that day's winner. Contestants with negative scores were not permitted to play Final Jeopardy, and more than once, that was the case for all three contestants.

Jeopardy!'s popularity (in its heyday it commanded 38 per cent of the viewing audience) cut across all age levels. Arthur Schlesinger, Jr., declared it to be his favorite show; college students cut classes—and lunch (*Jeopardy!* aired at noon on the East Coast) —to tune it in.

Neither of Griffin's other game shows, *Reach for a Star* and *One in a Million,* fared nearly as well. But *Jeopardy!* was *Jeopardy!* Beloved almost as much as the show itself was the *Jeopardy!* home game, which went through eleven editions, and which gave thousands of future contestants the chance to practice playing it before many of them traveled hundreds of miles to appear on the show. Practice makes perfect; *Jeopardy!*'s best players took part each year on the show's World Championship Tournament.

In 1975, *Jeopardy!* was canceled. It returned to NBC in the fall of 1978 refurbished sleeker, even better than before. In the new version, the lowest scoring contestant was progressively eliminated over the game's two rounds. The victorious remaining player now faced the "Super Jeopardy" board. If he could answer five questions in a row, without striking out, he won $5,000. Each subsequent day he faced the end game board added $2,500 to the stakes. As in the original game, champions could remain on the show for five days, at which point they retired undefeated.

For *Jeopardy!*'s all-star players, see page 16.
For the untimely demise of *Jeopardy!*, see pages 95–97.
For producer Bob Rubin's skill with question writing, see pages 56–58.

QUIZ

Here are some questions from the show, framed in inimitable "jeopardese."
How many do you know?

ODDS AND ENDS
A Mrs. Myra Franklin set a record by seeing this Julie
Andrews film more than 900 times.
What is The Sound of Music?

FAMOUS QUOTES
Caesar's three-word report after he routed Ponticus at first assault.
What is "Veni, vidi, vici?" (*I came, I saw, I conquered.*)

EMMY COMEDIANS
Bishop Sheen, dubbed "Uncle Fultie," competed with his show in fifties.
Who is Milton Berle?

$$$
The two bills scrambled by inept counterfeiter who puts Andrew Jackson
on face, Lincoln Memorial on back.
What are $20 and $5 bills?

ANIMALS
Weighing .000035 of an ounce as new embryo, it grows to twenty-nine tons
in first year.
What is a baby (blue) whale?

NOSTALGIA—THE SIXTIES
Ironically, he relayed his "message" thru "medium" of printed word,
not TV.
Who was Marshall McLuhan?

WOMEN
She was tagged "woman for all seasons" by husband's rival magazine in '71.
Who is Clare Boothe Luce?

----

32. Hollywood Squares

It's the longest-running game show currently on network television. *Hollywood Squares,* the larger-than-life game of tic-tac-toe, is played with comedy, bluff questions, and celebrities, and it's been getting belly laughs and giving away furs from Dicker and Dicker of Beverly Hills since October 1966. The game does have its rules, but it's been years now since anybody noticed either them, or the two contestants, or the prizes. Even host Peter Marshall races through the game-playing preliminaries at breakneck pace to get to the fun.

From the moment his merry "Hello, stars!" starts things off to the blatt of the "tacky buzzer," risqué ad libs fly while the two contestants jockey to distinguish clever bluff from outrageous fact. Whichever of them captures three celebrity-filled squares in a row wins the game. And, of course, there's that merchandise-laden "secret square" to locate along the way. Even better-known than the daily network game is the popular syndicated version of the show that airs in local markets several nights a week.

Hollywood Squares was not the first game show to have a tic-tac-toe format. The Barry-Enright game of *Tic Tac Dough* had one, too—while the show stayed on the air. It took a new packaging company formed by the producer-writer team of Merrill Heatter (once the producer of EPI's *The Big Surprise*) and Robert Quigley (host of an early local New York children's quiz, *Shenanigans*), to figure out how to play it straight. In the early sixties the two had come together to try to fill the vacuum left in the game show industry by the demise of the rigged companies.

Still, the decision to use tic tac toe again in a game show came slowly, and its evolution involved much trial and error. Heatter and Quigley's first collaboration, for example, was the short-lived (1960–62) *Video Village.* Memorable on two counts, *Video Village* introduced Monty Hall to America as a game show host; and it displayed Heatter-Quigley's first effort at constructing a larger-than-life environment for a game. On *Video Village,* contestants played the parts of tokens on an enormous board game, stashing the money they won into shoulder bags as they marched from square to square.

Undaunted by the cancellation of this show, Heatter and Quigley followed with *People Will Talk.* The innovation this time was to involve large numbers of people at a time, as fifteen non-celebrity contestants discussed their most embarrassing moments. Unfortunately, these moments were not highly embarrassing enough to attract high ratings, a problem Heatter and Quigley next tried to solve by using celebrities instead of civilians. *People Will Talk* became *Celebrity Game,* in which celebrities debated humorous topics, which were in turn voted upon by three civilian contestants. Still, the format was cluttered, and one reviewer singled out host Carl Reiner for special opprobrium, attacking everything from his toupee to his smile and dubbing him "just this side of vacuous." *Celebrity Game* aired for six months in 1964, and again briefly, in 1965.

It took Heatter-Quigley two more years to consolidate their winning format. Using tic-tac-toe allowed them to simplify what had until now been unwieldy, as they whittled the number of celebrities down to nine, the number of civilian contestants down to two. Still, there were other minor problems: the original pilot for *Hollywood Squares* employed Bert Parks as emcee, but before the show ever aired, Heatter-Quigley found a fresh, new face in Peter Marshall, late of the comedy team of Noonan and Marshall. Thanks to Marshall's straight-man training, he proved to be the perfect "master" to ride herd over the brilliant comics featured on the show. Marshall would learn, as time went on, how to move the game forward, when to dissolve into helpless giggles, and when to turn to the contestants to offer them strategic advice.

At long last, Merrill Heatter and Robert Quigley had their hit game show, one that was soon winning every Emmy in sight. In the early seventies, Peter Marshall would win three Emmys, the show's writers two, and its best celebrity player, Paul Lynde, one. In 1978, it won again, this time in the category of Outstanding Game or Audience Participation Show.

The set of *Squares* became the most desirable place to be in Hollywood on Sunday nights when the daytime version of the game is taped, and the show became an exclusive insiders' club for America's best comedians. Some of them, such Paul Lynde, Rose Marie, Jonathan Winters, and George Gobel, have been holding court in their own special cubicles for so long that each has turned his square into a cosy nest. On their chairs are their own cushions; on their desks are coffee cups; and always present is a box of Kleenex with which to surreptitiously pat a moist brow, as during tapings the low-ceilinged squares become intensely hot.

Famous Gobbledygook

"The areas of questions are discussed with each celebrity in advance. In the course of their briefing, actual questions and answers may be given or discerned by the celebrities." It's flashed on the screen at the end of every show but absolutely no one understands it.

Hollywood Squares is one of the most professionally conducted and highly regarded shows on television. Twice a year, though, it's time out for fun. That's when the stars, Rose Marie as Little Bo Peep and Paul Lynde as Georgie Porgie, dressed in nursery rhyme outfits, come out to play *Storybook Squares* with children contestants. The stars have to clean up their act some, but what the bleep.

To find out how the contestants for *Hollywood Squares* are chosen, see page 6.
For more about Peter Marshall, see page 24.
For more about the celebrities on *Squares* and how they're chosen, see pages 46–49.
Question-writing on *Squares* is an art; see pages 58–59.
There's more than fun and games to *Hollywood Squares*. To learn about its financial side, see page 90.

QUESTIONS FROM HOLLYWOOD SQUARES

They're the reason people watch the show. I'll give you a few of them, including the stars' ad-libs. You see if you can "discern" the correct answer.

1. According to police authorities, if you should ever be unfortunate enough to come face to face with a burglar, you should simply say to him "I'll . . ." what?
Paul Lynde: (wink) "I'll let you tie me up!"
   ANSWER: "I'll give you whatever you want."

2. According to Amy Vanderbilt, what is the maximum length of time you and your fiancé should be engaged?
Rose Marie: "Engaged in what?"
   ANSWER: Six months.

3. According to Raquel Welch, a woman's bust size should have nothing to do with her sex appeal. True or False?
Joan Rivers: "That's easy for her to say!"
   ANSWER: True.

4. According to Greek mythology, the god Apollo, in love with the maiden Daphne, pursued her through the forest. When he caught up with her, what did she change into?
Mel Brooks: "Something comfortable."
   ANSWER: A tree.

5. According to food experts, there are three things you should do to an item when shopping. First, look at it. Then feel it. What do you do next?
Jan Murray: "Buy it a drink."
   ANSWER: Smell it, of course.

6. To the ancient Romans it was the most prized and precious fruit of all. Which fruit was it?
Vincent Price: "Augustus Caesar."
   ANSWER: The apple.

Some fun . . .

7. Why is the booby bird called the booby bird?
Karen Valentine: "Because they have big . . . feet."
  ANSWER: Because they are so stupid.

8. Scientists describe it this way: "The excitation of surface nerves due to light stimulation, causing reactions of uneasiness or spasmodic movement."
Paul Lynde: "Levi's."
  ANSWER: Tickling.

----

and some nostalgic moments on *Squares* . . .

TOTIE FIELDS

with some time out for nursery rhymes.

Other Children's Games

Most producers have found that devising games for children isn't easy. Not that they haven't tried; including Heatter and Quigley themselves, with *Storybook Squares, Shenanigans,* and *Video Village, Junior.* Other misses were:

Birthday Party, seen locally in New York over WATV in 1957.

Choose Up Sides, with Dean Miller and later, Gene Rayburn. Seen both over CBS in 1953, and NBC in 1956.

Computer Quiz, seen over CBS on Saturday afternoons in 1967.

Do You Know? with Bob Maxwell, on CBS on Sundays in 1963.

50,000 Penny Jackpot, with Frann Weigle, aired locally in Chicago over WGN-TV in 1957.

Funny Boners, with Jimmy Weldon and Webster Webfoot. Shown on NBC on Saturday afternoons in 1954.

Giant Step, with Bert Parks, seen over NBC between 1956 and 1957.

It's a Hit, with Happy Felton; CBS on Saturdays, in 1957.

Just for Fun emceed by Sonny Fox and aired locally in New York over WNEW-TV in 1959.

Juvenile Jury, emceed by Jack Barry during 1949–53.

Magic Horseshoe, seen over NBC on weekday afternoons in 1953.

Make a Face, emceed by Bob Clayton. This show first aired in 1961 as an adult game, then over ABC in 1962 as a children's game.

My Secret Ambition, seen over NBC during the afternoons in 1953.

On Your Mark, emceed by Sonny Fox and seen locally over WNEW-TV 1961–62.

Quiz Kids, emceed by Clifton Fadiman from 1949–1953, again in 1957–58.

Runaround, Details unknown. Seen in 1969.

Tele-Kid Test, emceed by Bruce Eliot and Jim McCollough, aired locally in New York over WOR-TV in 1951.

What's My Name? with Paul Winchell and Jerry Mahoney, 1950–52.

The Best of the Seventies

Game shows got scarce for a while; for 1969 was the year of the great network game show purge. In 1971, the games were back, with new hard edges, flashy electronics and enormous floor-polishing bills. *Password* was the first to return, a harbinger of the trend for networks and packagers alike to show a great affinity for new games with old names: *The New Name That Tune, The New Break the Bank, The New Treasure Hunt, Match Game '73, The New Price Is Right*. And speaking of old names, thanks to syndication and the FCC's new public-access ruling, *they* were back as well—*really* old names like Ralph Edwards, and Barry-Enright. Local stations could show anything they wanted on this new first half hour of the evening: opera, ballet, public service, deep discussions: they gave us game shows. And as the things steal back into the evening once again, who knows what the next decade will bring, for it seems clear, doesn't it: like it or lump it, there will *always* be game shows?

33. Match Game

"Ugly Edna said, 'I'm all in a tizzy. At the airport today, as I went to board the plane, you'll *never* guess what happened. My BLANKS got caught in the propeller!' "

It's the Dr. Jekyll and Mr. Hyde of game shows. On the surface, the object of *Match Game* is to think of the word that the six celebrity panelists might most be apt to have thought of, too. But note, the studio audience has already begun to titter. The audience is thinking something suggestive, of course, for logic dictates a response referring to some part of "Ugly Edna's" anatomy. The payoff is: Will the contestant have the nerve to say just what *on television?* If he says, "Boobs," the audience will howl and catcall. If the contestant says, "Baggage, the audience will boo, even though that's a perfectly logical answer, too. The real game going on here is "Get the Contestant," few of whom seem up to the challenge of not being a patsy. Over and over, trying to be as witty and worldly as the panel, they give strange and tasteless answers until one of them wins the game by default.

Fascinatingly, *Match Game*'s nastiness all take place subliminally. Peel back its surrealism and you will find as staid and sober a game as you would ever hope to see, one that quietly chugs along independent of its uglier alter ego. Though it's easy to overlook when things get smarmy, the object of the game *is* to match the answers of six celebrities. To accomplish this, the first of the two contestants has host Gene Rayburn choose from an A or B joke question. While Rayburn reads it aloud, the six celebrities, using Magic Markers, write down their responses to the statement's missing word on a small card. Now Rayburn asks for the contestant's oral response to the question. One by one Rayburn polls the panel in search of matching answers. Now the second contestant tries to match the panel with a second question. Additional rounds follow until one contestant has accumulated six matches. To make his task more difficult, in the subsequent rounds the celebrities he has already matched abstain. Matching six celebrities now earns the winning contestant the right to play the two-stepped end game for up to five thousand dollars.

Match Game's "zaniness," to use producer Ira Skutch's word, evolved. The *Match Game* that first came into being in 1963 bore only the slightest resemblance to the show it is today. The original was a serious game played by two opposing teams comprised of one celebrity and two civilian contestants each. "Name a kind of muffin" was a typical question. If two teammates could achieve a match, their team would get 25 points. If all three matched, their team would get 50 points, with the first team to accumulate

100 points winning the game. There was also a telephone feature on the show in which a home viewer attempted to match a member of the studio audience. The early *Match Game* ran until 1969, the year CBS canceled all of its games.

When CBS revived *Match Game* in 1973 it had a refurbished and at first dignified format. However, within three weeks, the show's *double entendre* questions evolved to set America sniggering. Love it or hate it—that game, which is now in its sixth year, has become one of daytime's high-rated shows.

NBC page makes good. That's Gene Rayburn on the flashy *Match Game* set.

The game also airs in syndication. Known there as *Match Game, P.M.,* the stakes for matching two celebrities in the end game can run as high as $10,000.

Match Game's format is still evolving. After 1978, when the game's most popular player, Richard Dawson, no longer regularly appeared, the spin of a wheel of fortune determined the celebrity to be matched during both the network and the syndicated version of the endgame.

For more about *Match Game's* celebrities, see pages 44–45.

For question writing on *Match Game,* see page 60.

For an insider's look at the *Match Game* set, see page 71.

34. The $20,000 Pyramid

In the tensely hushed studio all eyes are focused on the Winner's Circle, upon the two chairs, one facing, one facing away, from the huge, looming structure called the $20,000 pyramid. There exists in human beings a compelling need, to push themselves beyond the limits of their endurance, past pain, past exhaustion, to aim at total perfection. Marathon runners have such a need, and Olympic athletes. So do the contestants on *The $20,000 Pyramid.*

"Ready," shouts host Dick Clark, retreating to the sidelines, "here's your first subject. Go!"

The first of *Pyramid's* six categories swings around. "A fedora . . ." says the celebrity partner facing the game board, straining against his chair's arm straps. "A beanie . . . a beret . . ."

"Types of hats," guesses his civilian partner, leaning forward in her seat the better to read every pore and line in her partner's famous face. For in giving clues he may only list examples in a category. He may not describe, use a form of the word, or make a gesture. Now five seconds have elapsed. In fifty-five more, if all goes well, his partner, a teacher, may win $10,000.

"I'm called the ship of the desert, and I've got two humps . . ."

"What a camel might say."

Tick tick tick.

"The clutch . . . the motor . . . the steering wheel . . ."

"Parts of a car!" Now the three easiest, the fifty dollar categories that form the pyramid's base, are out of the way. Players can expect the next two one-hundred-dollar categories that form the second tier to be more difficult, the last two hundred dollar category at the pyramid's top, the most amorphously abstract of all.

Inflation's caught up with *Pyramid* since this picture was taken. The stakes have doubled. Dick Clark and Joan Rivers cool out with a nice contestant.

"The sky . . . a baby boy's layette . . . your eyes . . ."

"Things that are blue!" Good. Four down without a hitch. Just two more.

"Your passport . . . your camera . . . luggage . . . your airplane ticket . . ."

"Things you take on a trip?"

Close, but not close enough. Perspiration rolls down the celebrity's face as he tries to pinpoint his clues more precisely. "Your passport . . . gambling money . . . resort wear . . ."

"Things you take on a vacation!"

An involuntary sigh of relief fills the studio, but the team has lost valuable seconds. Only one more category to go, but is there time? The audience has stopped breathing.

"Milk . . ." says the celebrity player . . . "no, *Bossy*'s milk . . . sand-box sand . . ."

"Liquids? Things children play with?" The contestant strains. So near yet so far away.

BUZZ! Time is up. The audience groans. Dick Clark rushes forward to see by hindsight what other clues might better have prompted the contestant to say, "Things in a bucket."

The teacher looks exhausted. Still, to stay champion, to earn the right to try again for stakes that will now be $15,000, she will, paired with the second celebrity player, have to play a qualifying round against a challenger just as good as she and fresher. All of her subsequent efforts to scale the pyramid after that will be worth $20,000. The record number of attempts on the part of one contestant before finally succeeding is seventeen.

The $20,000 Pyramid's qualifying game—there are two each day—is played by two teams comprised of one civilian and one celebrity. Contestants with the help of their celebrity partners each alternately play three rounds. First, the contestant must carefully select from the "small pyramid" category board what she hopes will be one of its easier subjects. The six categories on it are always deceptively labeled. For example, "X-Rated" will probably turn out to contain seven words beginning with "ex-." Now, the contestant must pray for good rapport with her new celebrity partner. For, having selected a category, the contestant has thirty seconds in which to try to convey to him the seven words, worth one point each, that flash one at a time on a small electronic screen. During this part of *Pyramid,* the contestant can gesture all she wants to, or can give a synonym, or both. But if she slips and uses a part of the word in her description, she hears a "cuckoo" sound effect disqualifying her from winning the point. If a word proves too difficult for her partner to guess, she must call for the next word to be flashed; she cannot return to it. All she can do is hope that her opponent will run afoul in his category as well. During the second round of play, clue givers become receivers and the screen slides over to them. In the third round, players can choose who will give, who receive. The team with the most points wins. Should play at the end of the third round result in a tie, contestants must select from special categories held in reserve. Play continues until the tie is broken. Pressure is intense. To lose a game on *Pyramid* is to lose. Unlike other shows where contestants play the best two out of three, here there are no rematches.

Famous Moments on Pyramid

The weeks two of the game's fiercest and most intense competitors, Odd Couple Tony Randall and Jack Klugman are pitted against each other, the fur always flies.

Ditto when Star Trekkers William Shatner and Leonard Nimoy face each other.

The day Sandy Duncan broke the straps on the chair in the winner's circle. These restraints, meant to keep *Pyramid* players from using their hands, during the final part of the game, have held fast for hulking men. It took five-feet-one-inch, ninety-seven-pound Sandy to rip them out by the roots.

The day Anita Gillette went overboard listing "Things that are stiff." Her answer was bleeped.

To further keep contestant adrenalin pumping, the game adds extra stimuli. In one of the two games of the day, a special card bearing a Big Seven is concealed behind one of the six categories on the small pyramid. If a team uncovers it and can successfully answer all seven words in the category, the civilian teammate wins a bonus of $500. Should a team manage to achieve a perfect score of 21 points, the civilian contestant wins $1,000. Should a team in the course of playing three perfect rounds coincidentally uncover the Big Seven, the contestant wins both bonuses.

The $20,000 Pyramid was created in 1973 by Bob Stewart, in business for himself since 1965 after leaving Goodson-Todman following the cancellation of the original *Price Is Right*. On his own, Stewart would quickly sell *Eye Guess* in 1966, *Personality* in 1967, and sprinkled throughout the seventies, *Three on a Match, Jackpot, Blankety—Blanks, Winning Streak, Shoot for the Stars,* and *Pass the Buck*. Nonetheless, *Pyramid* has been Bob Stewart's only major independent hit to date.

Known first as *The $10,000 Pyramid,* the game that has tested so many would itself be severely tested. After its ratings dipped two weeks in a row, CBS canceled the show in 1974. CBS's move proved premature, and in an act rare in television circles, ABC quickly stepped in and returned *Pyramid* to the air two weeks later. ABC has been repaid many times over both in ratings and prestige; and the game's director Mike Gargiulo has won four Emmys.

Pyramid airs in syndication as *The $25,000 Pyramid,* hosted by Bill Cullen. In this nighttime version, both contestants play for the entire half hour. Should one of them successfully scale the pyramid in the first round, he or she wins $10,000. Should he or she successfully scale it in the second round as well, he wins an additional $15,000. In the nighttime version of the game, the Seven bonus is worth $1,500.

For *Pyramid*'s high criteria for choosing contestants, see page 7.
For *Pyramid*'s celebrity players, see pages 50–51.
For *Pyramid*'s questions writing, see page 60.
For the special problem *Pyramid* presents to stagehands, see page 68.
For more about Bob Stewart's three other classic games, see pages 167–174, 181–184, and 221–225.

Some Things about Pyramid You Probably Never Thought to Ask

Off stage, those split-second rulings relayed from announcer Bob Clayton to host Dick Clark come from producer Anne-Marie Schmitt up in the control booth. She uses the show's instant replay to guide her on all close calls.

The show's cuckoo sound is stored in a tape cassette that is one continuous reel of nothing but cuckoo sounds. All a stagehand has to do is hit the button once and there's an instant cuckoo waiting.

The small pyramid is operated manually by two stagehands. It takes five to operate the big pyramid. All stagehands are hooked up to the control booth by earphones.

35. The New Treasure Hunt

The plump black woman in the housedress still hasn't recovered. Her hands flutter to her face, to her bosom. They clutch at Geoff Edwards, and then to her face again. All the while, she moans and twitches. All the while, tall, tan, curly-haired Edwards shakes his head in mock dismay, and the audience howls. She's just made it up on stage over four hundred other hopefuls, here on *The New Treasure Hunt,* "television's richest treasure."

One look at her, at the smirking Edwards, and then into your own voyeuristic heart, and you know that Chuck Barris has done it again. *The New Treasure Hunt* is the game critics most love to single out for calumny. The female contestants seem so needy; the prizes so opulent (they include Rolls-Royces, cabin cruisers, mink coats, and the cashier's check for $25,000) placed there at the beginning of the show by *Treasure Hunt's* famous bearded, bonded security agent, Emile Arturi); the suspense built into learning if you've won *at all* (your treasure hunt prize package could contain a klunk, you know) is so excruciating, so humiliating, so sadistic; that the show is painful to watch. Almost.

Get the Smelling Salts!

Vera Augenbach, a contestant on Chuck Barris' *New Treasure Hunt,* upon learning that she had won a new Rolls-Royce instead of being "klunked," fainted dead away right on camera. Later the size of the taxes on her elegant prize made her faint again. To afford them, she had to sell the car.

The plump black woman has been picked at random. Just a few minutes ago, she and two other women had found a qualifying slip inside the small, flat, gift-wrapped box handed out to everyone in the audience before the show. Only seconds ago, she'd selected one of the three jack-in-the-boxes Geoff Edwards had set before her. To her alone: the pop-up flower. Now the time has come to choose one of the thirty gaudily be-ribboned numbered boxes piled from floor to ceiling at the rear of the stage. Still shaking, the contestant is guided by Edwards back to the area where

The lady in the center now gets to go get one of the boxes behind her. The other two don't look as thrilled.

they all are so tantalizingly stacked. It is time for her to make her fateful choice. Pointing to the box she wants, for the rules of the game do not permit her to touch a prize package herself, she quavers, "Number Fifteen. That's how old my son is . . ." The show's two scantily clad models, Jane Nelson and Joey Faye, hand it to Edwards, who places it on a table at the front of the stage. He peers inside. He shuts the lid. Then he opens it again and reaches inside. "You've just won $1,305 in cash!" he shouts. Painstakingly he counts it all into her trembling hand. "It's yours to keep forever and ever. Or, you could give it all back to me and see what else is in the box. It could be a car, it could be a klunk, or it could be a check for $25,000! What do you want to do?"

Whichever she chooses doesn't matter. It is Edwards' job from here on in to make the contestant feel that she has wrongly chosen. It is a role Edwards plays to the hilt. He has been hired to be earnest and boyish and playful and, yes, a little cruel to these women who have come here with nothing and are so willing to be tormented. The structure of the *New Treasure Hunt* is designed to make Edwards' job a little easier. As soon as a contestant chooses a treasure box, the program breaks for a commercial. Edwards is then briefed backstage by the show's producer. "This one is the Chevy Camaro," the producer says. "The box has a flying hat and a scarf. Dont forget your music cue. And when you say the word, 'storm,' lightening will flash." Inside every treasure box are similar props that Edwards and a

---

Sorry Guys

Only women can be contestants on the *New Treasure Hunt*. It's not discrimination, it's logistics. *Treasure Hunt*'s staff deemed it easier to assemble the props for just one sex. *Which* sex to choose was no contest; women do make better contestants, you know.

---

group of *Treasure Hunt* staff actors will use to stage an elaborate series of pranks on the contestant to manipulate her into believing that she has been "klunked," that is, that she will receive only a dime-store prize. Before Edwards gets around to informing this contestant that she has indeed won the Chevy Camaro, he will have dressed the poor woman in the flying hat and scarf, and have her running around the stage vainly trying to fly a kite brought out by a Barris staffer playing the "Red Baron."

Edwards must memorize ninety such acts, one for each of the show's ninety possible prizes. In this one, for example, as in all of them, should the contestant choose the money, he must also know how to stage the routine backward. Edwards must know them all cold, because *Treasure Hunt*'s high stakes make the security surrounding it the tightest in television. No breaks in the taping are permitted on *Treasure Hunt;* there are no cue cards. More than once, Edwards has had to cover for a staff member who has forgotten his part.

Of the dozens of people who work on the show, only two of them, bonded security agent Emile Arturi and a member of CBS's Standards and Practices Department, know in which package the $25,000 check is hidden. Before each taping, the two are sequestered together in a room with the $25,000 check in a locked suitcase. There, the network representative holds out a hat containing thirty numbers, one for each of the thirty treasure boxes. Having made his selection, Arturi, accompanied by the CBS representative, carries the suitcase onto the set, which has been screened off from floor to ceiling. While the Standards and Practices representative watches, Arturi mounts the stairs at the rear of the set, locates the box that corresponds to the number he has drawn, removes the box's props, and replaces them with the check. If, as is usually the case, neither of the show's two contestants that evening selects that box, Arturi will appear on stage at the close of the show, dramatically to reveal, to excited murmurings of the audience, just where the money has been sitting all that time. If, however, a contestant should choose that box, the first time anyone on either the Chuck Barris staff or the technical crew, or even Edwards himself, is on camera, when Geoff Edwards actually opens the lid of the box and looks inside. At the precise moment the box is opened, the CBS Standards and Practices representative, now stationed in the control room, informs the game's director. Edwards now has the task of stalling the contestant so that the staff can get ready to stage the particularly torturous skit it has previously worked out for just this moment that will culminate in the appropriate fanfare.

The New Treasure Hunt is a far cry from Jan Murray's hit quiz show of the fifties. It didn't start out that way. When Chuck Barris bought the rights to *Treasure Hunt* from Murray, he had fully planned to include the original show's quiz segment; the question and answer format is, in fact, in the Barris pilot. When, however, playing the game that way, circa 1973, proved too slow-paced, it was duly decided to substitute the stunts and leave the choice of the boxes completely to chance, meaning that on *The New Treasure Hunt,* anything can happen. You'll be watching, won't you? After all, *Treasure Hunt* is still running in syndication.

For more about Jan Murray's original *Treasure Hunt,* see pages 179–180.
For more about host Geoff Edwards, see pages 24, 28.
For more about security measures taken on other game shows, see pages 7, 53–55, 77–80.

36. The Gong Show

From Hollywood, almost live, come nine scraggily-haired teen-aged girls, their bra straps peeking out of their pastel prom dresses, to tell America in earnest song that "people who need people are the luckiest people in the world." Except when they're off key.

Next, bandannaed and dressed in blue denim overalls, comes a male quartet of farmers who lay an egg—literally—while singing "Old McDonald."

Now comes a tap-dancing moppet in red satin and spangles whose obese mother and aunt provide backup at the piano. She's a "Yankee Doodle Dandy."

Something comes out in sneakers with its hair combed forward to completely cover its face; it is wearing glasses over its hair. In a flat mono-tone, it sings "Half Breed," a song once made popular by Cher.

GONG! Arte Johnson can take it no longer. He has seized the padded mallet and struck the golden gong to signify his displeasure. Jaye P. Morgan and Scatman Crothers of *Chico and the Man* cover their ears. The audience groans with relief as the faceless contestant is chased off the stage by a midget waving a butterfly net.

"Arte" says Chuck Barris, peering out from under his famous floppy hat, "Why did you gong Linda?"

"I just couldn't see it."

You might not consider it a game show until you realize that NBC's Standards and Practices department most definitely does. The network watchdogs are present at every taping with their stopwatches, making sure forty-five seconds elapse before a contestant does indeed get gonged. They're there adding up the number of points the celebrity panel awards each hopeful they like enough not to gong. And they're there to guarantee that the show's three celebrities have no contact with any "talent" before the show—even though only $516.32 is at stake. If Standards and Practices takes *The Gong Show* seriously, they are surely the only people in America who do.

The Gong Show is the nongame game that like any good game show breaks all the rules. It wasn't supposed to be a hit; the pilot tested abysmally. But ever since it first aired over NBC in 1976 and in syndication at night, first hosted by Gary Owens, later by Chuck Barris himself, no one in America has been able to stop talking about it. Instantly the word "gong" entered the language. Local clubs and groups across the country spontane-ously began staging their own gong shows. And in no time, this latest of Chuck Barris' offerings became the most outrageous show on television, as

Gongor . . . and

Gong-ees.

Barris, the brilliant maverick packager who had previously foisted upon America *The Dating Game, The Newlywed Game,* and *The New Treasure Hunt* from behind the scenes now came out of the closet to emcee it. And why not? After all, *The Gong Show* is open to everybody. And since it carries to the ultimate the yearning ordinary people have to be on television, who better than Barris to host his own game?

But Chuck Barris does more than emcee. He's behind the scenes carefully planning its every step. That's right, planning. Though it endeavors to look like a mélange, a mishmash, an unmade bed of mediocrity, *The Gong Show* auditions and screens all contestants, looking for an entertaining balance of the totally talentless amateurs (the "Oh my Gods," as the show refers to them); the very talented amateurs who will receive scores of 10 on the show and sometimes, though rarely, receive their first big break; and the union-card holding professionals who come to the show with such very funny acts as "recipe wrestling" (wherein two boxing trunk-clad actors proceeded to demolish each other with the ingredients of a soufflé). Barris has final approval of all acts booked onto the show. Most applicants are turned down outright if they are judged, according to the show's own code as SLAs (Sleazy Lounge Acts); NBDs (No Big Deals); WCs (Who Cares?); or YBMINADs (Your Basic Man in a Dress).

On a tape date, Barris arrives at the studio at 9 A.M. to spend the day rehearsing every contestant. The totally talentless are told in advance that they can expect to be gonged, and instructed how to exit gracefully.

Not Like a Trouper

Most contestants on *The Gong Show* take their fate with equanimity. Not so sixteen-year-old Lynn Turner. When she came out to sing "The Morning After," and was gonged by Arte Johnson, she burst into tears. "I couldn't help it," she said later. Neither could Arte.

Barris and his staff work right up to the very last moment at achieving the balance they seek. Even while taping is in progress, they are constantly shifting the order of acts and eliminating some altogether. In addition, all staff members have pre-rehearsed comic roles to play on the show, including wielding a huge gorilla paw or the giant padded baseball bat sometimes used to chase acts from the stage. Also seen on camera are *Gong Show* bandleader Milton de Lugg, stagehand "Gene Gene, the Dancing Machine," ad-lib writer Larry Spencer, resident midgets Jerry and Elizabeth Maren, model Siv Aberg, and Barris' daughter Della. The show's semi-regular celebrity panelists, Jamie Farr, Arte Johnson, Jaye P. Morgan, Rex Reed, Buddy Hackett, and Phyllis Diller, throw themselves into the general merriment, especially during the confetti-and-balloon celebration at the close of the show when the day's winner is announced.

Still, *The Gong Show* has one terrible worry. Finding "talent" that is "good" enough for the show gets tougher every passing day. If it gets much tougher, Chuck Barris may yet make good his frequent threat: to really retire from game shows once and for all. If he does, American television will be hard-pressed to find his cynical-sentimental floppy-hatted equal.

There's nothing novel about oddball contestants on game shows. See pages 16–17.
For more about Chuck Barris and his other outrageous shows, see pages 230–233; 233–237; 260–263.

Other, Alas, Serious TV Talent Shows

The Gong Show's a goof; *these* talent contests were unfortunately, dead in earnest—

Battle of the Ages, emceed by John Reed King and Morey Amsterdam. Seen both over Du Mont and CBS during 1952.

By Popular Demand, with Robert Alda and Arlene Francis and seen over CBS in 1950.

The Don Adams Screen Test, which aired in syndicated markets in 1975.

Hollywood Screen Test, with Neil Hamilton and seen over ABC in 1950.

Ladies' Choice, seen over NBC during the summer of 1953.

Live Like A Millionaire, emceed by Bob Russell and seen over CBS in 1950.

So You Wanna Lead a Band, emceed by Sammy Kaye, and seen during the summer over all three networks between 1950 and 1954.

Stage a Number, emceed by Bill Wendell and seen over Du Mont in 1953.

Tin Pan Alley TV, seen over ABC in 1950.

Try and Do It, emceed by Jack Bright and seen over NBC during 1948.

. . . and the granddaddy of all such shows, *Ted Mack and the Original Amateur Hour,* seen in the summer throughout the fifties.

---

37. Family Feud

Name a famous explorer.

If your first impulse was to say "Christopher Columbus," you would have matched 61 out of 100 people in one of *Family Feud*'s pre-show mailback surveys. Now, do you think that you and a team of four of your relatives can come up with seven other explorers? (say—Ponce de Leon, Admiral Richard Byrd, Marco Polo, Meriwether Lewis, William Clark, Hernando Cortez, and David Livingston)? Or do you think you might do better to pass the question to your opponents, another family team of five, and hope that they fail to match the remaining names in the survey? If you and your family elect to attempt to match the survey, you win a dollar for every person in the poll you match. If your family manages to stay in the game through all of the matches, you can win up to $25,000.

Family Feud would work without families. Any two teams of five unrelated people could play. But the game wouldn't be as good. It wouldn't tap the image of the ethnic American melting pot that is so important to the producers. Right up to the last minute, Goodson-Todman expected to have to tape the show in New York City, where such diversity abounds. To their delight, however, even in homogenized Southern California, the staff has been able to locate a seemingly endless supply of families of widely varied descent: German, French, Armenian, American Indian, East Indian, Italian, Chicano, Korean, Japanese, Jewish, Chinese, Irish, Black, and occasional WASP families, too. When the show isn't being ethnic, white-collar suburbanites have faced blue-collar working families; hardshell Baptists have faced Brahmins; matriarchs have faced patriarchs. And on certain special occasions members of ABC's soap opera "families" have faced off for charity. Using families as contestants proved such an affectionate notion to host Richard Dawson that whereas on all other game shows, the contestants kiss the host, on *Family Feud,* Dawson kisses the contestants. The practice began with the very first show, when Dawson spontaneously offered a kiss on the lips to each female family member, a handshake to male contestants in greeting them. Though nothing about Dawson's manner was lecherous, there was a storm of protest from some viewers, and even some hate mail. The uproar refused to ebb even when Dawson, the British-born former star of TV's *Hogan's Heroes,* explained on camera, "I'm a toucher. It's how we expressed affection in my own family, and it just comes naturally to me. My mother always said, you can't ever hate anyone you're on kissing terms with."

Finally, Dawson placed the matter in the hands of the viewers. He called for a write-in vote and promised to adhere to the verdict. The results were overwhelmingly in favor of Dawson's kissing: 14,600 to 704.

"Thank goodness," breathed the white-haired grandmother on the show the day it was announced. "I traveled all the way from Rhode Island just to be kissed by you." Richard kissed her on the air fourteen times.

Dawson has brought other innovations to this his first network hosting job. He begins each show by reading his mail from viewers or by making a witty topical comment. During the course of play he gently informs contestants when they have given an obviously stupid answer: "You've given me perhaps *the* number one answer; show us please, the dreaded . . ." Moreover, while he hosts Dawson openly plays along: "Oh, good answer! That's *sure* to be there, isn't it?" And he has frequently been known to console disappointed contestants with, "Come on, little darlin', don't feel badly. You haven't lost a limb, have you? This is only a game show!"

If *Family Feud* has any limitations, its questions can frequently be insulting and arbitrary. Name a Sound You Hear in a Barnyard; Give Me Another Name for Garbage; Name Something That Goes into Your Mouth That Isn't Swallowed may all be answerable by the lowest common denominator of contestant.

Still, *Family Feud* seems to work despite itself. From the very first week it aired over ABC in the summer of 1976 with its fiddle music and prim Whitman-sampler opening, it became an undisputed hit. In six months it was the number one rated show in daytime; in an unprecedented nine months it had won an Emmy. In 1978, host Richard Dawson won one, too. *Family Feud* began airing in syndication the fall of 1977.

For how *Family Feud* conducts its polls, see page 59.
For the workings of *Family Feud*'s electronic wizardry, see pages 67–72.
For more about Richard Dawson, see page 45.

"It's the star of *Family Feud* . . . Rrrr-ichard Dawson!"

FAST MONEY QUESTIONS FROM *FAMILY FEUD*

You have ten seconds to come up with the best answers to the following five questions. Then, give a friend or relative fifteen seconds to come up with five different answers. If your answers total 200 points (see below), you win $5000. (Try and collect.)

1. Name something you find at a picnic.
2. Name an Indian tribe.
3. Name a sport where gloves are worn.
4. Name something you adjust on a television set.
5. Name a year during World War II.

ANSWERS:

1. Ants 40   Barbecue 5   Chicken 3   Food 28   Hotdogs 5   Sandwiches 3
2. Apache 13   Blackfoot 8   Cherokee 15   Mohawk 2   Navajo 25   Sioux 27
3. Baseball 30   Boxing 53   Fencing 2   Golf 7   Handball 2   Hockey 6
4. Antenna 3   Color 33   Fine Tuning 10   Horizontal 2   Vertical 5   Volume 46
5. 1940 3   1941 4   1942 24   1943 27   1944 27   1945 14

Other Family Games

The family that plays together stays together? If that's the case, then these other family games must have helped:

The Baby Game, emceed by Richard Hayes, seen over ABC in 1968.

Balance Your Budget, with Bert Parks and "the horn of plenty" seen over CBS in 1952.

Everything's Relative, with Jim Hutton, seen over NBC in 1965.

The Family Game, emceed and owned by Bob Barker, seen over ABC during 1967–68.

The Generation Gap, emceed by Dennis Wholley, later Jack Barry, seen over ABC in 1969.

How's Your Mother-in-Law? emceed by Wink Martindale, seen over ABC in 1967–68.

Keep It in the Family, emceed by Bill Nimmo, Keefe Brasselle, seen over ABC in 1957–58.

Life Begins at Eighty, emceed by Jack Barry, seen over both NBC and ABC in the early fifties.

The Parent Game, emceed by Clark Race. Seen in syndication in 1972.

The Sam Levenson Show, seen over CBS in 1951.

There's One in Every Family, emceed by John Reed King, seen over CBS in 1952.

Wisdom of the Ages, emceed by Jack Barry and seen over NBC in 1952.

---

38. Pro-Fan

Okay, men. If you're the sort who swears that game shows are beneath you, fit only for silly women, I give you *Pro-Fan*. I *know* you've seen it. *Pro-Fan* is the little sports quiz that comes on before the big game. And even if you haven't seen *Pro-Fan*, I know you've seen one of its cousins, perhaps *Sports Challenge*. Whatever they're calling it this year, there will always be a *Pro-Fan*.

Hosted by Charlie Jones, *Pro-Fan* teams a star professional athlete with a layman sports fan. The athletes represent every field in sports from horse racing to boxing to football to field and track. Together star and fan oppose a similarly composed team. First the fan tries to answer a sports trivia question worth ten points: "Who is the youngest baseball player ever inducted into the Hall of Fame?" for example. If the fan knows the answer ("Sandy Koufax."), his professional athlete teammate must perform a physical feat outside his field in a sports competition held in the studio. Jockey Willie Shoemaker might have to sink a basket; boxer Ken Norton might have to sink a putt; baseball players might have to serve aces on the tennis court, and so on. The results are frequently amusing. Whichever of the two teams amasses the greater number of points by the end of the show wins up to $15,000 in merchandise prizes that include cars and trips.

Pro-Fan is shot in a massive Hollywood sound stage containing an ice hockey field, a bowling lane, putting green, basketball key and backboard,

Maybe Ken Norton should stick to boxing.

tennis court, pitching mound, goal posts, archery range, billiard table, and even a horseshoe area. Los Angeles *Herald-Examiner* sports writer Alan Malamud writes the trivia questions. Professional athletes on *Pro-Fan* have included among others track star Brian Oldfield, Harlem Globetrotter Meadowlark Lemon, baseball's Frank Tanana, Bobby Bonds, and Maury Wills, football's Fred Bilitnikoff, Pat Haden, George Atkinson, and Bob Klein, race-car driver Parnelli Jones, and women competitors pro basketball player Karen Logan, tennis star Rosie Casals, and track star Wyomia Tyus.

Yes, men, your every sports fantasy come true: you up there with the big guys. *Now* does anybody dare to dispute that there's no difference between a game show devotee's yelling "Take door number one!" at her TV and a sport fan's yelling "Block that kick!" at his? *Pro-Fan* is a syndicated game created by Sheldon Saltman and Lloyd Thaxton in association with Jerry Bender.

Other Sports Quizzes

Jock games and quizzes have abounded on TV. Remember any of these *or* fill in with the ones on *your* local station.

Batter Up, emceed by Joe Bolton, Hal Tunis, and Marion Carter. Seen locally in New York over WPIX-TV 1950–54.

Beat the Champions, emceed by Guy LeBow and seen locally in New York over WOR-TV in 1957.

Brains and Brawn, emceed by Jack Lescoulie. Seen over NBC in 1958.

Call the Play, emceed by Mel Allen. Seen over CBS in the fall of 1954.

Can Do, emceed by Robert Alda, seen over NBC between 1956 and 1957.

Clubhouse Quiz, emceed by Bob Edge and seen locally in New York over WOR-TV in 1950.

Fish and Hunt Club, emceed by Bill Slater and seen over Du Mont in 1949.

Hole in One, seen locally in New York over WPIX-TV in 1966.

Play Ball, emceed by Hal Tunis and seen locally in New York over WPIX-TV in 1951.

So You Know Football, emceed by Bill Mazer and seen over NBC in 1964.

So You Know Sports, seen over NBC in 1950.

Sports Challenge, with Dick Enberg and seen over CBS in 1970.

Sports Page, emceed by Stan Lomax and seen locally in New York over WOR-TV in 1952.

Stop the Experts, emceed by Sid Gordon and seen over CBS in 1955.

Touchdown, seen over NBC in 1950.

Touchdown Quiz, emceed by Guy LeBow and seen over ABC in 1954.

What Is It?, with cartoonist Marvin Stein. Seen locally in New York over WOR-TV in 1950.

---

39. The New Price Is Right

"C'MON DOWN!"

The mellow male voice of Johnny Olson crackles with manipulative mellifluousness. The frenzied buzz in the orange, blue, and brown Hollywood studio is suddenly punctuated by delirious shrieks of recognition and frantic scrambling up front! over there! now way over there! Johnny Olson has just called the first four names of the day on this television's only hour long game show, the incredible, incomparable *New Price Is Right,* the show that offers "a fortune in fabulous" prizes in exchange for bids, rounded off to the nearest dollar, which come closest to their retail price without going over.

"Geneva Maynard, COME ON DOWN!!!"

In the fourth row, the camera pans, then locates a plump face with a California tan, and a tinted red hairstyle cut a little too short. Earlier that day, without ever realizing it, Geneva Maynard had caught the attention of show's producer, Jay Wolpert, on his stroll down the line outside the CBS studio where she and 229 other housewives, retirees, work-skippers, hooky-players, and tourists, had been waiting for four hours. Wolpert had liked her warmth, her poise, her lack of desperation and had secretly so signaled his clipboard-wielding assistant. Then she, having checked Geneva Maynard's name in CBS's computerized contestant book, had typed it in the number-four position on the list she placed on Olson's podium before the show. Now hearing her name read aloud, Geneva Maynard's face registers nothing, then shock. And as this Van Nuys housewife with three children, married to a mechanic, COMES ON DOWN! to her coveted spot on Contestants' Row, she displays to all of daytime America a body perhaps twenty

"Too bad! You've gone over by four dollars." Remember when cars were $2,500?

pounds overweight that still looks okay in her pink slacks and printed overblouse.

"I can't believe it," she shrieks, rocking back and forth at the podium from which she will bid against the three others. It's not like this woman to shriek (or to rock). But with the heat of the studio lights, the gaze of the four insinuating cameras with their snaky cables, her proximity to the famous face of Bob Barker, and the high-pitched lilting of the *Price Is Right* theme song—well, there seems nothing else to do.

The item going up for bids is a pool table, and if Geneva Maynard can estimate its price more exactly than the other three contestants can without overbidding, she will win both it and the opportunity to join Bob Barker up on stage to play one of the *Price Is Right*'s thirty-four pricing games for still more merchandise, including, if she is lucky, one of the two cars the show offers its six contestants each day. Geneva Maynard has no idea what a pool table costs; thankfully, neither do either of the three contestants who have also just arrived. "Six hundred fifteen dollars," she hazards, then holds her breath. Three-point five seconds of suspense pass before Bob Barker's fingers tear open the envelope, before his dry warm voice reads the neatly typed figure on the card within. The pool table is hers. Had she exactly guessed its retail price, a special bell would have sounded to indicate that the bonus one-hundred-dollar bill in Bob Barker's right front suit jacket pocket was hers to reach in and take.

To this day, Geneva Maynard cannot remember how she made it up onto the stage or much of what followed. She will see by videotape when the show is aired three weeks later that she traveled through the crisscross of lights over the polished blue stage to grab Bob Barker in a huge, hysterical hug. She'll see him, still smiling and talking to the camera, gently but firmly disengage himself and get her to stand on legs that tremble like the coming California earthquake. Dimly she will see Janice Pennington wheel out and hear Johnny Olson describe the Alpo, Riceroni, Downy Fabric Softener, TV-Time Popcorn, Drano, and Hawaiian Punch to be used in the Grocery Game. She will hear her wavering voice somehow speak up over the baying studio audience to purchase $6.89 worth of groceries and fall safely between the $6.75 and $7.00 limit to win a Broyhill living room worth $1,635.

As exciting as the game has been so far, Geneva Maynard is by no means finished. She has yet to spin the Big Wheel in the show's half-time competition to determine which of the first three contestants today will win the opportunity to bid upon one of the *Price Is Right*'s two lavish showcases in the final round of the game. The Big Wheel contains twenty numbers ranging from $.05 to $1.00. Each contestant can spin twice to achieve a score as close to $1.00 as possible. Players spinning more than $1.00 are eliminated. Tie scores are broken by one additional spin each. As a bonus, any contestant achieving $1.00 on the wheel wins $1,000. Leading a charmed life today, Geneva Maynard spins $.80, a score which forces the other two contestants to overspin in their efforts at bettering her. Geneva Maynard's berth in the showcase is assured.

Some twenty minutes, three more pricing games, and one more "showcase showdown" later, and it's time for *The Price Is Right*'s climactic moment, during which she and a slightly built medical student from Thailand will compete to make the most accurate single bid on a multiple grouping of prizes presented to them in the form of an amusing skit.

Each day there are two such showcases. After the first has been presented, the contestant who has won the most merchandise that day in the preliminary rounds has the option, without yet having seen the second showcase, of bidding on it or awaiting the presentation of the second showcase. In the event that he elects to wait, the second contestant must place his bid at this time. Now, as the top winner of the day, standing on stage beside her opponent at twin podiums, Geneva Maynard readies herself for her decision as model Holly prepares to take the contestants on one of the popular visits to *The Price Is Right* "department store." Before she is finished, the showcase elevator doors will open upon a microwave oven, a bedroom set, a game room with color TV and pinball machine, and a redwood hot tub. Geneva is strongly tempted, but experience born of faithful viewing tells her that second showcases are generally even more lavish. She passes the prize package to the medical student, who bids $8,500.

In sixty seconds, Geneva Maynard is glad she waited. Today, *The Price Is Right* staff has readied one of their Flakey Flicks, "Socky," a prize-filled parody of the Academy Award-winning movie *Rocky*, acted out by all three models, Johnny Olson, and an inflatable bounce-back balloon who eventually kayos Olson in a boxing ring. Included in the skit for Geneva's consideration are an aquarium, exercise equipment, $1,000 in cash, a trip for two to Philadelphia, and a Cadillac Seville. It's so much to keep track of that Geneva's mind goes blank and Bob Barker must prompt her several times before, to her horror, she hears herself make a rattled, far-too-low bid of $3,500. Still, once again, fortune has smiled. Geneva's opponent has overbid on his showcase, and even though Geneva Maynard's bid is more than $10,000 off the mark, she wins all the prizes in her showcase. Had both contestants overbid, neither would have won any showcase prizes. Had either contestant's bid been within $100 of the retail value of the showcase without going over, he would have won all the prizes in both showcases. And as the credits begin to crawl up the screen and the final applause sign flashes to the audience, Bob Barker escorts Geneva Maynard over to see the winnings of one hour, worth, all told, more than her husband makes in a year.

Though it looks smooth and effortless to its viewers, *The Price Is Right* is the most complicated and difficult show to produce on television. Not even the most elaborate prime-time variety show compares to the effort that goes into mounting it. A month's planning goes into each of the six shows taped a week. Moreover, every six months, *The Price Is Right* introduces a new pricing game which must be planned and rehearsed. By the time the six shows are finally ready to be taped at CBS's studio 33, the *Price Is Right* takes up an entire floor. As far as the eye can see, cluttering the halls outside the studio are the hundreds of prizes and set walls for each of the three shows that will be taped today. The prizes, from Buick Regals to refrigerators to Rolaids, lie around on dollies, ready to be moved into place behind one of the show's three doors, mounted on the turntable, tacked to the wall, wheeled in on a game cart, inserted into the "clam," or concealed behind the show's rising price tag. All must be gotten on and off stage on the show's split-second time schedule. After acts three and six each taping, stagehands must move the Big Wheel into place. In addition to its two cars each taping, *The Price Is Right* has given away airplanes, boats, vans, and trailers, each of which has to be shown on camera. For its famous skits, *The Price Is Right* has mounted a full sea battle with authentic special effects. Timing on the show is so tight that prizes are wheeled away before contestants have even finished bidding on them.

Fibber McGee's Closet

Getting all those prizes *on* stage on cue is only half the battle on the *Price Is Right*. Getting them off fast is the other. How do they do it? The answer is, they *don't*. All the prizes are unceremoniously dumped on dollies behind Door Number One, right on stage, until a taping is over. Then they're wheeled back to the *Price Is Right* warehouse that sits right behind the CBS studio.

The New Price Is Right did not begin life as an hour-long show. The original Bob Stewart version of the show, which had aired over NBC and ABC in both daytime and nighttime version from 1956 to 1965, (see pages 181–184) had been like all game shows, a half-hour show. And in 1972, almost ten years later, that was what CBS had in mind when daytime vice-president Bud Grant called Mark Goodson to revive it. Goodson was delighted; his company had been in eclipse for four years; obviously a lot would be riding on how well they could do in remounting *The Price Is Right*. To his dismay, it took Goodson all of one week to realize that the old game, the original concept for *The Price Is Right*, no longer worked. Having contestants spend six or seven minutes making three bids on a modestly priced coffee table in these inflated times was boring; yet no show could afford to give away prizes expensive enough to make three bids interesting. Too, today the original game, seemed far too predictable; you always knew that eventually each contestant would win something. A better game would continually leave in doubt whether anyone would win anything. Goodson told Grant his reluctant conclusion: "Unless you want a whole new show, we're going to have to cancel our deal," he said.

"No," said Grant. "Go ahead. I trust you. Overhaul it from top to bottom if you have to."

For the next three months, seven days a week, twelve hours a day, the Goodson-Todman staff would work at coming up with a game that would contain within it many mini-games. Every detail of the new show was thoroughly tested and retested. It would take three full days just to figure out how to make the selection of contestants a complete surprise to them.

At last, the half-hour show was ready, but it was a bare skeleton of the game it would yet become. The game that premiered on September 4, 1972, summoned forth only three contestants a day to play a handful of pricing games. There was no Big Wheel. Showcases were downright dour. As austere as it was, by today's standards, *The Price Is Right* instantly commanded a forty share. Would it do as well in the afternoon? Bud Grant experimented to find out, but *The Price Is Right* faltered there. Still, no one could fail to notice that even as its ratings dipped, exciting innovations were beginning to take place on the afternoon show. In the spring of 1974, *The Price Is Right* created its first showcase skit, "Little Red Riding Hood," performed by the show's two models at the time, Janice and Anitra, with Johnny Olson playing the big bad wolf. Gradually new pricing games were added to the show. More and more men began to appear as contestants. And always there was Bob Barker, masterfully drawing his players into games that excited without demeaning. It seemed clear that *The Price Is Right* was not dying, it was suffering from claustrophobia.

It took an act of courage to make the next logical step. When CBS returned *The Price Is Right* to the morning, it expanded the game to an hour, doubling the number of prizes and contestants. *The Price Is Right* has been thriving ever since. A half-hour version of *The Price Is Right* still airs in syndication, originally hosted by Dennis James. In 1977, Bob Barker assumed the job as nighttime host.

To find out how contestants are selected on *The New Price Is Right*, see pages 12–14.

For Bob Barker's contribution to the show, see pages 21–24.

To read about the *Price Is Right*'s unique audience warm-ups, see page 18.

To learn how the *Price Is Right* acquires and stores its prizes, see pages 82–83.

COME ON DOWN FOR *THE PRICE IS RIGHT* QUIZ:

1. At the time of this writing, the *Price Is Right* has in its repertoire thirty-seven pricing games for contestants who've won their way up on stage.

a) There are twelve games in which it is possible to win a car on the show. How many can you name?

ANSWER:

Any Number	The Money Game
The Card Game	Golden Road
5 Price Tags	Lucky 7
The Dice Game	Ten Chances
Three Strikes	Switcheroo
Temptation	Hole in One

b) Now try to recall all twenty-five prize-package (*not* showcase) games on the show in which merchandise prizes other than cars can be won:

ANSWER:

The Shell Game	One Right Price
The Hurdles Game	The Race Game
Danger Price	Extra Digit
Most Expensive	Secret X
The Clock Game	The Grocery Game
The Range Game	Give or Keep
Finish Line	Hi-Lo
The Bonus Game	Double Prices
The Bull's Eye Game	Poker Game
Cliff Hangers	Safe Crackers
Take Two	Squeeze Play
It's Optional	Penny Ante
	Punch-A-Bunch

2. Nine showcases on *The Price Is Right* have become more or less regular features on the show. How many can you name?

ANSWER:

The Trip Down Main Street	A Tribute to a Great American
The Visit to TPIW Department Store	A Salute to Famous Brothers
The Man of the World	Johnny's School House
Something for Every Room in the House	A Tribute to a Deserving TPIW Staffer
Flakey Flicks	

3. Bonus question. We've already mentioned two of TPIW's special bonuses on the show: $100 for bidding exactly on a "one-bid" price and $1000 for spinning $1.00 on the big wheel. Can you name the third?

> ANSWER: A bonus of $500 goes to the contestant in The Shell Game who, having guessed correctly the prices of all four prizes, thereby automatically winning the game, can also guess under which shell the ball is hidden.

---

40. The New High Rollers

Game shows come and game shows go, and, at the time of this writing, it is too soon to judge the staying power of *The New High Rollers*. Still, it is not too soon to see that it's the first television game accurately to capture the excitement of casino gambling.

Not that people in game shows haven't tried; in fact, it's been practically an obsession. Packagers have trotted out TV-tailored versions of bingo, slot machines, wheels of fortune, horse-race wagering, pinball, such card games as acey-deucy, high-low, poker, and at least two versions of blackjack. Between 1974 and 1975 there was even an *Original High Rollers* dice game with Alex Trebek and Ruta Lee. All have seemed strangely sterile, and cluttered, too full of rules and gadgetry.

The elements of *The New High Rollers,* on the other hand, are breathtakingly simple: two contestants, a large pair of dice, the crap table, and "the numbers." The pacing is fast, the prizes tantalizingly difficult to win, and the pot as high as your luck will take you sometimes more than $50,000. Players vie to gain control of the dice by buzzing in first with the correct answer to a multiple-choice question. The questions are tricky: "James Coburn, James Garner, James Coco . . . who played a hard-bitten detective in . . ."

BUZZ! "James Garner!?"

Trebek and magic dice.

"I'm sorry, that's wrong. Your anticipation got the best of you. If you'd waited until I'd read the question completely, I would have said, 'in *The Dane Curse.*' The correct answer is James Coburn."

When a player is right, he has the option of rolling the dice or passing them to his opponent; wrong, the option falls to his adversary. A player rolls the dice in hopes of matching one or more of the nine numbers that appear in random order on the three-columned game board. Say, for example, in this particular game, that the numbers have appeared on the board as follows:

$$2 \quad 1 \quad 4$$
$$7 \quad 3 \quad 8$$
$$5 \quad 6 \quad 9$$

and a player rolls a ten. He can now claim whatever combination of numbers he chooses that add up to ten: 9–1; 8–2; 7–3; 6–4; 5–2–3; 1–2–7; 1–2–4–3. Better still, he can "clear a column" by calling for 1–3–6, and provisionally claim for himself whatever prizes are listed below the column. Though these prizes now electronically move to his side, he does not actually learn whether he has in fact won them until a game has been completed. Once he has made his choice, the numbers 1, 3, and 6 are now removed from play. Since the board now reads:

$$2 \quad \quad 4$$
$$7 \quad \quad 8$$
$$5 \quad \quad 9$$

should a player roll a three, he will automatically lose. Six, four, and ten remain "safe" rolls, however, since they can still be made in other combinations. Rolling doubles earns a player an "insurance marker" for a free roll. Players continue to compete for questions, electing to roll the dice or pass them, until as the numbers on the board diminish, one player is forced to roll an unmakable combination, to lose the game. If the winning player has prizes on his side, they now officially become his. Prizes on the losing players' side return to their columns where they are joined by three new prizes. The first player to win two games wins the match and the right to play the big money end game, whether or not he has collected any prizes that round.

In the end game, the champion again confronts the numbers 1 through 9. Again he rolls the dice, this time collecting $100 for each safe roll. If he can clear all nine numbers from the board without crapping out, he wins $5,000 in cash and a new car. In either case, he can continue as champion until he is defeated.

The appealing simplicity of *The New High Rollers* goes beyond its rules. Contestants on the game are graciously introduced to each other by Becky Price and Linda Hooks, the two least artificial, most lighthearted models on any game shows to date. Unfettered by a podium, players sit side by side, free to jostle and joke during play, each to display his own individual style of rolling and responding to the dice. Once play has begun, things happen fast. Games are over in minutes. As in a casino, luck plays an exciting role; one player needs a 2 to stay in the game, and thrillingly, and there it is! The music, too, differs from the usual automated tinkling; instead "the numbers" flash on the board to an upbeat drum roll. Other times, jazz plays in the background. Even "the numbers" have their own personality, appearing each game in a different type face and color. The trips offered as prizes on the show are innovatively presented to viewers not as still pictures tacked up in front of the camera but instead as action film clips, of, say, the waves rolling up on the beach of Tahiti. Other prizes offered on the show are equally fresh and creative, including such desirable fare as one-of-a kind antiques, a fully-staffed catered dinner in your own home for fifty of your friends, twelve portable televisions for yourself and all your friends, a Picasso lithograph, tickets to the Kentucky Derby with a $100 bet on every horse, and assorted $1,000 shopping sprees along Beverly Hills' plush Rodeo Drive.

The New High Rollers bowed over NBC during the spring of 1978, hosted by Alex Trebek. As the most natural, wholesome-looking game show airing to date, it can only be regarded as one of Heather-Quigley's greatest triumphs.

Other Gambling Games

The New High Rollers is the crown jewel in a long string of lesser gambling games, namely:

Beat the Odds, emceed by Johnny Gilbert and seen over ABC in 1969.

Big Showdown, emceed and Jim Peck and seen over ABC in 1975.

Bingo at Home, emceed by Monty Hall and seen over Du Mont in 1958.

Card Sharks, emceed by Jim Perry and first seen over NBC in 1978.

Celebrity Sweepstakes, emceed by Jim McKrell and seen over NBC from 1974 through 1977.

Dealer's Choice, emceed by Jack Clark, and seen in syndication in 1974.

Fast Draw, emceed by Johnny Gilbert and seen in syndication in 1968.

Gambit, emceed by Wink Martindale, with Elaine Stewart, and seen over CBS between 1972 and 1977.

Gamble on Love, emceed by Denise Darcel, and seen over Du Mont in 1954.

Go for the House, emceed by John Reed King and seen over ABC in 1948.

I'll Bet, emceed by Jack Narz, and seen over NBC in 1965.

It's Your Bet, emceed by Hal March, Tom Kennedy, Dick Gautier, and Lyle Waggoner and seen over NBC in 1969.

Jackpot Bingo, emceed by Marty Allen and Steve Rossi and seen in syndication in 1967.

The Joker is Wild, emceed by Jack Barry and seen first over CBS, later in syndication from 1972 through the time of this writing.

Lucky Pair, emceed by Richard Dawson and syndicated in 1969.

Lucky Partners, emceed by Carl Cordell and seen over NBC in 1958.

Money Makers, a syndicated game airing in 1969.

On the Money, emceed by Bob Braun and seen in syndication in 1973.

Pay Cards, emceed by Art James and seen in syndication in 1968.

Second Chance, emceed by Jim Peck and seen over ABC in 1977.

Take a Chance, emceed by Don Ameche and seen over NBC in 1950.

Twenty-One, emceed by Jack Barry. See pages 198–210.

Wheel of Fortune, emceed by Todd Russell and seen over CBS between 1952 and 1953.

Wing-O, emceed by Bob Kennedy and seen over NBC in 1958.

Winner's Circle (later called *Win With a Winner*), emceed by Sandy Becker and seen over NBC during the summer of 1958.

Wizard of Odds, emceed by Alex Trebek with Marty Pom. Seen over NBC between 1973 and 1974.

QUIZ

High Rollers' questions sound easy, but note how they withhold information as long as possible to rattle contestants into buzzing in too soon:

1. New York, San Francisco, Los Angeles. Which city provided the setting for the movie *Chinatown?*
   ANSWER: Los Angeles
2. Are you tall, quiet, or lazy if you're laconic?
   ANSWER: Quiet.
3. Was Benjamin Disraeli the Prime Minister of England, Germany, or Israel?
   ANSWER: England.
4. If you're baking an upside-down cake, do you actually turn the cake upside down?
   ANSWER: Yes.
5. Are you a bachelor or married if you're living in connubial bliss?
   ANSWER: Married.

The contestants on the show all missed. But *you* didn't did you?

Gambit, an almost successful gambling game in progress.

The Ten Worst Game Shows

You think picking them was easy? Not when there have been shows where people dragged in the contents of their attic to have them appraised, where panelists tried to read each other's minds, guess each other's signs, and match the right lackey with his celebrity boss. There have been games where contestants earned their vacations, parsed their Bibles, ran through mazes and up papier-mâché volcanoes, and even hooked themselves up to aptimeters and "Galvanic skin response" machines. To put myself in the proper frame of mind for my decision, I furrowed my brow. I stammered, I patted my forehead, I tensely listened to think music from inside an unventilated isolation booth. I even over skipped some and returned to them later. And now, I offer you for your consideration;

1. *Comeback Story.* George Jessel emceed this appalling talent contest whose do-gooder aim was to give a humiliating second chance to celebrities whose careers were on the skids. After they performed their pathetic acts, the audience decreed their fate via applause meter. Seen briefly over ABC during the fall of 1953.

2. *Dream House.* On this game, you didn't just get merchandise to put *in* your house, you got the house, room by room. Contestants could win either a minihouse worth $20,000 or a $40,000 job to be built "anywhere in the U.S.A." *Dream House* was created by Don Reid, the same man who created *G. E. College Bowl.* The show, which aired over ABC between 1968 and 1970 was hosted by Reid's cousin, Mike Darrow.

3. *Finders Keepers.* Speaking of houses, this game was actually televised in the contestant's home. Every day, the show would hide a prize in the contestant's living room, set up the cameras, and let viewers watch him tear the

place apart looking for it. Emceed by Fred Robbins, *Finders Keepers* first aired over NBC in 1951, then returned to the air to be seen over Du Mont during the fall of 1954.

4. *Make Me Laugh.* Contestants were confronted by three nightclub comedians, Sid Gould, Buddy Lester, and Henny Youngman, who attempted to make them laugh. If the contestant could refrain, he won a prize. Robert Q. Lewis was the host. The show aired over ABC between March and June of 1958, then returned in 1979 as a syndicated show as dim-witted as ever, hosted by Bobby Van.

5. *100 Grand.* Lavishly publicized in *Life* and *Look* magazines as the game that would bring back to TV the honest big-money quiz, this show had two contestants write their own questions while the audience watched. One contestant was an amateur, chosen by his local chamber of commerce, the other an expert in his field. Watching them, encased in a large, bubble-shaped isolation booth, scribbling out obscure minuti from an encyclopedia proved deadly dull. Besides, in the first go-round, the expert missed all the questions. *100 Grand* aired twice before sinking into oblivion. Jack Clark hosted the show, which, if you caught it, was seen over ABC in 1963.

6. *Sense and Nonsense.* This one *really* stank, calling as it did for contestants to use their five senses. Even its producer seemed embarrassed. "Maybe mothers can use the show to get kids to eat, their carrots," he said dubiously. If they hadn't already lost their appetites. Hosted by Bob Kennedy, assisted by Vivian Farrar, *Sense and Nonsense* aired over NBC in 1953.

7. *Supermarket Sweep.* Three housewives equipped with shopping carts and abetted by a fleetfooted aide of their choosing, were set loose in a super-market. Racing against the clock, the couple who managed to load the cart up with the pickings worth the most money got the chance to race again. The show set up bleachers for the audience near the checkout counter "finish line," where red-aproned clerks tallied the score. The Grand Champion of the game, as of July 22, 1966, was Mrs. Harold Rathson, who accumulated and got to keep thirty-five turkeys, twenty-two lawn chairs, and one hundred pounds of meat and canned goods. Bill Malone hosted the game, which aired over ABC between December 1965 and July 1967. David Susskind (you read right) owned the show.

8. *Treasure Isle.* Millionaire John D. MacArthur constructed an elaborate tropical setting behind his Palm Beach hotel, then built a grandstand for spectators. The show furnished two couples with rubber rafts. The husbands were required to paddle, blindfolded, across a lagoon, while their

Ticky tacky! It's Mike Darrow in front of someone's "dream house."

wives attempted to scoop up floating foam-rubber jigsaw-puzzle pieces. When they reached their island destination, they had to solve the puzzle on a billboard. The puzzle spelled out an impossible riddle, the answer to which floated in the lagoon attached to a buoy. Husbands were steered to the buoy by remote-control devices their wives operated from shore. The first couple to return to shore and ring a ship's bell hung on an artificial palm tree now earned the right to partake in an end game: a search for merchandise concealed on a second island. John Bartholomew Tucker was the host of the show which aired over ABC from the close of 1967 through the first thirteen weeks of 1968.

9. *With This Ring.* On this amazing show, engaged couples submitted themselves to the inspection of a panel of marriage counselors who publicly mulled over whether they were a good bet. Couples who passed muster won a free honeymoon. Hosted by Bill Slater, *With This Ring* aired over Du Mont in 1951.

10. *You're in the Picture.* Games get canceled all the time, but rarely, voluntarily, by their hosts. Jackie Gleason emceed this bomb which required contestants to stick their heads through holes in carnival cutouts, then try to guess the scene depicted upon them. Viewers who tuned into the show's third broadcast saw, however only a bare stage containing an armchair in which "The Great One" sat. "I apologize for insulting your intelligence," Gleason told his astonished viewers. "From now on I promise to stick to comedy." *You're in the Picture* aired over CBS between January 20, 1961, and January 27th at 9:30 P.M. Friday night.

They didn't seem too bad to you? That's because, my friends, in game show land, the difference between the best and the worst, a hit and a flop is always a *very* thin line.

Appendix

EVERY GAME SHOW EVER

An Annotated Chronological Listing

Key: R = Radio
   T = Television
   S = Syndicated

PROTOTYPES (FOR GAMES TO FOLLOW)

1924

R   *The Pop Question.* Radio news quiz sponsored by *Time* magazine.

1928

The successful experimental telecast of the image of Felix the Cat.

1932

R   *Vox Pop,* originally called *Sidewalk Interview,* emceed by Parks Johnson and Jerry Belcher, later by Wally Butterworth and Warren Hull. First heard over NBC, later CBS. The show changed its format to a quiz after 1936. Still on the air in 1948.

1934

R,T   *Major Bowes and His Original Amateur Hour,* emceed by Major Edward Bowes, later Ted Mack. Heard over WHN in 1934, NBC in 1935, CBS in 1936, and ABC in

---

* With apologies to any elusive locally-aired games, the games of Canada, Japan, and other far flung places. Any additions submitted by readers will be excitedly received.

1948. The show enjoyed a long run on early television. Closely related, the *Major Bowes Family Hour,* featuring Belle "Bubbles" Silverman, later known as Beverly Sills.

1936

The quiz show is born.

R   *Professor Quiz,* emceed by Craig Earl. Heard over CBS.
R   *Uncle Jim's Question Bee,* emceed by Jim McWilliams, later by Bill Slater Heard over NBC Blue.

1937

R   *Doctor Dollar,* heard over NBC.
R   *Let's Play Games,* heard over Mutual.
R   *Melody Puzzles,* emceed by Fred Uttal, with Harry Salter and his orchestra. Heard over NBC Blue.
R   *Dr. Peter Puzzlewit,* heard over NBC.
R,T   *The National Spelling Bee,* emceed by Paul Wing, later Joe Gannon. Heard over NBC Blue at 8:30 P.M. This long-running radio hit also pioneered on very early television in 1939 over NBC.

1938

The Du Mont television network placed its first commercial television sets on the market. This year, both Du Mont and CBS telecast the first experimental television quizzes.

R   *The Ask-it Basket,* emceed by Jim McWilliams, later by Ed East. Heard over CBS. Sponsored by Colgate.
R   *Battle of the Sexes* with Frank Crumit and Julia Sanderson, Walter O'Keefe and Jay C. Flippen. Heard over NBC.
R,T   *Information, Please,* emceed by Clifton Fadiman, with Franklin P. Adams, John Kieran, Oscar Levant, Russel Crouse, Hendrik Willem van Loon. Owned by Dan Golenpaul. Heard over NBC Blue. This show aired unsuccessfully over CBS television during the summer of 1952.
R,T   *Kay Kyser's Kollege of Musical Knowledge,* emceed by Kay Kyser. Heard over NBC Radio. This show made a successful transition to television in 1949, where it aired in the summers until 1955. During its last years it dropped its quiz segment and was emceed by Tennessee Ernie Ford.
R   *True or False,* emceed by Harry Hagen, later Eddie Dunn and Bill Slater. Heard over NBC Blue. Still on the air in 1948.
R   *What Would You Have Done?* emceed by Ben Grauer. Heard over NBC Blue.
R,T   *What's My Name?* with Wilbur Budd Hulick and Arlene Francis. Announced by Ralph Edwards. Heard over Mutual. Originally owned by Ed Byron, this game was acquired in 1948 by Louis G. Cowan and returned to the air that year hosted by Bert Parks. The game came to NBC television in 1950, hosted by ventriloquist Paul Winchell and Jerry Mahoney, and enjoyed a three-year run.

1939

RCA President David Sarnoff's speech at the 1939 World's Fair became the first televised news event. That year, President Franklin D. Roosevelt, opera, and sports events were televised for the first time. There were probably no more than five hundred sets in operation in the country at the time. A program called Visiquiz *aired over NBC television along with Paul Wing's* National Spelling Bee.

R   *Colonel Stoopnagle's Quixie Doodle Contest.* Heard over Mutual.

R   *Doc Rockwell's Brain Trust,* heard over NBC Blue.

R,T   *Doctor I.Q.,* emceed by Lew Valentine, later by Jim McClain and Stanley Vainrib. Heard over NBC Blue. Sponsored by Mars Candy. Seen briefly on ABC-TV the fall of 1953, hosted by Jay Owen, then again by McClain. Revived for television in 1958, hosted by Tom Kennedy.

R,T   *Doctor I.Q., Jr.,* a spin-off for children, heard over NBC. This show was also seen locally in New York over WWJ-TV in 1948.

R   *Guess Where?* heard over Mutual. Sponsored by Philip Morris. Owned by Milton Biow.

R   *Gag Busters,* emceed by Milton Berle. A comedy quiz.

R   *Name It and Take It,* heard over Mutual. Owned by Milton Biow.

R   *Name Three,* heard over Mutual. Owned by Milton Biow.

R   *People's Rally Fun Quiz,* heard over Mutual.

R   *Pot O' Gold,* emceed by Rush Hughes, later by Ben Grauer. Heard over NBC. Broadcasting temporarily interrupted by WWII, the show returned to radio in 1946.

R   *So You Think You Know Music.* No other information.

R   *We, the Wives, Quiz.* First heard over NBC Red, later Mutual.

R   *Word Game,* heard over CBS. Sustaining.

R   *Youth vs. Age,* emceed by Cal Tinney. Heard over NBC Blue.

1940

The year marked the birth of a couple of quiz show classics and a slew of pre-war jackpots.

R   *Answer Auction,* heard over CBS.

R   *Beat the Band,* emceed by Marvin Miller, Tom Shirley, and "the incomparable Hildegarde." Heard over NBC.

R,T,S   *Can You Top This?* emceed by Peter Donald, later Ward Wilson, and Dennis James. Panelists "Senator" Ed Ford, Harry Hershfield, and Joe Laurie, Jr. This was a joke contest, the best determined by a "laugh meter." Heard over Mutual, and on ABC television between 1950 and 1951. Syndicated in 1970 hosted by Wink Martindale and Dick Gautier.

R   *Cash on Delivery,* heard over Mutual.

R   *Crackpot College,* heard over CBS.

R   *Dealer in Dreams,* heard over CBS.

R   *Dixie Treasure Chest,* a jackpot quiz, with the orchestra of Horace Heidt. Heard over NBC Red. Sponsored by Tums.

R,T   *Double or Nothing*, emceed by Walter Compton, later Todd Russell, Walter O'Keefe, and John Reed King. This comedy quiz was heard over Mutual, and seen over CBS-TV at 2 P.M. beginning in 1952. Hosted by Bert Parks, eventually owned by Walt Framer.

R   *Especially for You*, a jackpot quiz.

R   *Fame and Fortune*, a jackpot heard over NBC Blue.

R   *Hollywood Grabbag*, heard over Mutual.

R   *Marriage Club*, emceed by Haven MacQuarrie. Heard over CBS.

R   *Melody Treasure Hunt*, emceed by Pat Ballard, Charlie Henderson.

R   *Musico*. Heard over CBS.

R   *The Philip Morris Musical Game*, heard over CBS. Owned by Milton Biow.

R   *Pin Money Party*, heard over NBC Red.

R   *Play Broadcast*, emceed Bill Anson. A comedy quiz featuring Marvin Miller as Jack the Crackpot. Heard over Mutual.

R,T   *Quiz Kids*, emceed by Joe Kelly. Heard over NBC. Sponsored by Alka-Seltzer. Owned by Louis G. Cowan and John Llewellen. In 1949, the show made its television debut, emceed by Clifton Fadiman, and enjoyed a long, but irregular run over all three networks until 1953. *Quiz Kids* returned again in 1957, and was seen over CBS.

R   *Santa Cataline Fun Quiz*, heard over CBS.

R   *Sing for Your Money*, heard over Mutual.

R   *The Sears Grabbag*, a jackpot quiz.

R   *Songo*, a jackpot quiz.

R   *Spelling Beeliner*, heard over CBS.

R   *Sports Pop-offs*, heard over CBS.

R   *Stillicious Kids Quizeroo*, heard over CBS.

R   *Take It or Leave It*, emceed by Phil Baker, later by Bob Hawk, Garry Moore, Jack Paar, and Eddie Cantor. Owned by Milton Biow. Sponsored by Eversharp Pencils. Heard over CBS. See *The $64 Question*, 1950.

R,T,S   *Truth or Consequences*, emceed and owned by Ralph Edwards. Heard over NBC. Sponsored by Procter and Gamble. *Truth or Consequences* fought a tenacious, and eventually winning battle with television. It aired unsuccessfully in 1950, hosted by Edwards, tried again in 1954, hosted by Jack Bailey, and again in 1955. Not until 1958, under the guidance of Bob Barker, did the show become a viable television game. It ran on network television until 1965, and has been in syndication ever since. First hosted by Bob Barker, later by Bob Hilton. See pages 166–167.

R   *Where and When?* heard over NBC.

R   *Who Are You?* heard over Mutual.

R   *Who Knows?* heard over Mutual.

R   *Your Dream Has Come True*, emceed by Ian Keith with his "wishing well." Heard over NBC Red. Sponsored by Quaker Oats.

R   *Your Happy Birthday*, emceed by Edmund "Tiny" Ruffner, with Helen O'Connell.

1941

The coming of World War II brought the network airwaves under government control. Most existing quizzes remained on the air, but the jackpot games became security risks because of their use of open microphones and left the air until after the war. Most experimental television programming halted, the Du Mont network being the only one of the four to continue broadcasting on a regular basis. However, NBC aired Irene Wicker and Her Telewizzers, *a quiz in which schoolchildren acted out charades and answered questions mailed in by famous people and* Play the Game, *emceed by Dr. Harvey Zorbaugh of New York University. New radio quizzes:*

R   *Gold If You Find It,* emceed by James Fleming. Heard over CBS.

R   *Here's the Clue,* heard over CBS.

R   *Pull Over Neighbor,* emceed by Art Baker, owned by John Guedel. Heard locally in Los Angeles over NBC, this show was the prototype for *People Are Funny.*

R   *Quiz of Two Cities,* emceed by Bud Collyer, and worked on by both Dan Enright and Bill Todman.

R   *Quizzer Baseball,* with Budd Hulick as "pitcher" and Harry Von Zell as "umpire." Heard over NBC Red.

R   *Talk Your Way Out of This One,* heard over CBS. Toward the end of its run in 1948, called *Talk Your Way Out of It.*

R   *You're the Expert,* emceed by Fred Uttal. Heard over CBS.

1942

R   *Are You a Genius?* emceed by Ernest Chappell, this children's quiz was heard over CBS.

R   *Auction Quiz,* heard over NBC Blue. Sponsored by Standard Oil of Indiana.

R   *Battle of the Boroughs.* This quiz marked Mark Goodson's arrival in New York and his debut into quizzes . . . as emcee.

R,T   *The Better Half.* Husbands versus wives. Heard over Mutual. This quiz returned after the war and aired locally on television in New York over WOR-TV in the winter of 1951 hosted by Frank Waldecker.

R   *The Bob Hawk Show,* a comedy quiz heard over CBS before and after the war.

R,T,S   *It Pays to Be Ignorant,* emceed by Tom Howard with George Shelton, Lulu McConnell, and Harry McNaughton. A parody of *Information, Please,* this fully scripted comedy quiz was first heard over WOR, later WABC and WNBC, then on over both the CBS and NBC networks. The quiz also enjoyed a berth on early television, over CBS in 1949 and 1950 and over NBC in 1951 when it replaced *You Bet Your Life* in the summer. A syndicated version aired in 1973 in local television markets.

R   *Jack Dempsey's Sports Quiz,* emceed by Mark Goodson.

R   *Mr. Adam and Eve.* Husband and wife quiz.

R,T,S   *People Are Funny,* emceed by Art Baker and Art Linkletter, later by Linkletter alone. Owned by John Guedel and Art Linkletter. Heard over NBC. *People Are Funny* came to television over NBC in a three-million-dollar, two-year deal the fall of 1954. It ran in prime time for the next seven years, and in syndication thereafter. See pages 168–170.

R   *Singo,* emceed by Welcome Lewis. A servicemen's quiz involving three song titles that formed clues to a story.

R   *Thanks to the Yanks,* emceed by Bob Hawk. Heard over CBS.

1943

R,T   *Blind Date,* emceed by Arlene Francis and Kenneth Roight. Heard over NBC.

Originally a game for servicemen, this show also enjoyed a long run on early television, on ABC, NBC and Du Mont from the summer of 1949 through 1953. A prototype for Chuck Barris' *The Dating Game,* servicemen and college students attempted to woo models and coeds through a partition speaking to them over a phone. Winners received a date at the Stork Club and a Gruen watch. In its last years, the game was hosted by Jan Murray.

R   *Grand Slam,* emceed by Irene Beasley. A musical quiz based on the rules of bridge. This show returned to the air in 1946 and was heard as late as 1951.

R,T   *Guess Who?* emceed by Peter Donald. Heard locally in New York over WOR, this game, emceed by Happy Felton later aired over NBC television on Sunday evenings in 1949.

R   *The Quiz Quotient,* heard over CBS.

R   *Take a Card,* emceed by Wally Butterworth, with Margaret (Honey) Johnson. Heard over Mutual.

R   *Yankee Doodle Quiz,* emceed by Ted Malone. Heard over ABC.

1944

R   *Coronet Quick Quiz,* heard over NBC Blue.

R,T,S   *General Electric's House Party,* emceed by Art Linkletter. Owned by John Guedel and Art Linkletter, this beloved audience-participation stunt show first aired over CBS radio and was first seen on television over CBS during the fall of 1952. It remained on the air for twenty-six years, until 1970. See pages 168–170.

R,T   *Ladies Be Seated,* emceed by Johnny and Penny Olson. Heard over ABC. This audience-participation show with door prizes simulcasted over ABC-TV the following year. Later in the early fifties, it moved to Du Mont.

R   *Money on the Line,* heard over CBS.

R,T   *Quick as a Flash,* emceed by Ken Roberts, Win Elliott, Bill Cullen, with Ray Bloch and his orchestra. This long-running game was the first to employ flashing lights as special effects and featured mystery guests from detective shows. Heard over Mutual. Seen on TV the spring and summer of 1953 at ten-thirty Thursday nights, emceed by Roberts and Bobby Sherwood, the televised version of the game called upon contestants to identify film clips.

R   *Stop That Villain,* emceed by Jack Bailey and Marvin Miller. This comedy quiz was heard over Mutual. Miller later played the character of Michael Anthony on *The Millionaire,* a TV hit in the late fifties.

R   *Two on a Clue,* heard over CBS.

R   *What's the Name of That Song?* emceed by Bud Williamson and Bill Gwinn. Broadcast from Hollywood and heard over Mutual.

R   *Which is Which?* emceed by Jan Murray, his first game. Heard over CBS and sponsored by Old Gold Cigarettes.

1945

Two new experimental television games made their appearance as the war drew to a close. They were Telequizzicals, *seen over WBKB in Chicago and* Thanks for Looking, *seen over Du Mont. And new on the radio:*

R,T,S   *Break the Bank,* emceed first by John Reed King, later by Johnny Olson, Bert Parks, and Bud Collyer. Originally heard over Mutual, this quiz moved to ABC in

1948 and simulcast over ABC television, becoming one of television's first quiz show hits. In the fall of 1949, it moved to NBC and aired until 1953, then returned to ABC the following year. In 1956, the game returned to the air as *Break the $250,000 Bank*. In 1976. Jack Barry acquired the rights to the show's name from its later owner Walt Framer and revamped it for network and syndicated viewing. See pages 127–131.

R,T *Bride and Groom,* emceed by John Nelson. Not technically a quiz or a game, this show was popular for actually marrying couples on the air and lavishing them with luxurious honeymoon merchandise. Heard over ABC. It moved to daytime television in 1951 over CBS and in 1954 became one of the first audience-participation shows to be seen in color.

R,T *County Fair,* emceed by Win Elliot and Jack Bailey. This quiz featured stunts and prizes with a country theme. CBS revived the show on television the summer of 1959. Bert Parks emceed.

R *Detect and Collect,* emceed by Fred Uttal and Wendy Barrie. Heard over ABC.

R,T,S *Give and Take,* emceed by John Reed King. Contestants selected the prize they wanted from a table, then had to answer questions to win it. Heard over CBS, sponsored by Chef Boyardee. The show came to daytime TV in the spring of 1952, sponsored by Cannon Towels, then returned to the air again in 1975 as a daytime show over CBS, hosted by Jim Lange. It entered syndication that same year.

R,T *Leave It to the Girls,* emceed by Maggie McNellis with Eloise McElhone, Dorothy Kilgallen, Harriet Van Horne, and Florence Pritchett. Guest male "defendants" faced a panel of women. Heard over Mutual, the panel later aired over NBC television beginning in the spring of 1949. Viewers received ten dollars for every question accepted.

R,T,S *Queen for a Day,* emceed by Jack Bailey. Heard over Mutual, this unbelievable show was first televised locally in Los Angeles over KTLA in 1950. It came to network television over NBC in January 1956 and aired until October 1964. A version of *Queen for a Day* aired in syndication in 1970. The show, which was seen in the late afternoon, divided its home base between Los Angeles and New York. See pages 174–176.

1946

The war was over! There were six thousand television sets in use. If you owned one of them you saw:

T *Face to Face,* seen over NBC and sponsored by Standard Brands.

T *King's Party Line,* seen over CBS.

T *Play the Game,* seen over Du Mont, sponsored by Alexander's Department Store.

T *Visi-Quiz,* seen over Du Mont, sponsored by Sears, Roebuck.

More likely, you heard on the radio that year:

R *By Popular Demand,* owned by Walt Framer and Jack Rubin. Mutual.

R *Heart's Desire,* emceed by Ben Alexander. Heard over Mutual.

R *Hope Chest,* heard over CBS.

R *Hollywood Jackpot,* emceed by Bill Cullen. Owned by Louis G. Cowan. Heard over CBS.

R,T,S   *Juvenile Jury,* emceed by Jack Barry. Owned by Jack Barry and Dan Enright. This children's panel featured celebrity guests Eddie Cantor, Red Skelton, and Milton Berle. It simulcast on NBC-TV the following year, sponsored by General Foods, and ran throughout the early fifties. A related panel, *Kidding Around* aired locally in New York over Channel 13, in 1961, marking Barry's first effort to return to the air after the scandals. *Juvenile Jury* entered the syndication market in 1971.

R,T   *Missus Goes A'Shoppin',* emceed by Bill Cullen, later John Reed King. Heard over CBS, the show simulcast on CBS television in 1947.

R   *Pick and Pat Time,* owned by Walt Framer. Heard over Mutual. Sponsored by Helbros watches.

R,T   *So You Wanna Lead a Band?* emceed by Sammy Kaye. This talent contest simulcast over NBC, CBS, and ABC in the summer from 1950 to 1954.

R   *Surprise Party,* emceed by Stu Wilson. Heard over CBS. Sponsored by American Home.

R   *Try 'n' Find Me,* owned by Walt Framer. Heard over ABC. Sponsored by Wesson Oil.

R,T   *Twenty Questions,* emceed by Bill Slater, with Fred Van Deventer, Florence Rinard, Herb Polesie, and Johnnie McPhee. Heard over ABC. Sponsored by Ronson. This popular game moved to television in 1949 where it was heard first over ABC, then WOR-TV, then Du Mont, and back to ABC its last years, between 1954 and 1955. See pages 137–138.

R   *What's Doin', Ladies?* emceed by Jay Stewart. Heard over ABC.

R,T   *Winner Take All,* emceed by Bill Cullen, Ward Wilson, Bud Collyer, with Dolores "Roxanne" Rosedale. Owned by Mark Goodson and Bill Todman, their first collaboration. Heard over CBS. The game began to simulcast on television in the summer of 1948, then enjoyed a four year run first on CBS in prime time then over NBC moving to daytime in 1951 and 1952 where it was hosted by Barry Gray. See pages 123–124.

1947

There were 142,000 television sets in operation, showing:

T   *Act It Out,* emceed by Bill Cullen. A charade game seen over Du Mont.

T   *Amadee Quiz,* seen over KSD-TV St. Louis.

T   *Cash and Carry,* emceed by Dennis James. Seen over Du Mont.

T   *Fun Time,* seen over KSD-TV, St. Louis.

T   *Let's Face It,* seen over WBKB-TV, Chicago.

T   *Let's Pop The Question,* seen over WFIL-TV, Philadelphia.

T   *Pantomime Quiz,* emceed by Mike Stokey. Seen over KTLA, Los Angeles. This early game went "network" over CBS in 1949, thanks to "kinescope," where it aired until 1954, mainly in the summers; moved to ABC in 1955 and aired again in 1958–59. See *Stump the Stars,* the name of the later incarnation of the game, under the 1962 games. See also pages 125–127.

T   *Seven Arts Quiz,* seen over NBC in New York.

T   *Telequizcalls,* seen over KSD-TV in St. Louis.

T   *Television Party,* seen over WWJ in Detroit.

And on the radio that year:

R   *The Big Break,* heard over CBS.

R   *Darts for Dough,* heard over ABC and sponsored by Dr. Pepper.

R   *Don't You Believe It,* heard over ABC.

R   *Free for All,* heard over CBS.

R   *Glamour Manor,* owned by Walt Framer. Heard over Mutual, ABC.

R   *Hint Hunt,* heard over CBS.

R   *Meet the Missus,* heard over CBS.

R,T   *Stop Me if You've Heard This One,* heard over Mutual, this joke contest came to television over NBC in 1949, emceed by Morey Amsterdam.

R,T   *Stop the Music.* First heard over CBS and owned by Harry Salter, this show would not become a big hit until brought to Louis G. Cowan in 1948 by Mark Goodson and Howard Connell. Emceed by Bert Parks. Heard in 1948 over ABC; simulcast over ABC television. *Stop the Music* aired irregularly over ABC until the summer of 1956.

R,T,S   *Strike It Rich,* emceed by Todd Russell, later Warren Hull. Owned by Walt Framer, his first big hit. The show came to CBS daytime television in May 1951, and ran until the summer of 1958. During some summers it also aired during prime time. Syndicated in 1973, Tom Kelly emceed. See pages 158–159.

R   *Your Surprise Package,* emceed by Jay Stewart. Heard over ABC.

R,T,S   *You Bet Your Life,* emceed by Groucho Marx. Owned by John Guedel. This beloved quiz would first be filmed and edited for television in October 1950. It ran until the fall of 1961. The quiz entered syndication in 1963, known as *The Best of Groucho.* It is still running. See pages 141–147.

R   *Your Sports Question Box,* heard over ABC.

1948

There were 977,000 television sets in use. By now every local station realized how easy and profitable quiz shows were to mount—and dismount—many of these aired no more than once. New TV games and quizzes of the year:

T   *Adam vs. Eve,* seen locally over WTMJ, Boston.

T   *Americana Quiz,* seen in the summer over NBC, also in 1949.

T   *Cartoon-a-Quiz,* seen locally over WMAL-TV, Washington.

T   *Charade Quiz,* emceed by Bill Slater and sponsored by United Cigars and Whelan's. Seen over Du Mont.

T   *Cross-Question,* seen locally over WGN-TV, Chicago.

T   *Did You Find It?* seen locally over WTTG-TV.

T   *Doorway to Fame,* emceed by Johnny Olson. Seen over Du Mont.

T   *The Drawing Game,* emceed by Rube Goldberg. Seen over NBC.

T   *It's a Hit,* seen locally over KSD-TV, St. Louis.

T   *Let's Have Fun,* seen locally over WCAU-TV, Philadelphia.

T   *Movieland Quiz,* emceed by Arthur Q. Byron and Patricia Bright. Seen the last two weeks of August over ABC. Staged on movie theater set.

T   *Now I'll Tell One,* seen locally over WBKB-TV, Chicago.

T   *Open House,* seen locally over KPIX-TV, San Francisco.

T   *Party Game,* seen over CBS, sponsored by Mennen.

T   *Picture This,* seen over NBC, sponsored by Vicks.

T   *Prime Ribbing,* seen locally over KTSL-TV, Hollywood.

T   *Prize Party,* emceed by Bill Slater. Seen over CBS at 7 P.M., Tuesday nights. Sponsored by Messing's Bread.

T   *Quarterback Quiz,* seen over CBS, sponsored by Mennen.

T   *Quizdom Class,* seen over WJZ-TV, the local ABC affiliate in New York.

T   *Quizette,* seen locally over WRGB-TV, Schenectady.

T   *Quizzing the News,* emceed by Allen Prescott. Seen over ABC into the spring of 1949. A panel tried to guess the identity of pictures of newsmakers camouflaged with false mustaches and other disguises.

T   *Stars Are Bright,* seen locally over KTTV, in Washington, and also locally in Los Angeles.

T   *Stop the Clock,* seen locally over WCAU-TV, Philadelphia.

T   *Try and Do It,* emceed by Jack Bright. Seen over NBC in the spring. Stunt show staged on picnic set. Sponsored by Maxwell House Coffee.

T   *You Name It,* seen locally over WNBW-TV, Washington, D.C.

Note this year the proliferation of radio jackpots and giveaways meant to combat the increasing encroachment of television. Truth or Consequences *was now staging its* Walking Man *and* Hush Contests, *and* Stop the Music *was red hot.*

R   *Easy Does It,* emceed by Ed East. Heard over CBS.

R   *Everybody Wins,* emceed by Phil Baker. Owned by Milton Biow. Heard over CBS.

R,T *Fish and Hunt Club,* emceed by Sanford Bickart, later by Bill Slater. Heard over Mutual, this sports-oriented show gradually evolved into a quiz that telecast over Du Mont on a hunting lodge set in 1949. Sponsored by Mail Pouch Tobacco.

R   *Go for the House,* emceed by John Reed King. Heard over ABC.

R   *Hit the Jackpot,* emceed by Bill Cullen with the Al Goodman Orchestra and the Ray Charles Singers. Owned by Goodson-Todman. Heard over CBS.

R,T *Life Begins at Eighty,* emceed by Jack Barry. Owned by Barry and Enright. Heard over Mutual, this comedy panel featuring old-timers came to NBC television in February 1950 where it was heard at 9:30 P.M. on Fridays. Later that year it switched to ABC television for an extended run.

R   *Second Honeymoon,* emceed by Bert Parks. Heard over ABC.

R,T *Sing It Again,* emceed by Dan Seymour, with Ray Bloch and his orchestra. Heard over CBS through 1950, when this music quiz moved to television over CBS on Saturday nights at 10:30 P.M.

R   *Spin to Win,* emceed by Warren Hull. Owned by Goodson-Todman. Heard over CBS.

R   *Take a Number,* emceed by Al "Red" Benson. Heard over Mutual.

R   *There's Money in Your Name,* emceed by Frank Small.

R   *Three's a Crowd,* emceed by John Reed King. Heard over Mutual.

R   *Time's A'Wastin',* emceed by Bud Collyer. Owned by Goodson-Todman. Heard over CBS. See *Beat The Clock,* under the 1950 heading.

R,T,S *This Is Your Life,* emceed by Ralph Edwards. This surprise party show began on radio this year, moved to TV in 1952, picking up two Emmys and remained on network TV until 1960. It returned to the air in the early seventies to air in local markets. See pages 163–165.

R   *Treasure Salute,* heard over CBS. Owned by Goodson-Todman.

R   *What Makes You Tick?* emceed by John K. M. McCaffery. Heard over CBS.

R,T *Who Said That?* emceed by Robert Trout. Heard over NBC, this panel news quiz began simulcasting over NBC television the following year on Saturday evenings. On the panel: Robert Ruark, Burl Ives, Gypsy Rose Lee, and John Cameron Swayze. Writer: Fred Friendly.

R *Who's Next?* emceed by Ed East. Heard over CBS.

R,T *Yours for a Song,* emceed by Bert Parks. First heard over Mutual, this music game moved to ABC where it was heard on Tuesday nights. It would be revived for television in 1961, seen irregularly both in prime time and daytime until September of 1963.

1949

With 3,660,000 television sets in use, more games and quizzes than ever moved to TV. Simulcasting are Winner Take All, Break the Bank, Stop The Music, Juvenile Jury, Life Begins at Eighty, What's My Name?, Quiz Kids, *and* Twenty Questions.

T *Auctionaire,* emceed by Jack Gregson and Charlotte "Rebel" Randall, this game was seen over ABC on Friday nights. Contestants bid Libby canned goods labels for merchandise and tried to identify a "mystery chant" delivered in "auctionese" by Gregson.

T *Auction Night,* seen locally over WXYZ-TV in Detroit.

T *Beat the Band,* seen locally over WHEN-TV in Syracuse and locally in New York over the ABC station WWJ-TV.

T *Draw Me a Laugh,* emceed by Walter Hurley. Seen over ABC.

T *Dress and Guess,* seen locally over WEWS-TV, Cleveland.

T *The Eyes Have It,* emceed by Douglas Edwards. This early panel game went through several incarnations and several names. First seen over NBC, it then became known as *Stop, Look, and Listen,* emceed by Paul Gallico over KECA-TV in Hollywood. It then traveled back to New York where it was called *Riddle Me This,* emceed by Conrad Nagel and seen over CBS. In its best-known incarnation, the show became *Celebrity Time,* emceed by Conrad Nagel with John Daly, Cornelia Otis Skinner, John Carradine, Ilka Chase, and others. *Celebrity Time* aired over ABC in 1949 on Sunday nights featuring a film clip quiz and arch conversation. Gradually the show, now permanently called *Celebrity Time,* veered from quiz to variety format and became the prototype for all later talk shows. Long running.

T *Fun and Fortune,* emceed by Jack Lescoulie. Seen over ABC. Contestants received four clues in which to guess what merchandise prize sat behind a curtain.

T *Fun for the Money,* emceed by Johnny Olson. Seen over ABC. In an effort to be "visual" this quiz pitted men against women and dressed everyone in baseball uniforms.

T *Grab Your Phone,* seen locally over KLAC-TV, Hollywood.

T *Headline Clues,* emceed by George F. Putnam, and later, in 1951, by Bill Slater. Seen in prime time over Du Mont. A daytime version of this quiz was hosted by Don Russell.

T *Here's a Clue.* Seen over Du Mont on Thursday nights.

T *Hold It, Please,* emceed by Gil Fates. Seen over CBS. A phone-in game to identify the spinning picture of a celebrity, with Cloris Leachman and others.

T *The John Reed King Show,* featuring Don Richards, baritone. Seen locally over WOR-TV, New York, this loose-format show included parlor tricks, interviews, and quizzes.

T   *King's Court,* emceed by John Kerr, and later Bill Edmonds. Seen locally over WATV, New York.

T   *Let's Play Pyramid,* seen locally over WTVJ-TV, Miami.

T   *Let's Pop the Question,* seen locally over WAAM-TV, Baltimore.

T   *Majority Rules,* emceed by Myron Wallace. Seen over ABC Friday and later Sunday evenings.

T   *Make It and Take It,* seen locally over WXYZ-TV, Detroit.

T   *Meet Your Match,* emceed by Jan Murray. First seen locally in New York over WOR-TV, this game aired again during the last week of August 1952 over NBC.

T   *Minute Mysteries,* seen locally over WPIX-TV, New York in the fall.

T   *Name the Star,* seen locally over KNBH and KTLA, Hollywood.

T   *Okay, Mother,* emceed by Dennis James. One of the first daytime games. Seen over Du Mont. James initiated his "trademark" practice of giving away his necktie to some lucky woman each day on this show.

T   *Photo-Crime,* seen over ABC on Wednesday nights at 8:30 that year.

T   *R.F.D., America,* seen in the summer that year over NBC. Short lived.

T   *The Rube Goldberg Show,* seen locally over WPIX-TV, New York on Thursday nights. Charade format.

T   *Say It with Acting,* emceed first by Bill Berns, later by Maggie McNellis and Bud Collyer. This long-running show pitted the casts of Broadway plays in charade matches. Seen on weekend evenings.

T   *Shopper's Guide,* seen locally over WTVJ-TV, Miami.

T   *Show-off Club,* seen locally over WTCN-TV, Minneapolis.

T   *Sing My Name,* seen locally over WPTZ-TV, Philadelphia.

T   Spell with Isbell, seen locally over WGN-TV, Chicago.

T   *Spiegel's Quiz,* seen locally over WGN-TV, Chicago. Sponsored by the Spiegel Catalog Company.

T   *Spin the Picture,* emceed by Carl Caruso, Eddie Dunn, and Kathi Norris with Jerry Shad's Quartet. Originally called *Cut,* this show aired over Du Mont on Saturday nights.

T   *Stop, Look, and Learn,* seen locally over WGN-TV, Chicago.

T   *Talent Jackpot,* emceed by Vinton Freedley and Bud Collyer. Seen over Du Mont. The winner was determined by audience applause.

T   *Tel-a-Vision,* seen locally over WPIX-TV, New York on Wednesday nights. A local phone-in quiz.

T   *Tele-Charades,* seen locally over WBKB-TV, Chicago.

T   *The Telephone Game,* emceed by Durwood Kirby and Toby Deane. Seen over ABC in the afternoons, viewers played bingo with phone numbers.

T   *They're Off,* seen over Du Mont on Thursday nights.

R,T   *Think Fast,* emceed by Dr. Mason Gross, and later by Rex Stout, with Gypsy Rose Lee. This panel game, seen over ABC on Friday nights at 9:30, simulcast on radio this and the following year.

T   *Toon-a-Vision,* emceed by Artie Malvin. Seen locally over WOR-TV on Friday nights in the fall. A cartoon quiz.

T   *Treasure Hunt,* seen locally over WGN-TV, Chicago.

T   *Treasure Quest,* emceed by David Broekman, Leon Janney, and Eloise McElhone. Seen over ABC on Sunday and Friday nights.

T   *Tricks and Treats,* seen locally over KTLA-TV, Los Angeles.

T   *Viz Quiz,* seen locally over WDTV-TV, Pittsburgh.

T   *What Happens Now?* also called *What Happens Next?* emceed by John Dahl, and later Nelson Olmstead. Seen locally over WOR-TV, New York, and later over ABC. Viewers mailed in examples of sticky situations for which actors had to improvise a solution. The show moved to CBS-TV in 1951, where it became known as *The Ad-Libbers* and was hosted by Peter Donald. Jack Lemmon was one of the show's regulars.

T   *What's It Worth?* emceed by Sig Rothschild. Seen over CBS. Viewers sent in art objects for appraisal.

T   *What's New Ladies?* seen locally over WBAP-TV, Fort Worth.

T   *Your Lucky Star,* emceed by Candy Jones. Seen locally over WPIX-TV, New York. Telephone quiz.

And new on the radio that year:

R,T   *Chance of a Lifetime,* emceed by John Reed King. This show enabled deserving members of the audience to perform stunts and answer questions to win a jackpot worth up to $5,000. The show came to television in 1950, emceed at times by King, Dick Collier, Russell Arms, and in 1952, by Dennis James. Seen over ABC.

R   *Free For All,* heard over CBS radio.

R   *Hollywood Calling,* emceed by George Murphy. This jackpot quiz with movie trivia questions was the summer replacement that year for Jack Benny.

R   *Hollywood Quiz,* heard over Mutual.

R   *Ladies Fair,* emceed by Tom Moore. Heard over Mutual.

R   *Name the Movie,* emceed by Marvin Miller with Clark Dennis, the singing host, and Peggy Mann and the Starlighters. Heard over ABC.

R   *Pass the Buck,* heard over CBS. Sponsored by Roman Meal Bread.

Radio games and quizzes of the forties, dates unknown:

R   *Anniversary Club,* emceed by Ben Alexander.

R   *Auction Gallery,* emceed by Dan Elman.

R   *Cliché Club,* emceed by Walter Kieran and panelists.

R   *Correction, Please,* emceed by Jim McWilliams.

R   *Crossword Quiz,* emceed by Allen Prescott.

R   *Fun Fair,* emceed by Jay Stewart. Built around people and their pets.

R   *Game Parade,* emceed by Arthur Elmer. Children's quiz.

R   *The March of Games,* emceed by Arthur Ross.

R   *Stop and Go,* emceed by Joe E. Brown.

R   *Tello Test,* a syndicated radio game owned by Walter Schwimmer.

R   *Tune Test,* also owned by Schwimmer.

R   *Watch and Win,* owned and emceed by Ben Alexander.

R   *Whiz Quiz,* emceed by Johnny Olson.

1950

There were 9,732,000 television sets in use. Enough for You Bet Your Life *and* Truth or Consequences *to take the plunge. New shows:*

T   *All Sports Quiz,* seen locally over WPIX-TV, New York.

T   *Animal, Vegetable, or Mineral,* this local version of *Twenty Questions* was seen locally over WMAR-TV, Baltimore.

T   *Anniversary Party,* seen locally over WSPD-TV, Toledo.

T   *Around the House,* seen locally over WNBK-TV, Cleveland.

T   *Batter Up,* emceed by Joe Bolton, Hal Tunis, and Marion Carter. Seen locally over WPIX-TV, New York during baseball season up to 1954. Telephone quiz.

T,S   *Beat the Clock,* emceed by Bud Collyer with Dolores "Roxanne" Rosedale. This classic stunt game came to television over CBS on March 3, 1950 and ran over that network until February 1958. ABC picked up the game in October of that year and carried it until 1962. *Beat the Clock* entered the syndication market in 1969 and ran until 1975, hosted by Gene Wood, with a celebrity guest performing the duties originally performed by Roxanne. Best-known time: Saturday nights at 7:30. Best-remembered sponsor: Sylvania. See pages 138–141.

T   *Broadway to Hollywood,* emceed by George Putnam. Seen over Du Mont during the summer on Wednesday nights.

T   *By Popular Demand,* emceed by Robert Alda and Arlene Francis. Seen over CBS in the summer. Talent-evaluation format.

T   *Clubhouse Quiz,* emceed by Bob Edge, featuring "the mystery Dodger of the week and guests." This sports trivia quiz aired during baseball season over WOR-TV in New York. Similar shows aired in all Major League cities.

T   *Dollar Derby,* seen locally over WLWC-TV, Columbus.

T   *Golden Game.* This Bible quiz aired once over ABC, on a spring Sunday afternoon.

T   *Guggenheim,* emceed by John K. M. McCaffery. This short-lived word game aired locally over WPIX-TV in New York on Thursday evenings.

T   *Hold That Camera,* emceed by Jimmy Blaine. Seen over Du Mont. On this strange show, the home audience directed the camera over the phone. Seen on Sunday eves.

T   *Hollywood Screen Test,* emceed by Neil Hamilton. Talent show seen over ABC.

T   *Johnny Olson's Rumpus Room,* emceed by Johnny and Penny Olson. Seen over Du Mont at 12:30 P.M. for the next three years. Featuring "Stumpers Day."

T   *Life with Linkletter.* Several years before *People Are Funny* and *House Party* would come to television, Guedel and Linkletter tested the waters with this shortened version of the shows. Seen for fifteen minutes a day over ABC this year, and again the next. *House Party* bowed on daytime TV in 1952; *People Are Funny* in prime time the fall of 1954.

T   *Music Can Be Fun,* emceed by Bob Brown, Rick Mardell, and Jana Commodore, this local New York phone-in quiz soon changed its name to *Musical Jackpot.* Seen on Sunday afternoons then daily over WATV-TV into 1954, when it was hosted by Paul Brenner. Viewers submitted postcards in hopes of winning $1000 in merchandise.

T   *Photo-Test,* soon known as *Foto-Test,* emceed by Bruce Eliot and Dan McCullough. Seen locally over WOR-TV in New York, this quiz aired first in the early evening, then in daytime into 1951.

T   *Premium Quiz,* seen locally over KECA-TV, Hollywood.

T   *Prizes and Presents.* Seen locally over WXYZ-TV, Detroit.

T *Quick on the Draw*, emceed by Eloise McElhone and Bob Dunn, later by Robin Chandler. This popular panel game first aired over NBC, and later over ABC. Regular panelists were Louis Untermeyer and Betty Furness. The game was in some ways a prototype for *Concentration* in that panelists had to solve the message contained in a cartoon puzzle. Seen on Thursday nights.

T *Remember This Day*, emceed by Bill Stern with vocalist Jet McDonald, this quiz first bowed on Thanksgiving and had a brief run over NBC thereafter.

T *Riddle in the Middle*, emceed by Bill Goodwin, seen during the afternoon over NBC.

T *Sit or Miss*. This television version of musical chairs was seen over ABC on Sunday evenings.

T *So You Know Sports*. Seen over NBC.

R,T *Songs for Sale*, emceed by Jan Murray, later by Steve Allen, with panelists Rosemary Clooney, Tony Bennett, and others. Simulcast on radio over CBS and CBS-TV, in this talent contest winners received $100 and had a song published by BMI.

T *Take A Chance*, emceed by Don Ameche. Seen over NBC in the fall. Contestants were permitted to keep their money or bet it against the next question for one thousand bars of Sweetheart soap and one thousand dollars.

T *Tin Pan Alley TV*, emceed by Johnny Desmond and the composer of the week. Another talent contest that year. Seen over ABC in the summer.

T *Touchdown*, seen over NBC in the fall, this was a football quiz.

T *Two Grand*, seen locally over WBZ-TV, Boston.

T *Variety Quiz*, later called *Midnight Snack*, emceed by Jack Lescoulie, Sandy Becker, and Bob Sherwood. Seen over CBS on Monday nights, this film clip quiz evolved into an early talk show.

T *V-I-D-E-O*. Seen locally over WHEN-TV, Syracuse.

T *We Take Your Word*, emceed by John K. M. McCaffery with John Daly and Abe Burrows. Seen over CBS on Saturday nights, on this word discussion game, the celebrity panel played for charity.

T *What Am I Bid?* seen locally over WOR-TV during the summer.

T *What Is It?* emceed by cartoonist Marvin Stein, this sports quiz was seen locally over WOR-TV, New York.

R,T,S *What's My Line?* emceed by John Daly, with panel. First seen in January 1950, it took all year for this great classic to hit its stride and find its famous time slot at 10:30 P.M. on Sunday nights, where it would stay for seventeen years until the fall of 1967. *What's My Line* entered the syndication market in 1968 and ran there until 1974, hosted first by Wally Bruner and then by Larry Blyden. In 1952, the show simulcast on radio. See pages 135–138.

T *What's Offered?* emceed by Al "Red" Benson. Seen locally over WOR-TV during the summer on Wednesday nights.

T *What's the Record?* Local New York sports quiz seen over WPIX-TV.

T *Yes or No?* later called *Answer Yes or No*. Emceed by Moss Hart and Arlene Francis. Seen over NBC on Sunday nights. This psychological parlor game was the *Tattletales* of its day as celebrities discussed what they would do in complicated hypothetical situations.

While on radio that year, these shows bowed:

R,T *Live Like a Millionaire*, emceed by Bob Russell, later by Jack McCoy. First heard over NBC, this show soon moved to CBS that year where it simulcast over CBS-TV. Seen on alternate Fridays, on it children served as talent scouts for their parents to win, by audience acclamation, diamond watches, a week's vacation, and one week's interest from a million dollars.

R *Rate Your Mate,* emceed by Joey Adams. Owned by Goodson-Todman. Heard over CBS. A husband-vs.-wives game.

R *Share the Wealth.* Heard over ABC.

R *Shoot the Moon.* A late-bowing jackpot quiz. Network unknown.

R *The Sixty-four Dollar Question.* Still owned by Milton Biow, the quiz formerly called *Take It or Leave It* officially changed its name this year, paving the way for Louis G. Cowan's TV extravaganza five years later.

1951

There were 15,782,000 TV sets in use and lots of new, not-so-good TV games.

T *Battle of the Boroughs,* emceed by Durwood Kirby, Ted Brown. Seen over CBS on Tuesday nights in the summer of the year. Contestants representing each of New York's five boroughs vied for savings bonds by performing stunts. Unrelated to a radio game of the same name emceed by Mark Goodson nine years earlier.

T *Darts for Dollars,* seen locally over WXEL, Cleveland.

T *Down You Go,* emceed by Bergen Evans. First seen over Du Mont on Thursday nights, the popular panel game moved to ABC during the fall of 1953 and ran until the summer of 1956. Based on the game of Hangman, with clues in the form of dreadful puns.

T *Finders Keepers.* First bowing over NBC during the daytime, this game returned to the air over Du Mont during the fall of 1954 hosted by Fred Robbins. On it, contestants allowed cameras into their homes, then attempted to locate a valuable object the show had hidden there. Seen at 7:30 P.M.

T *Go Lucky,* emceed by Jan Murray, his first television game. Seen over CBS during the summer, it featured celebrity guests and was based on the parlor game of Coffeepot. Seen in the evenings.

T *Guess Again,* emceed by Mike Wallace, his first game show. Seen over CBS over the summer, this comedy panel game with Claire Booth Luce, Victor Jory, and Glenda Farrell, was played with members of the audience who answered questions based on skits.

T *Happiness Exchange,* emceed by Big Joe Rosenfield. Seen over Du Mont. A phone quiz for charity in which participants split a $100 jackpot.

T *Hold Everything,* emceed by Hal Tunis. Seen locally over WOR-TV, New York during the summer.

T *In Record Time,* emceed by Art Ford. This show aired once over NBC in the fall.

T *It's in the Bag,* emceed by Win Elliot, Bob Russell. Seen first over Du Mont during the day, this show moved to NBC in 1952 where it aired on Monday afternoons.

T *It's News to Me,* emceed by John Daly. Owned by Goodson-Todman in an effort to trade upon the success of *What's My Line?* This news panel game aired over CBS until 1955, usually at 9:30 P.M., e.s.t. on Monday nights.

T *Ladies Before Gentleman,* emceed by Ken Roberts, and later Steve Allen. Seen first over ABC, later over Du Mont, this panel was the mirror image of the then popular *Leave It to the Girls.*

T   *The Name's the Same,* emceed by Robert Q. Lewis, with Abe Burrows, Meredith Wilson, Joan Alexander, Gene Rayburn, and others. Seen over ABC through 1954. Owned by Goodson-Todman, again copying their own *What's My Line?,* the shtick here was for the panel to guess a contestant's famous name, e.g., Abraham Lincoln.

T   *Play Ball,* emceed by Hal Tunis, with Marilyn Davies. Seen locally over WPIX-TV in New York this pre-game quiz offered prizes worth up to $2,700.

T   *Pop the Question,* seen locally over WAVE-TV, Louisville.

T   *Prize Performance,* seen locally over WPIX-TV, New York.

T   *Q.E.D.* emceed by Fred Uttal, Doug Browning. Seen through the summer over ABC on Tuesday evenings, this show presented to a panel the plot to a murder mystery for them to guess the solution.

T   *The Real McKay,* seen during the day over CBS, this was a local New York house-wife stunt show.

T   *Ring the Bell,* emceed by Hal Tunis and Jacqueline Susann. A telephone quiz seen over Du Mont weekly at 11 P.M.

T   *Ruth Lyons' 50–50 Club,* seen during the day over NBC, this variety show which originated in Cincinnati offered door prizes to the studio audience drawn daily by lot.

T   *The Sam Levenson Show,* seen over CBS, this folksy comedy show offered one "gamey" feature: the audience voted each week over whether they sympathized with the point of view of the parents or a child. The show thereby became the prototype of many a Chuck Barris game of the sixties.

T   *Tag the Gag,* emceed by Hal Block. Seen over NBC in the summer. Best-caption contest.

T   *Take the Break,* emceed by Don Russell. Seen over CBS during the day. Stunts and door prizes.

T   *Take Your Pick,* emceed by Al "Red" Benson. Seen locally over WPIX-TV, New York. Seen at the first of the year.

T   *Tele-Kid Test,* emceed by Bruce Eliot and Dan McCullough. Seen locally over WOR-TV. Children phoned in to answer questions to win bicycles and other prizes. Seen daily at 5:30 P.M.

T   *This Could Be You,* emceed by Bill Gwinn. Seen over ABC on Monday Nights. On this nostalgia game couples described how a favorite song had changed their lives for the better.

T   *Town and Country Quiz,* seen locally over WDAF-TV, Kansas City, Missouri.

T   *Video Venus,* emceed by Herb Sheldon. Seen over ABC on Friday evenings. Beauty contest.

T   *Viz-Quiz,* emceed by Jack McCarthy. Seen locally over WPIX-TV.

T   *What's the Story?* emceed by Walter Kieran, Al Capp. Seen over Du Mont during the summer through 1953. News quiz.

T   *Who's Whose?* emceed by Phil Baker. Seen over CBS during the summer. A celebrity panel attempted to correctly match spouses.

T   *With This Ring,* emceed by Bill Slater. Seen over Du Mont during prime time. Engaged couples submitted themselves to the advice of a marriage counselor in exchange for a free honeymoon. Another pre-Barris concept.

And one lone new radio game that year:

R *Health Quiz.* Sponsored by the American Protam Corporation. Heard over Mutual, and CBS.

1952

There were 21,782,000 television sets in use, and for the first time, no new radio games.

T *Answer Me This,* emceed by Tom Romano. Seen locally over WNHC-TV, New Haven.

T *Are You Positive?* emceed by Bill Stern, Frank Coniff with panelists Frank Frisch and Lefty Gomez. Summertime quiz in which the celebrity panel attempted to guess the identity of guest celebrities from their baby pictures.

T *Ask Me Another,* seen over NBC.

T *Ask The Camera,* emceed by Sandy Becker. Seen over NBC. This show originated as a film-clip quiz, then shifted to a phone-in viewer information service. Barbara Walters assisted in 1953. Seen daily at 6:15 P.M.

T *Away You Go,* emceed by Bob Haymes. Seen during the summer, on Sunday nights over ABC after the 11 o'clock news.

T *Balance Your Budget,* emceed by Bert Parks, "the keeper of the horn of plenty" and Lynn Connor. Seen over CBS, this quiz netted couples enough cash to better run their households.

T *Battle of the Ages,* emceed by John Reed King and Morey Amsterdam. Seen first over Du Mont, later that year over CBS on Saturday nights, this for-real prototype to *The Gong Show* pitted new and old talent against each other in a contest.

T *The Big Idea,* emceed by Donn Bennett. Seen over Du Mont. Amateur inventors submitted their ideas to businessmen for evaluation and door prizes.

T *The Big Payoff,* emceed by Bert Parks, Randy Merriman, Mort Lawrence, and Robert Paige, with Bess Myerson, Betty Ann Grove, Denise Lor, and Dori Ann Grey. This quiz dominated the afternoon over CBS from January of 1952 until 1960, and even aired in prime time some summers over NBC. For more, see pages 160–162.

T *Birthday Party,* seen locally over WTMJ-TV, Boston.

T *Buyer For A Day,* seen locally over WJZ-TV, the local ABC affiliate in New York.

T *Calling All Women,* emceed by Jack Kilty. Seen locally over WPIX-TV, New York. Seen during the daytime in the spring.

T *Club Matinee,* emceed by Jim Fair and Joe Biviano, the accordionist. Seen over ABC from May through the summer. Daytime giveaway.

T *Draw to Win,* emceed by Henry Morgan with Abner Dean, Bill Halman, Eve Hunter, and Sid Hoff. Seen on Tuesday nights in the spring. Comedy cartoon quiz.

T *Food for Thought,* seen over Du Mont during the afternoon. Food quiz.

T *Fur Fun,* seen locally over KNXT-TV, Hollywood.

T *Guess What?* emceed by Dick Kollmor. Seen over Du Mont on Tuesday nights during the summer. With Virginia Peine, Quentin Reynolds, Mark Hanna, Cliff Norton, and others.

T *Guess What Happened?* emceed by John Cameron Swayze, Ben Oliver, Ben Grauer, and panel. News quiz seen on Thursday nights during August.

T *High School Quiz,* seen locally over WNHC-TV, New Haven.

T *Housewives' Jamboree,* emceed by Johnny Olson. This daytime game aired only once, over ABC.

T *It's a Fact,* seen locally over KNON-TV.

T,S *I've Got a Secret,* emceed by Garry Moore, Steve Allen, with panel. Seen from June 26, 1952 through September 3, 1967. Best-remembered time: Wednesday nights at 9:30 P.M. The game entered syndication in 1972 and ran until 1975, emceed by Steve Allen. For more, see pages 147–151.

T *The Johnny Dugan Show.* NBC daytime quiz.

T *Kitchen Kapers,* emceed by Tiny Ruffner. Seen during the day over ABC. Phone quiz for merchandise prizes.

T *Ladies' Date,* emceed by Bruce Mayer. Du Mont daytime audience participation show, seen again in 1954.

T,S *Masquerade Party,* emceed by Peter Donald, Douglas Edwards, Bud Collyer, Bert Parks, Eddie Bracken, Robert Q. Lewis. Based in Los Angeles, this irregularly but long-running game first aired in July over NBC and every year thereafter over CBS, ABC, and in 1958 over CBS again. A syndicated version of *Masquerade Party* bowed in 1974 hosted by Richard Dawson. For more information, see pages 151–153.

T *Midway,* emceed by Don Russell. This summer quiz aired over Du Mont. Russell posed questions to passersby at New Jersey amusement park Palisades Park.

T *Movie Quiz.* First seen locally over WPIX-TV, New York in the fall at 7:15 P.M. on week nights, the show moved to ABC in 1953 where it was seen at 12:40 P.M. during the day hosted by Ed Cooper.

T *PDQ I.* Seen one time over ABC in January. *For PDQ II,* see, 1965.

T *Pud's Prize Party,* emceed by Todd Russell. This children's game show, sponsored by Fleer's Double Bubble Gum, aired over ABC in the summer on Saturday mornings.

T *The Ralph Edwards Show.* When *Truth or Consequences* failed to catch on in early television in prime time, this version of the game briefly aired over Monday, Wednesday, and Friday during the afternoon over NBC.

T *Sense and Nonsense,* emceed by Ralph Paul, Bob Kennedy, and Vivian Farrar. This game incorporating the five senses first aired over NBC on weekday evenings. In 1954, the game moved to Du Mont, and Peggy O'Hara replaced Vivian Farrar.

T *Shoot the Works,* seen locally in Cincinnati. Station unknown.

T *Sports Page,* emceed by Stan Lomax. Seen locally over WOR-TV, New York. Sports quiz between races.

T *Talk to the Stars,* emceed by Happy Felton. Seen locally over WOR-TV, New York. Phone-in sports quiz.

T *The Ted Steele Show,* seen locally over WPIX-TV, New York during the day, featuring the "Money Melody" scoreboard.

T *That Reminds Me,* emceed by Arlene Francis, with panel. Seen over NBC, this show was a New York version of *Masquerade Party.*

T *There's One in Every Family,* emceed by John Reed King. This audience-participation show first aired during the late morning over CBS in September.

T *Trash—Or—Treasure?* emceed by Sigmund Rothschild, Nelson Case, and Bill Wendell. Seen over Du Mont. Viewers brought in items from their attic for evaluation. Seen over Du Mont, in 1953, the show changed its name to *Treasure Hunt,* no relation to the Jan Murray or the Chuck Barris games of the same name.

T *TV Auction Club,* emceed by Johnny Olson. Seen locally over WOR-TV, New York, in May on Wednesday nights.

T *TV Crossword Puzzle* with Larry Stevens, Anne Burr, Gouvernor Paulding, and John Duff Stradley. Seen locally over WPIX-TV, New York during the summer.

R,T *Two for the Money,* emceed by Herb Shriner, with Dr. Mason Gross, later by Sam Levenson. Owned by Goodson-Todman. First seen over NBC, this popular prime-time quiz moved to CBS during the summer of 1953 where it stayed until 1956. Modeled after *You Bet Your Life,* the Hoosier comic first presented a comedy monologue then emceed a serious quiz with an end game that required contestants to list as many items as they could in a category within a time limit. The first year of its run, the show simulcast over NBC radio.

T *Up to Paar,* emceed by Jack Paar. This news quiz aired over NBC during the summer.

T *What Happened?* emceed by Ben Grauer with Lisa Ferraday, Maureen Stapleton, Roger Price, and Frank Gallup. This news quiz aired over NBC in prime time during the summer.

T,S *What in the World?* emceed by Dr. Alfred Kidder, Dr. Carlton Coon, Dr. Schuler Common, and Froelich Rainey. Seen over CBS on Sunday afternoons, this game challenged museum experts to identify artifacts, sort of an egghead *Liar's Club.* The show briefly aired again in 1971, in New Haven.

T *Wheel of Fortune I,* emceed by Todd Russell. Seen over CBS, in Los Angeles during prime time, in New York on Friday mornings. For *Wheel of Fortune II,* see 1975 heading.

T *Where Was I?* emceed by Dan Seymour, Ken Roberts. Seen over Du Mont. Panel photo quiz.

T *Who Knows?* News panel quiz with Chet Huntley, Alex Gottlieb, Sterling Holoway and Hilary Brooke. Seen briefly over ABC on Sunday evenings. The panel guessed the answers through pantomimed clues.

T *Who's My Parent?* seen over ABC during the summer on Tuesday evenings.

T *Who's There?* Celebrity panel game. The panel guessed the identity of mystery guests through articles of clothing presented to them. Seen over CBS in the fall. With Arlene Francis, Bill Cullen, Paula Stone, and Robert Coote.

T *Why?* emceed by John Reed King, Bill Cullen. Seen over ABC on Monday nights beginning in December. Another news panel. The panel has to guess the "why" of a story, having been furnished with the "who," "what," "when," and "where."

T *Wisdom of the Ages,* emceed by Jack Barry. Seen over NBC. Barry-Enright combined the generations on this panel.

T *Your Lucky Clue,* emceed by Basil Rathbone. Seen over CBS during the summer on Sunday night. Two celebrity teams attempted to solve a mystery.

T *Your Surprise Store,* emceed by Lew Parker with Jacqueline Susann. Seen over CBS daytime in the spring. Stunts and merchandise prizes from the "surprise store."

1953

As prime time TV dramas and comedies began to establish themselves, most new quizzes appeared in the summer, when regularly-programmed live shows went on vacation. More and more quizzes began to appear during one day this year where they competed with the variety shows of Arthur Godfrey and Garry Moore.

T *Anyone Can Win,* emceed by Al Capp, with Laraine Day, Wendy Barrie, Jackie Cooper, and mystery guests. This panel game first aired over CBS on Tuesday evenings in the summer. In 1957, it was revived over Du Mont during the day, emceed by Herb Sheldon and quickly evolved into a nonquiz format called *The Herb Sheldon Show.*

T *Back the Fact,* emceed by Joey Adams and Al Kelly. Seen over ABC. Contestants were abruptly challenged by an offstage voice to prove various details about their identity.

T *Bank on the Stars,* emceed by Jack Paar, Bill Cullen. This film-clip quiz first aired during the summer on Saturday evening over CBS. It returned to the air the following summer with Cullen. Paar was never a good game-show host.

T *Call the Play.* Sports quiz seen locally over WPIX-TV, New York.

T *Choose Up Sides,* emceed first by Dean Miller, later by Gene Rayburn. Seen first over CBS in the late afternoon, this children's quiz pitted teams of cowboys against space rangers. NBC picked up the game in 1956 airing it on Saturday mornings with Rayburn in charge. The show marked Rayburn's first hosting berth.

T *Comeback Story,* emceed by George Jessel. Seen over ABC briefly. The show offered has-been celebrities the chance to make a "comeback."

T *Dollar a Second,* emceed by Jan Murray. First seen over Du Mont on Sunday evenings, this stunt show aired over ABC in the fall of 1954 where it ran until the summer of 1956, and returned briefly during the summer of 1957. The show resembled *Beat the Clock.*

T *Follow the Leader,* emceed by Vera Vague. Seen on Tuesday nights over CBS.

T *Freedom Rings,* emceed by John Beal. Seen over CBS during the afternoons during the spring. Phone—in quiz with prizes for stunts.

T *Fun with Food,* emceed by Martin E. Lamont, this game soon changed its name to *Name the Dish.* Seen locally over WPIX-TV, New York at 11 P.M. during the summer.

T *Glamour Girl,* emceed by Harry Babbitt. Seen over NBC, mornings during the summer. The show offered women a chance for a new wardrobe and vacation.

T *Hail the Champ.* Seen over ABC. Sports quiz.

T *Judge for Yourself,* emceed by Fred Allen, Dennis James. Owned by Goodson-Todman. Allen was terrible on this talent evaluation show that aired over NBC that summer on Tuesday nights.

T *Know Your Bible,* seen over NBC on Sunday mornings. Brief run.

T *Ladies' Choice,* host unknown. Seen over NBC daytime in June. Ladies' clubs voted on their favorite talent acts.

T *Magic Horseshoe,* emcee unknown. This children's quiz which aired over NBC with a Western theme, later became *Silver Horseshoe.* Seen on Thursday afternoons.

T *Make a Million,* emceed by Jerry Lester. Seen very briefly over Du Mont during the summer on Tuesday night.

T *My Secret Ambition.* Kids audience participation. Seen over NBC in the fall.

T,S *Name That Tune,* emceed by Al 'Red' Benson, Bill Cullen, George DeWitt, with Vicki Mills. Owned by Harry Salter. This show bowed over NBC in July, ran through 1954 emceed by Benson, then moved to CBS emceed by Cullen, where it ran until 1960. DeWitt replaced Cullen in 1955. In 1970, Ralph Edwards acquired the rights to the game for syndication. The Edwards version next aired over NBC daytime from January 1974 until June 1975, hosted by Tom Kennedy. A syndicated version of the show, called *$100,000 Name That Tune,* hosted by Kennedy, is still airing in syndication at the time of this writing. See pages 153–157.

T *On Your Account,* emceed by Eddie Albert, Win Elliott, Dennis James. Seen over NBC daytime through the fall of 1954.

T   *On Your Way,* emceed by Bud Collyer, John Reed King. Seen over Du Mont on Wednesday nights. Contestants answered four easy questions to arrive at a "destination" shown on a large map.

T   *Personality Puzzle,* emceed by John Conte, Robert Alda. Seen over ABC on Thursday nights. As with *Who's There?* of the previous year, a panel attempted to guess the identity of a celebrity from a personal belonging.

T   *Place the Face,* emceed by Jack Smith, Jack Paar, Bill Cullen. First seen over NBC in the summer, this game ran through August of the following year, then returned to the air in the summer of 1955. Broadcast from Hollywood, contestants tried to pinpoint the identity of someone from their past. Owned by Ralph Edwards.

T   *Shenanigans,* emceed by Bob Quigley, later by Stubby Kaye. First seen locally over WPIX-TV during the first quarter of the year, this children's show returned to the air over ABC between 1964 and 1965 at 10 A.M. on Saturdays.

T   *Stage a Number,* emceed by Bill Wendell. Prospective amateur directors got a chance to try their hand at mounting a variety act. Seen over Du Mont in the spring on Wednesday nights.

T   *Take a Guess,* emceed by John K. M. McCaffery with Ernie Kovacs, Joan Crawford, and Dorothy Hall. Seen over CBS in the summer on Thursday nights, this show marked the first time celebrities and civilians played on the same team.

T   *Turn to a Friend,* emceed by Dennis James. Seen over ABC in the afternoons, needy contestants shared their sob stories for merchandise prizes.

T   *What Have You Got to Lose?* emceed by John Reed King. Seen over ABC daytime television during the summer.

T   *What's the Pitch?* emceed by Peter Donald, with panel. Seen over ABC in the late afternoon, during the fall.

T   *What's Your Bid?* emceed by John Reed King, Robert Alda, and Leonard Rosen. Seen over ABC on Saturday nights. Charity auction held by celebrities.

T   *Your Big Moment,* emceed by Melvyn Douglas. Seen over Du Mont. Douglas arranged blind dates and other requests for contestants who wrote in to him. Seen during the spring on Tuesday nights.

T   *Your Claim to Fame,* emceed by Jay Stewart. Seen over ABC.

This year marked the last gasp of radio quizzes. See if you can spot the only one with a future.

R   *Fun for All,* emceed by Bill Cullen. Heard over CBS, ABC. Sponsored by Toni.

R,T *G.E. College Bowl,* emceed by Allen Ludden, later by Robert Earle. Owned by Moses-Reid-Cleary. Heard over NBC, this quiz came to television in January of 1959 and ran through 1966 on Sunday afternoons at 5:30 P.M. For more about it, see pages 184–187.

R   *I'll Buy That,* heard over CBS.

R   *Make Up Your Mind,* emceed by Bill Sterling. Heard over CBS.

R   *Movie Quiz.* Heard over Mutual. Sponsored by Kix Cereal.

R   *Second Chance.* Heard over NBC. Sponsored by Tums.

R   *Walk a Mile,* emceed by Bill Cullen. Heard over CBS.

R   *Wizard of Odds.* Heard over CBS. Sponsored by Toni.

1954

The coast-to-coast network hookup had been completed, bringing order to nighttime schedules and, in effect, squeezing Du Mont out; the following year it began to sell the few affiliates it had. The great quizzes and games of the period, What's My Line?, Name That Tune, I've Got a Secret, Beat the Clock, You Bet Your Life, had settled into unshakable niches. Even daytime was less volatile, given over as it was to variety shows, serials, movies, and such quizzes and games as Walt Framer's Strike It Rich, The Big Payoff and G. E. House Party. Television schedules changed now mainly in the summer in this pre-videotape, pre-rerun era. When regular shows took a summer vacation, the networks temporarily replaced them with quiz shows. But change was in the wind. The Supreme Court finally ruled that tuning into a jackpot quiz did not constitute gambling. The heat, on for almost fifteen years, was off quiz shows at last, and their stakes, until then modest, were about to grow big, big, big.

T   *Art Linkletter and the Kids.* Linkletter and Guedel again tested the TV waters with this popular fifteen-minute segment of *People Are Funny* to see what viewer reaction would be to finally bringing their radio hit to television. Reaction was favorable. *People Are Funny* began its eight-year run on television that fall.

T   *Be My Guest.* This brief-running local New York show (network unknown) made history by running out of prizes.

T   *Call the Play,* emceed by Mel Allen and seen over CBS on Saturday afternoons through the fall of the following year. This sports quiz used film footage and phone calls to home—viewer quarterbacks.

T   *Come Closer,* emceed by Jimmy Nelson. Seen over ABC on Monday nights in the fall.

T   *Droodles,* emceed by Roger Price. Seen briefly over NBC during the summer on Monday nights, this game employed Price's comic drawings, then in vogue.

T   *Earn Your Vacation,* emceed by Johnny Carson with former Miss America Jackie Lougherty and Millie Sinclair. Seen over CBS during the summer on Sunday nights. Contestants qualified by indicating through an essay "where in the world I want to go and why." If they could answer four questions that took them up an "airplane ramp" on the set, they won a trip and were welcomed aboard the show's "plane." Not Carson's brightest moment.

T   *Feather Your Nest,* emceed by Bud Collyer with Lou Prentiss and Janis Carter. This popular daytime quiz ran from October through June of 1956 and distinguished itself by giving away rooms full of furniture, each day from a different period. Seen at 12:30 P.M.

T   *Funny Boners,* emceed by ventriloquist Jimmy Weldon and Webster Webfoot. Seen over NBC on Saturday mornings, this children's quiz unsuccessfully attempted to recapture the popularity Paul Winchell and Jerry Mahoney had had on early television with former radio hit, *What's My Name?* (See 1938 heading.)

T   *Gamble on Love,* emceed by Denise Darcel. Seen over Du Mont during the summer. Three couples competed against a wheel of fortune for the chance to answer "Cupid's question."

T   *I Made the News,* emceed by Johnny Olson. Seen locally over WPIX-TV, New York. Allen Ludden was a panelist on this news quiz. Seen in the fall on Sunday evening.

T   *It's About Time,* emceed by Bergen Evans. Seen over ABC during the summer on Thursday evenings.

T *Manhattan Honeymoon,* emceed by Neva Patterson. Seen from February through April over ABC at 10 A.M.

T *One Minute Please,* emceed by John K. M. McCaffery. Seen over Du Mont on Tuesday evenings in the summer. The idea was based on a British show. Panelists had to talk on a subject for one whole minute. Most diverting panelist: Hermione Gingold.

T *Photo Quiz,* seen locally in New York over WATV-TV, during the summer.

T *Sky's the Limit,* emceed by Gene Rayburn, with Marilyn Cantor and, later, Hope Lange. Seen over NBC at 6:30 P.M. daily during the fall.

T *Time Will Tell,* emceed by Ernie Kovacs. Seen over Du Mont during the late summer, Fridays at 10:30 P.M.

T *Touchdown Quiz,* emceed by Guy LeBow. Seen over ABC during football season.

T *Town Hall Party,* emceed by Jay Stewart. Seen locally over KTTV-TV, Los Angeles.

T *Travel Quiz,* emceed by Ben Grauer, Horace Sutton. Seen over NBC on Saturday afternoons in the summer.

T *Treasurama,* seen locally over WOR-TV in the summer at 4:30 P.M.

T *TV-Auction,* emceed by Sid Stone. Seen during the summer over ABC on Saturday night.

T *Two in Love,* emceed by Bert Parks. Seen over CBS during the summer at 10:30 P.M., Saturday night.

T *What Do You Have in Common?* emceed by Ralph Story. Seen over CBS during the summer on Thursday night. Three contestants competed to discover their hidden relationship with a fourth party: they all had the same doctor, say.

T *What's Going On?* emceed by Lee Bowman. Contestants were taken to a location outside the studio and their teammates tried to guess where. Seen over ABC that summer.

T *What's in a Word?* emceed by Clifton Fadiman, Mike Wallace. Rhyming game played by Faye Emerson, Audrey Meadows, Carl Reiner, and Jim Moran. Seen on Thursday evenings into 1955 over ABC.

T *Where Have You Been?* emceed by Horace Sutton. Riddle clues for panel to solve. Seen over NBC.

T *Who's the Boss?* emceed by Walter Kieran. A celebrity panel quizzed secretaries in an effort to guess which young lady "belonged" to which boss. Seen over ABC on Friday nights during the spring.

And one lone radio game:

R *It Happens Every Day,* emceed by Bill Cullen. Heard over Mutual.

1955

That year a summer replacement quiz struck paydirt.

T *Contest Carnival,* seen over CBS.

T *Have a Heart,* emceed by John Reed King. Seen over Du Mont beginning in April. Two teams played for a home-town charity. Seen on Tuesday nights.

T *It Pays to Be Married,* emceed by Bill Goodwin. From Hollywood. Seen over NBC during the summer. Couples related how they overcame marital problems, then competed in a quiz for prizes.

T   *Let's See,* emceed by John Reed King. Seen over NBC on Thursday night that summer. Broadcast from Atlantic City, this show imitated *I've Got a Secret.*

T   *Love Story.* Seen over CBS during the day, the show offered contestants a trip to Paris and $500. An imitation of *The Big Payoff.*

T   *Make The Connection,* emceed by Jim McCay, with Betty White, Eddie Bracken, and Gene Klavan. The panel had to guess how two contestants' paths had crossed. Seen over NBC in the summer on Thursday night.

T   *Musical Chairs,* emceed by Bill Leyden. Seen over NBC on Saturday night during the summer. With Johnny Mercer, Bobby Troup, and Mel Blanc.

T   *$100,000 Big Surprise,* emceed by Jack Barry, Mike Wallace. Produced by Merrill Heatter. Owned by EPI. This show aired in October on Saturday nights and went through many transformations, none of which ironed out its kinks.

T   *Penny to a Million,* emceed by Bill Goodwin. Owned by Walt Framer. Two panels of five contestants each vied to win a million pennies. Seen over ABC from May through September.

T   *The $64,000 Question,* emceed by Hal March. Seen over CBS Tuesday evenings at 10 P.M. Owned by EPI. The show aired until November 2, 1958. One of the biggest television hits *ever.* See pages 189–216.

T   *Stop the Experts,* emceed by Sid Gordon. Seen over CBS. Sports quiz.

T   *What's the Joke?* emceed by Paul Killian with panelists Joey Adams, Henny Youngman, Dagmar, and Betty Kean. Seen over ABC during the summer. The panel first observed a dramatic skit, then tried to guess the punchline to a joke based on what they'd witnessed. Seen on Sunday nights.

1956

Some of the best game shows there ever were bowed that year . . .

T   *Can Do,* emceed by Robert Alda. Seen briefly over NBC on Monday nights. From isolation booths, contestants tried to anticipate whether celebrities could perform the stunts they said they could, as in Mickey Mantle hitting five out of five pitches. Played for a jackpot of $50,000.

T   *Dove Son Nato?* seen locally over WATV-TV, New York. An Italian version of *The $64,000 Question.*

T   *Do You Trust Your Wife?* emceed by Edgar Bergen, later Johnny Carson. (See also *Who Do You Trust?* 1958. Owned by Art Stark. Seen over CBS on Tuesday nights at 10:30 P.M. from January until March of the following year. It returned to the air over ABC during the day that fall with Carson. The show did not officially change its name until 1958. See also pages 176–179.

T   *Giant Step,* emceed by Bert Parks. Owned by EPI. Seen over NBC from November until May of 1957. Children's quiz.

T   *High Finance,* emceed by Dennis James. Seen over CBS on Saturday nights that summer.

T   *It Could Be You,* emceed by Bill Leyden. Seen during the day over NBC during the summer. Surprise-party format. From Hollywood. Owned by Ralph Edwards.

T   *Million Lira Quiz,* emceed by Lew Danis. Another ethnic version of *The $64,000 Question* seen locally over WATV-TV, New York. The show changed its name to *Win a Million Lire* with John Myers. Seen Sundays at 5:30 P.M.

T *Pluvio de Oro (Rain of Gold)* seen locally over WATV-TV, New York. Spanish version of *The $64,000 Question.*

T *The (Original) Price is Right,* emceed by Bill Cullen. Owned by Goodson-Todman. Created by Bob Stewart. This show first aired on daytime TV over NBC in November, ran simultaneously for a time in prime time, then ran exclusively in daytime again until September 1963. ABC picked up the game one week later and carried it through 1965. Best-remembered time: 10:30 A.M. See pages 181–184.

T *The $64,000 Challenge,* emceed by Sonny Fox, Ralph Story. Owned by EPI. Seen over CBS from April 1956 on Sundays at 10 P.M. See pages 189–216.

T *Stand Up and Be Counted,* emceed by Bob Russell. Seen over CBS during the summer at 11 A.M. Advice show with audience voting.

T *Tic Tac Dough,* emceed by Jack Barry, Bill Wendel. Seen over NBC, daytime, beginning in August and running through 1959. Owned by Barry—Enright.

T,S *To Tell the Truth.* A rough version of this show, called *Nothing but the Truth,* aired earlier in the year emceed by John Cameron Swayze over CBS. In its final version, this classic panel game was hosted first by Bud Collyer, later by Garry Moore. Seen in prime time between December 1956 and 1967. Seen during the day between 1962 and 1968. The game entered the syndication market from 1973 to 1979 hosted by Garry Moore and Joe Garagiola. Owned by Goodson-Todman. Created by Bob Stewart. See pages 167–174.

T *The (Original) Treasure Hunt,* emceed and owned by Jan Murray. First seen over ABC in prime time between the fall of 1956 and the summer of 1957, this game found its niche over NBC during the day between 1957 and 1960. For more, see pages 179–180.

T *Twenty-One,* emceed by Jack Barry. Owned by Barry-Enright. Seen on Wednesday nights at 10:30 P.M. over NBC between September 1956 and October 1958. See pages 189–216.

T *You're on Your Own,* emceed by Steve Dunne. Owned by Barry-Enright. Seen over CBS. Contestants were asked three questions based on their backgrounds, the answers to which could be found within the studio, or they could phone whomever they thought might know. Played against the clock.

1957

T *Beat the Champions,* emceed by Guy LeBow. Seen locally over WOR-TV, New York. This phone-in sports quiz aired at midnight.

T *Birthday Party,* seen locally over WATV-TV, New York. Surprise party for children.

T *50,000 Penny Jackpot,* emceed by Frann Weigle. Seen locally over WGN-TV, Chicago. Children answered questions for bikes and the like.

T *Hidden Treasure,* emceed by Robert Q. Lewis. This quiz aired one time as a special. Seen locally over WPIX-TV, New York on April 5. The background for singing clues was provided by Ray Bloch and his orchestra.

T *High Low,* emceed by Jack Barry. Seen over NBC on Thursday nights between 1957 and 1958. Contestants tried to guess which experts were "high" in the number of questions they knew the answers to, which were low. Owned by Barry-Enright.

T *Hold That Note,* emceed by Bert Parks. Seen over NBC on Tuesday nights, this show replaced *Break the $250,000 Bank.*

T *Hollywood Jackpot,* seen locally over WATV-TV, New York. This summer quiz aired at 11:30 A.M., Sunday.

T *It's a Hit,* emceed by Happy Felton. Summer children's quiz seen on Saturdays.

T *Keep It in the Family,* emceed by Bill Nimmo, Keefe Brasselle. Seen over ABC from October to February of the following year. Literally a quiz for the whole family. Merchandise prizes.

T *Spell and Tell,* seen locally over WATV-TV, New York. Limerick quiz.

T *What's It For?* emceed by Hal March, then making $9000 a week. Seen over NBC October through January. Inventors and their descendents faced a celebrity panel.

T *Where Was I Born?* seen locally over WATV-TV, New York, Sunday afternoons.

1958

Rumors of rigging did not stop a whole new crop of quizzes from being born, and a classic game or two.

T *Anybody Can Play,* emceed by George Fenneman. Seen over ABC from July through December. Sunday nights. Panelists had to guess the identity of a concealed object.

T *Bid 'n' Buy,* emceed by Bert Parks. Seen over CBS briefly during the summer.

T *Big Game,* emceed by Tom Kennedy, his first show. Seen over NBC between June and September, on Friday nights.

T *Bingo at Home!* emceed by Monty Hall. Seen locally in New York over Du Mont. This was only one of many TV bingo games that aired this year, many of them syndicated and owned by Martin and Allan Stone. One such game was called *Teloh* in Iowa, another, *Play Marko* in Oklahoma.

T *Brains and Brawn,* emceed by Jack Lescoulie. Seen Saturday nights over NBC in the fall.

T *Chance for Romance,* emceed by John Cameron Swayze. Seen during the day over ABC the fall of 1958.

T,S *Concentration,* emceed by Jack Barry, Hugh Downs, Art James, Bill Mazer, Ed McMahon, Bob Clayton. Originally owned by Barry-Enright, subsequently by NBC, and still later by Goodson-Todman. First seen in August 1958, in the mornings over NBC, *Concentration* also briefly aired in prime time during 1961. The daytime version of the network game aired until March 1973. *Concentration* entered syndication in 1973, hosted by Jack Narz. See pages 219–221.

T *Dotto,* emceed by Jack Narz. This show aired over NBC between January and August when in abruptly left the air. Before its demise it aired briefly in prime time during the summer. Contestants tried to complete the dots by answering questions.

T *Dough Re Mi,* emceed by Gene Rayburn. Owned by Barry-Enright. Seen over NBC between February 1958 and December 1960 in the morning. Contestants got to hear three musical notes, then could bid and buy more to identify songs.

T *End of the Rainbow,* emceed by Art Baker. Owned by Ralph Edwards. Seen over NBC on Saturday nights, this show traveled from city to city to lend a helping hand to deserving people.

T *ESP,* emceed by Vincent Price. Seen briefly over ABC on Friday nights during the summer. Contestants attempted to identify the suit and value in exact order of masked playing cards.

T *For Love or Money,* emceed by Bill Nimmo. Seen during the daytime over CBS during the summer.

T *Gags to Riches,* emceed by Joey Adams. Seen locally over WATV-TV, New York, during the fall on Thursday evenings.

T *Haggis Baggis,* emceed by Fred Robbins, Bert Parks, Art Linkletter in the daytime version, Jack Linkletter and Dennis James in the evening. The daytime version of the game aired over NBC between June and September 1958, the prime time version until June 1959. Contestants attempted to win haggis—luxury prizes, or baggis—utility prizes.

T *How Do You Rate?* emceed by Tom Reddy. Seen over CBS Monday through Thursday mornings between March and June. Contestants revealed hidden aptitudes with the help of an "aptimeter."

T *Jig Saw,* emceed by Allen Kent. Seen locally over WOR-TV, New York. Phone-in quiz.

T *Keep Talking,* emceed by Merv Griffin, Monty Hall. First seen over CBS between July 1958 and September 1959, ABC then carried the game until May 1960. On this panel game with Ilka Chase, Joey Bishop, Danny Dayton and Morey Amsterdam, Paul Winchell, Peggy Cass, and Pat Carroll, contestants tried to work a secret phrase into an ad-libbed situation.

T *Lucky Partners,* emceed by Carl Cordell. Seen over NBC during the afternoons in the sumer. On this game, home viewers could write the last 5 serial numbers of bills in their wallet under the letters LUCKY and hope for matches for cash.

T,S *Make Me Laugh,* emceed by Robert Q. Lewis and comedians. Seen over ABC between March and June. Contestants attempted to refrain from laughing at jokes. Revived as a syndicated game in 1979, hosted by Bobby Van.

T *Mother's Day,* seen during the day over ABC.

T *Music Bingo,* emceed by Johnny Gilbert. Seen over NBC between June and December 1958, over ABC through 1959.

T *The News Game,* emceed by Pat Herndon. Seen locally over WATV-TV, New York, Monday evenings during the spring.

T *Play Your Hunch,* emceed by Merv Griffin, Robert Q. Lewis. Owned by Goodson-Todman. Seen both during the day and in prime time, over CBS between June 1958 and June 1962, over NBC between June 1962 and September 1963. Contestants and panelists attempted to use their intuition to separate fact from fiction.

T *Put It in Writing,* emceed by Sandy Becker. Seen over Du Mont on Tuesday evenings. A panel of handwriting experts attempted to match writing samples with contestants.

T *Top Dollar,* emceed by Toby Reed, Bergen Evans. Seen over CBS in the spring and summer of 1958 on Saturday nights. Based on the parlor game Ghosts.

T *Who Do You Trust?* emceed by Johnny Carson, Woody Woodbury. The game of *Do You Trust Your Wife?* changed name and format in this daytime show, seen with this new name between July of 1958 and December of 1963.

T *Win-Go,* emceed by Bob Kennedy. Seen over NBC during the spring. Contestants answered hard questions for stakes worth up to $250,000.

T *Winner's Circle,* soon called *Win with a Winner,* emceed by Sandy Becker. Seen over NBC during the summer. Based upon the rules of horse racing. Similar to *Celebrity Sweepstakes* years later.

1959

With trouble brewing in game show land, the new games of the year all had low stakes and non-controversial formats. Mass cancellations of suspect quizzes began to occur toward the close of the year.

T *Across the Board,* emceed by Ted Brown. Seen over ABC at noon during the summer. Crossword-puzzle format.

T   *Cinderella Weekend,* emceed by Joe Francis and Fedora Bontempi. Seen locally over WNHC-TV, New Haven. Contestants won a weekend in New York.

T   *Double Cross,* emceed by Allyn Edwards. Seen locally over WATV-TV, New York. Crossword-puzzle game.

T   *Just for Fun,* emceed by Sonny Fox. Seen locally over WNEW-TV on Saturdays. Children's game.

T   *Laugh Line,* emceed by Dick Van Dyke. Seen over NBC in the spring and summer. Panelists Mike Nichols and Elaine May and Orson Bean thought up comic captions for real-life cartoons acted by local actors. Seen on Thursday nights.

T   *Split Personality,* emceed by Tom Poston. Owned by Goodson-Todman. Seen during the fall. Panelists attempted to guess two sides to a given celebrity's life. Seen over NBC.

T   *Take a Good Look,* emceed by Ernie Kovacs with Edie Adams, Cesar Romero, and Carl Reiner. Seen during the fall over ABC on Thursday nights. Film clip quiz.

T   *Who Pays?* emceed by Mike Wallace with panelists Celeste Holm, Sir Cedrick Hardwicke, and Gene Klavan attempting to match maids, valets, and the like with their celebrity employers. Seen over NBC during the summer on Thursday nights.

1960

With the exposure of quiz show rigging and sensational congressional hearings, quiz shows fell from favor . . . during prime time anyway. Still, as the networks discovered their popularity had remained high with daytime viewers, they began slowly to steal back onto the airwaves, with strict new controls and minimal stakes. New only three:

T   *About Faces,* emceed by Ben Alexander. Owned by Ralph Edwards. Seen over ABC between January 1960 and June 1961 during the day.

T   *Charge Account,* emceed by Jan Murray. Essentially a variety show, Murray introduced a game segment to this NBC daytime show that aired between September 1960 and September 1962.

T   *Video Village,* emceed by Jack Narz, Monty Hall. Heatter-Quigley's first collaboration. Seen over CBS between the summer of 1960 and the summer of 1962, in the mornings.

1961

1961 saw a marked resurrgence of the programs now determinedly called "game shows." Most would prove mediocre, one, distinguished.

T   *Camouflage,* emceed by Don Morrow. Seen over ABC. Contestants searched for an object hidden in a cartoon.

T   *Don't Call Us,* emceed by Ted Steele, Clay Cole. Seen locally over WATV-TV, New York. Daytime phone game.

T   *Double Exposure,* emceed by Steve Dunne. Seen over CBS in the mornings. A copy of *Concentration.* Contestants tried to solve a jigsaw puzzle.

T   *Face the Facts,* emceed by Red Rowe. Seen over CBS in the afternoons. Contestants served on a "jury" for merchandise prizes.

T   *Make a Face,* emceed by Bob Clayton. Contestants tried to identify a celebrity's face formed by three revolving wheels. Seen over ABC in the fall of 1961 into the spring of 1962, and a gain in a children's version in the fall of 1962.

T   *Number, Please,* emceed by Bud Collyer. Seen over ABC, this word game which resembled Hangman, replaced *Beat the Clock.* It ran through 1961 at 12:30 P.M.

T   *On Your Mark,* emceed by Sonny Fox. Seen locally over WNEW-TV, New York on Saturday mornings, this was a career-oriented quiz for children.

T,S   *Password,* emceed by Allen Ludden. Owned by Goodson-Todman, created by Bob Stewart. This classic game aired first over CBS in October and ran until May 1967. It also aired briefly in prime time. Upon its cancellation, it entered the syndication market. In 1971, ABC received the game which ran until February 1975. In 1979, the game updated again, aired over NBC, known as *Password Plus.* Ludden again emceed. See pages 221–226.

T   *Say When,* emceed by Art James. Seen over NBC in the mornings. Similar in format to *The Price Is Right.*

T   *Seven Keys,* emceed by Jack Narz. Seen over ABC in the afternoons until the spring of 1964. If contestants could answer seven straight questions they earned a "key" and an opportunity to unlock a merchandise showcase.

T   *Teen Quiz,* emceed by Clay Cole. Seen locally over WATV-TV, New York week day afternoons.

T   *Video Village, Junior,* emceed by Monty Hall. Owned by Heatter-Quigley. A children's version of *Video Village,* this show aired Saturday mornings.

T   *Your Surprise Package,* emceed by George Fenneman. Seen over CBS in the mornings.

T   *You're in the Picture,* emceed by Jackie Gleason. Seen very briefly over CBS on Friday nights. After the second airing of this show, which required four contestants to stick their heads into cutout pictures and try to guess the setting depicted in the picture, Jackie Gleason pulled up a chair and publicly apologized to America for it. Thereafter, the show ran out its thirteen weeks with a variety format.

1962

T,S   *Match Game,* emceed by Gene Rayburn. The original version of this Goodson-Todman game aired over NBC between December 31, 1962, and September 1969. See also: *Match Game '73,* under the 1973 heading.

T,S   *Stump the Stars,* emceed by Mike Stokey. Seen over CBS from fall of 1962 to fall 1963, this updated version of *Pantomime Quiz,* entered syndication during 1969.

T   *Tell It to Groucho,* emceed by Groucho Marx with Patty Harmon, Jack Wheeler, and George Fenneman. Seen over CBS on Thursday nights, this was an unsuccessful attempt to return Marx to television after the cancellation of *You Bet Your Life.*

T   *Window Shopping,* emceed by Bob Kennedy. Seen over ABC in the afternoons, this was a memory test for merchandise prizes, with William A. Wood, a Columbia journalism professor, as referee.

T   *Your First Impression,* emceed by Bill Leyden. Owned by Monty Hall, Stefan Hatos, Nat Ligerman, and Art Stark. Seen over NBC between January 1962 and April 1964. Panelists Dennis James, Linda Darnell, and George Kirbo had five chances to guess a mystery guest.

1963

Hey, a couple of these games were good!

T   *Alumni Fun,* emceed by John K. M. McCaffery. Seen over ABC on Sunday afternoons. Similar in format to *G.E. College Bowl.*

T   *Do You Know?* emceed by Bob Maxwell. Seen locally over WCBS-TV, New York on Sunday afternoons; a schoolbook quiz for children.

T   *It's Academic,* emceed by Art James. Seen locally over WNBC-TV, New York on Sunday afternoons, this show featured local New York high schools in a *College Bowl* type quiz. Long-running.

T   *The John Dando Quiz,* seen locally over WFSB-TV, Hartford, on Tuesday nights. Foreign-country quiz.

T   *Laughs for Sale,* emceed by Hal March. Seen over ABC on Sunday nights.

T,S   *Let's Make a Deal,* emceed by Monty Hall. Owned by Hatos-Hall. Seen over NBC between December 1963 and December 1968, and over ABC from December 1968 through the summer of 1976. A nightime version of this classic game aired between 1969 and 1971. The show is still airing in syndication, taped in Las Vegas. See pages 226–230.

T   *Missing Links,* emceed by Ed McMahon. Owned by Goodson-Todman. Seen over NBC between fall of 1963 and spring of 1964. Panelists had to fill in a missing word to complete a story.

T   *The Object Is,* emceed by Dick Clark. Seen over ABC in the fall of 1963.

T   *$100 Grand,* emceed by Jack Clark. Seen very briefly over ABC on Sunday nights in the fall.

T   *People Will Talk,* emceed by Dennis James. Owned by Heatter-Quigley. Seen over NBC during the day in the summer, the show consisted of man-in-the-street interviews for the studio audience to debate and vote upon for merchandise prizes.

T   *Picture This,* emceed by Jerry Van Dyke. Seen over CBS in the summer during prime time on Tuesday nights.

T   *Take Two,* emceed by Don McNeill. Seen over ABC on Sunday afternoons in the summer. Celebrity and civilian teams vied to identify pictures.

T   *Tell Us More,* emceed by Conrad Nagel. Seen over NBC in the afternoons. Armchair psychology as a panel discussed the life of celebrities such as Elizabeth Taylor and Marilyn Monroe. Short-lived.

T   *Word for Word,* emceed and owned by Merv Griffin. Seen over NBC during the morning through the fall of 1964.

T,S   *You Don't Say,* emceed by Tom Kennedy. Owned by Ralph Andrews. Seen over NBC in the afternoons between the spring of 1963 and the fall of 1969. It aired briefly in prime time in 1964. The game entered syndication in 1970, returning in 1975 and again in 1978 and 1979, hosted by Jim Peck. Closely related to *Password.*

1964

T   *The Celebrity Game,* emceed by Carl Reiner. Seen over CBS in prime time on Sunday evenings in the spring and summer of 1964. Owned by Heatter-Quigley.

T   *Get the Message,* emceed by Frank Buxton, Robert Q. Lewis. Owned by Goodson-Todman. Seen over ABC in the mornings between March and December.

T,S   *Jeopardy!* emceed by Art Fleming. Owned by Merv Griffin. Seen over NBC between April 1964 and January 1975, *Jeopardy!* aired in syndication during the fall of 1974. In 1979, the show, updated returned to the air. Fleming continued to host. See pages 238–242.

T   *Made in America,* emceed by Bob Maxwell, with Hans Conreid, Don Murray, and Jan Sterling. Seen over CBS on Sunday nights. The panel explored the lives of self-made contestants.

T *So You Know Football,* emceed by Bill Mazer. Seen over NBC on Saturday after-noons, during the fall.

T *Spread the Word,* emceed by Bill Nimmo. Seen locally over WPIX-TV, New York on Monday nights in the fall.

T *What's This Song?* emceed by Win (later known as Wink) Martindale. Seen over NBC in the morning. Celebrity-civilian teams vied to identify song titles.

1965

Holy Moley! Who let Chuck Barris in? And David Susskind?

T *The Bible Story Game,* emceed by Buddy and Beverly Piper. Seen over NBC on Sunday mornings. Local New York Sunday schools vied.

T *Call My Bluff,* emceed by Bill Leyden. Owned by Goodson-Todman. Seen over NBC in the spring and summer of 1965 at noon.

T,S *The Dating Game,* emceed by Jim Lange. Owned by Chuck Barris (his first). Seen over ABC during the afternoons between December 1965 and July 1973, *The Dating Game* also aired in prime time between October 1966 and July 1973. The game entered syndication in 1977. See pages 230–233.

T *Everything's Relative,* emceed by Jim Hutton. Seen over NBC in the afternoons. Members of families predicted what one of their members would do.

T *Fractured Phrases,* emceed by Art James. Owned by Stu Billett and Art Baer. Seen over NBC in the mornings. Figuring out phrases from nonsense syllables. Short-lived.

T *Hall of Fun,* emceed by Fred Hall. Seen locally over WNEW-TV, New York during the summer.

T *I'll Bet,* emceed by Jack Narz. Seen over NBC during the afternoon. Show-business husbands and wives vied.

T *Let's Play Post Office,* emceed by Don Morrow. Seen over NBC between September of 1965 and July of 1966. Contestants tried to guess the identities of famous people from their correspondence.

T,S *PDQ,* emceed by Dennis James, Bill Cullen. Owned by Heatter-Quigley. Seen over NBC in 1965 and again in 1970, when it was revised and known as *Baffle.* Word game in the *Password* genre.

T *The Rebus Game,* emceed by Jack Linkletter. Seen over ABC during the spring in the afternoon.

T *Supermarket Sweep,* emceed by Bill Malone. Owned by David Susskind. Seen over ABC between December of 1965 and July of 1967.

1966

One game that bowed this year is still airing on network TV, another's still active in syndication. Note too, the arrival of Bob Stewart as an independent packager.

T *Chain Letter,* emceed by Jan Murray. Owned by Hatos-Hall. Seen in the summer and fall of 1966.

T *Dream Girl of '67,* emceed by Dick Stewart, Paul Petersen, Wink Martindale. Owned by Chuck Barris. Seen over ABC between December 1966 and December 1967 during the afternoons. Beauty-contest format.

T   *Eye Guess,* emceed by Bill Cullen. Seen over NBC in the mornings between January 1966 and September 1969. Memory game. Owned by Bob Stewart—his first independent venture.

T   *The Face is Familiar,* emceed by Jack Whitaker. Seen over CBS between the spring and fall during prime time on Tuesday nights. Scrambled-photo game.

T   *Food Buyers' Quiz,* with Betty Furness, George Kirby, Joyce Brothers, and Boots Randolph. Seen locally over WNDT-TV, New York as a special on November 17, 1966.

T   *Hole in One,* seen locally over WPIX-TV, New York during the summer on Sunday nights. Three amateur golfers and one pro vied at targets on golf courses around New York.

T,S   *Hollywood Squares,* emceed by Peter Marshall. Owned by Heatter-Quigley. Seen during the day over NBC from October 17, 1966 up to the present. *Hollywood Squares* entered syndication in 1972. See pages 243–249.

T,S   *The Newlywed Game,* emceed by Bob Eubanks. Owned by Nick Nicholson, Roger Muir, and Chuck Barris. First seen over ABC during the afternoons in July 1966 up until December 1974, *The Newlywed Game* also aired during prime time in the late sixties. It is still airing in syndication. See pages 233–237.

T   *Show Down,* emceed by Joe Pyne. Owned by Heatter-Quigley. Seen during the summer over NBC in the morning. Featuring preteen rock group, The Bantams.

T   *Surprise Show,* seen locally over WPIX-TV, New York in the afternoons.

1967

Daytime America was about to go three years without a single new blockbuster game show, culminating in massive network axing at the close of 1969.

T   *Computer Quiz,* seen locally over WCBS-TV on Saturday afternoons, grade-school children answered questions posed by a robot.

T   *Everybody's Talking,* emceed by Lloyd Thaxton. Seen over ABC from February 1967 to the fall of 1968 in the afternoon. Film-clip game.

T,S   *The Family Game,* emceed by Bob Barker. Owned by Chuck Barris. Seen over ABC between June 1967 and July 1968. Three teams of parents attempted to guess whose children said what.

T   *Honeymoon Race,* emceed by Jim McKrell. Owned by David Susskind. This refurbishment of *Supermarket Sweep* moved to Florida but continued to air over ABC between July 1967 and April 1968.

T   *How's Your Mother-in-Law?* emceed by Wink Martindale and panelists. Seen over ABC during the mornings in the fall and spring. Owned by Chuck Barris.

T   *It's Your Move,* emceed by Jim Perry. This charade game was seen over ABC during the fall in the late afternoon.

S   *Jackpot Bingo,* emceed by Marty Allen and Steve Rossi.

T   *Matches and Mates,* emceed by Art James. Seen over ABC into 1968 in the mornings.

T   *One in a Million,* emceed by Danny O'Neill. Owned by Merv Griffin. Seen over ABC in the mornings that spring. Contestants attempted to guess which panelists had amazing unique talents.

T   *Perfect Match,* emceed by Dick Enberg. Seen over ABC in the fall. Computer date game.

T *Personality*, emceed by Larry Blyden. Owned by Bob Stewart. Seen over NBC in the summer of 1967 until the fall of 1969. Celebrities vied to discover how well they knew each other.

T *Reach for a Star*, emceed by Bill Mazer. Owned by Merv Griffin. Seen over ABC in the mornings. Stunt format.

T *Snap Judgment*, emceed by Ed McMahon, Gene Rayburn. Owned by Goodson-Todman. Seen in the mornings between April 1967 and the spring of 1969.

T *Temptation*, emceed by Art James. Seen in the mornings over ABC between the late fall of 1967 and the summer of 1968. James played the role of a riverboat gambler in this game which resembled *Let's Make a Deal*.

T *Treasure Isle*, emceed by John Bartholomew Tucker. Seen during the afternoons over ABC into 1968. Couples struggled to complete a real-life treasure hunt set in a Florida lagoon and island.

1968

T *The Baby Game*, emceed by Richard Hayes. Owned by Chuck Barris. Seen over ABC the first six months of the year, in the afternoons.

T *Dream House*, emceed by Mike Darrow. Owned by Don Reid. Seen during the afternoons from the spring of 1968 until January 1970. Couples vied to win an entire house, room by room.

S *Fast Draw*, emceed by Johnny Gilbert.

T *Funny You Should Ask*, emceed by Lloyd Thaxton. Seen over ABC during the fall. Celebrity matching game.

S *Pay Cards*, emceed by Art James.

T *Wedding Party*, emceed by Al Hamel. Seen over ABC in the spring during the afternoon. Engaged couples competed for prizes. Knock-off of *The Newlywed Game*.

S *Win with the Stars*, emceed by Allen Ludden. Owned by Walter Schwimmer.

1969

The networks refused to buy any new games the following year, forcing packagers to become resourceful to survive. They discovered if they paid their own production costs without network support, then sold their games locally, station by station, they could realize unlimited profits—provided their game was any good to begin with. Ralph Edwards' Truth or Consequences, *Goodson-Todman's* What's My Line?, I've Got a Secret, Beat the Clock, *though off the network schedules now for a couple of years, and new G.T. game,* He Said! She Said!, *all thrived in syndication, and indeed, actually kept Goodson-Todman afloat through a couple of very lean years.*

T *Anniversary Game*, emceed by Al Hamel. Seen in the mornings over ABC.

T *Beat the Odds*, emceed by Johnny Gilbert. Seen during the mornings over ABC.

S *Game Game*, emceed by Jim McKrell. Owned by Chuck Barris. Celebrities gave candid answers to personal questions.

T *Generation Gap*, emceed by Dennis Wholley, Jack Barry—his first time back on the air. Seen over ABC on Friday nights between February and May.

S *Guess My Sign*, with a celebrity panel including Alan Alda and Larry Blyden.

S *He Said! She Said!* emceed by Joe Garagiola, Johnny Olson. This game became the prototype for *Tattletales*. See 1973 heading.

T   *It Takes Two,* emceed by Vince Scully. Seen over NBC in the mornings between March 1969 and August 1970. Three celebrity couples estimated facts and the studio audience bet upon who was closer.

T   *It's Your Bet,* emceed by Hal March, Tom Kennedy, Dick Gautier, Lyle Waggoner. Seen over NBC, afternoons. Husband-vs.-wife game.

T,S   *The Liar's Club,* emceed by Rod Serling, Bill Armstrong. Seen locally over KTLA-TV, Los Angeles during the fall of 1974, syndicated 1969, 1975, 1976. Owned by Ralph Andrews. Panel bluff game incorporating unusual objects.

S   *Lucky Pair,* hosted by Richard Dawson; owned by Bob Barker, seen locally in Los Angeles.

S   *Money Makers.* Details unknown.

S   *The Movie Game,* emceed by Sonny Fox, Larry Blyden. Film-clip game.

T   *Name Droppers,* emceed by Al Loman, Roger Barkley. Seen over NBC from the fall of 1969 until the spring of 1970. The game featured studio audience members attempting to guess which "name dropper" knew which celebrity. Seen in the afternoons.

T   *Runaround.* A children's game, other details unknown.

T,S   *Sale of the Century,* emceed by Jack Kelly, Joe Garagiola. Seen over NBC from the fall of 1969 until the summer of 1973, whereupon it entered syndication. Owned by Ron Greenburg. Three contestants vied for a chance to win a valuable piece of merchandise at a bargain-basement price. The highest bidder won a choice of five bargains.

S   *Spending Spree,* emceed by Al Hamel.

S   *Storybook Squares.* This was a syndicated dress-up version of *Hollywood Squares* for children, emceed by Peter Marshall. No longer seen regularly. *Hollywood Squares* usually takes two weeks a year out of its schedule to play this version of the game.

T   *Who, What, Where Game,* emceed by Art James. Seen over NBC in the afternoons between December 1969 and January 1974. Owned by Ron Greenburg.

T   *You're Putting Me On,* emceed by Bill Leyden, Bill Cullen, with panel. Seen over NBC in the afternoons through the fall. Celebrity acting game with Peggy Cass, Larry Blyden, Ann Meara, and others as panelists.

1970

Only two new game shows bowed this year, and one of those was syndicated.

S   *Sports Challenge,* emceed by Dick Enberg. Pro athletes competed in a sports quiz.

T   *Words and Music,* emceed by Wink Martindale. Seen during the afternoon over NBC between September and February of the following year, the only new game of 1970 on all three networks.

1971

Though down for the count, game shows revived this year with:

S   *All About Faces,* emceed by Richard Hayes.

T,S   *Anything You Can Do,* emceed by Gene Woods. A Canadian stunt show that aired stateside over ABC during the winter.

T   *Joe Garagiola's Memory Game,* seen over NBC during the afternoons between February and July.

T   *The Reel Game,* emceed and owned by Jack Barry. Seen over ABC during the evenings in the winter and spring. Film clips and celebs.

T   *Three on a Match,* emceed by Bill Cullen. Owned by Bob Stewart. Seen over NBC in the afternoons between the summer of 1971 and the summer of 1974.

1972

ABC's success with their revival of Goodson-Todman's Password *in 1972 led CBS to reconsider game shows for their daytime schedule, which had been full of reruns and serials. They had Goodson-Todman dust off* The Price Is Right, *with phenomenal success.*

T   *Amateur's Guide to Love,* emceed by Gene Rayburn. Owned by Heatter-Quigley. Seen over CBS in the spring. Celebs and film clips.

T   *Dialing for Dollars.* Seen locally over WTNH-TV, New Haven. Emceed by Bob Norman.

T   *Gambit,* emceed by Wink Martindale with Elaine Stewart. Owned by Heatter-Quigley. Seen over CBS in the mornings between September 1972 and January 1977.

T,S   *The Joker Is Wild,* emceed and owned by Jack Barry. Seen over CBS in the mornings from the fall of 1972 into the summer of the following year. This game entered syndication in 1974 and has been running ever since.

S   *The Parent Game,* emceed by Clark Race. Owned by Chuck Barris.

T,S   *The New Price Is Right,* emceed by Bob Barker. Seen over CBS through various schedule changes from September 1972 until the present. Television's only hour-long game show also airs in a syndicated half-hour version, originally hosted by Dennis James, more recently, since 1977, by Bob Barker. See pages 276–283.

T   *Split Second,* emceed by Tom Kennedy. Owned by Hatos-Hall. Seen during the afternoons over ABC between the spring of 1972 and the summer of 1975.

1973

More revivals of earlier games followed. Then Bob Stewart clicked with The $10,000 Pyramid, *a name which in a year or so inflation doubled. During the summer, the first "Lin Bolen" game bowed, one of several over the next few years that, with the premature cancellation of* Jeopardy! *and* Concentration, *changed the look of game shows but nearly destroyed NBC's daytime schedule, already weakened in 1968 with its loss to ABC of* Let's Make a Deal.

T   *Baffle,* emceed by Dick Enberg. Seen over NBC in the mornings, this revitalized version of *PDQ* aired between the spring of 1973 and that fall. Owned by Heatter-Quigley.

T   *Hollywood's Talking,* emceed by Geoff Edwards. Owned by Jack Barry. Seen over CBS in the spring during the afternoon.

T,S   *Match Game '73,* emceed by Gene Rayburn with celebrity panel. Owned by Goodson-Todman. Completely revamped from its 1963 version, this comedy matching game, which yearly updates its name, airs in syndication under the name of *Match Game P.M.* See pages 253–255.

S   *The New Treasure Hunt,* emceed by Geoff Edwards. Owned by Chuck Barris. "Television's richest treasure" was an outrageous, and some thought sadistic, update of the Jan Murray game. Seen throughout the late seventies. See pages 260–263.

S *On the Money,* emceed by Bob Braun.

T,S *$10,000 Pyramid,* emceed by Dick Clark, soon to be referred to as *The $20,000 Pyramid.* Owned by Bob Stewart. Originally seen over CBS from the spring of 1973 until the spring of 1974. Upon cancellation, ABC bought the game. It is still running. Seen in syndication as *The $25,000 Pyramid,* hosted by Bill Cullen. See pages 255–259.

T *The Wizard of Odds, II,* emceed by Alex Trebek with Marty Pom. Owned by Burt Sugarman. The first "Lin Bolen" game. Seen over NBC during the mornings between July 1973 and the following summer.

1974

Through this year and the next, the networks once again indiscriminately cluttered their daytime schedules with mediocre game shows.

T *The Big Showdown,* emceed by Jim Peck. Seen over ABC from December 1974 until July of the following year. Featured tossup questions and a category board. The game aired in the afternoons.

T,S *Celebrity Sweepstakes,* emceed by Jim McKrell. Owned by Burt Sugarman. Seen over NBC until 1977, this horse-race-odds game with a celebrity panel aired in syndication in 1974.

S *Dealer's Choice,* emceed by Jack Clark. Taped in Las Vegas.

T *The Girl in My Life,* emceed by Fred Holliday. Seen over ABC during the winter in the afternoons.

T,S *High Rollers,* emceed by Alex Trebek with Ruta Lee. Owned by Heatter-Quigley. Seen over NBC during the mornings from July of 1973 until 1975. A nighttime version of the game also aired in syndication. Full of kinks until revised in 1978 as *The* highly—successful *Newsletter Rollers.* See pages 283–289.

T *Jackpot!* emceed by Geoff Edwards. Owned by Bob Stewart. Seen over NBC between January 1974 and September 1975. This game replaced *Jeopardy!*

T *Money Maze,* emceed by Nick Clooney. Seen over ABC between December 1974 and July of the following year.

T *Now You See It,* emceed by Jack Narz. Owned by Goodson-Todman. Seen over CBS from April 1974 into 1975. Word game.

T,S *Tattletales,* emceed by Bert Convy. Owned by Goodson-Todman, the network version of *He Said! She Said!* (See 1969 heading.) Seen over CBS from the spring of 1974 until the spring of 1978. Seen in syndication in 1977.

T *Winning Streak,* emceed by Bill Cullen. Owned by Bob Stewart. Seen over NBC in the mornings from July through December.

1975

S *Almost Anything Goes,* emceed by Charlie Jones, Regis Philbin. Communities vied in this stunt show.

T *Blank Check,* emceed by Art James. Owned by Jack Barry. Seen the first thirteen weeks of 1975. ESP game with audience involvement.

T *Blankety-Blanks,* emceed by Bill Cullen. Owned by Bob Stewart. This word game was seen the second cycle of the year.

S *The Cross—Wits,* emceed by Jack Clark. Owned by Ralph Edwards. The crossword game features celebrities partnered with civilians. Still airing.

T *Diamond Head Game,* emceed by Bob Eubanks with Jane Nelson. Owned by Fisherman-Freer. Seen over NBC during the afternoons the first quarter of 1975. Shot in Hawaii, the game featured a *papier-mâché* volcano set on Waikiki Beach.

S *Don Adams Screen Test.* Hopeful amateurs attempted to play famous Hollywood roles.

T *The Magnificent Marble Machine,* emceed by Art James. Owned by Heatter-Quigley. Seen over NBC during the third quarter. Celebrity-civilian word game with pinball-machine end game.

T *Musical Chairs,* emceed by Adam Wade. Seen over CBS form June through October.

T *The Neighbors,* emceed by Regis Philbin. Seen over ABC from the end of December through the following April. Gossip game.

T *Rhyme and Reason,* emceed by Bob Eubanks with Nipsey Russell. Owned by W. T. Naud. Seen briefly over ABC.

T *Show-offs,* emceed by Bobby Van. Owned by Goodson-Todman. Pantomime game. Seen the third cycle.

T *Spin Off,* emceed by Jim Lange. Owned by Nicholson-Muir. Briefly seen over CBS.

T *Three for the Money,* emceed by Dick Enberg. Owned by Hatos-Hall. Seen over NBC during the fourth quarter of the year.

T *Wheel of Fortune, II,* emceed by Chuck Woolery with Susan Stafford. Owned by Merv Griffin. Seen over NBC in the mornings, this game which began airing during the fourth quarter of the year is still running.

1976

Not until this year did any solidly ground-breaking new games appear. Meanwhile, Jack Barry and Dan Enright, reunited for the first time since the scandals; Ralph Edwards; Bob Stewart; and Chuck Barris challenged Goodson-Todman for the lucrative syndication market.

T *Double Dare,* emceed by Alex Trebek. Seen over CBS from the fall of the year through the following spring, this game featured contestants in isolation booths and an end game in which the winner faced three Ph.D. "spoilers." Owned by Goodson-Todman.

T,S *Family Feud,* emceed by Richard Dawson. Owned by Goodson-Todman. First seen over ABC during July. Still running. The game entered syndication during the fall of 1977, and occasionally aired in 1978 as a prime time special, played by soap-opera "families" for charity. See pages 269–273.

T *Fifty Grand Slam,* emceed by Tom Kennedy. Owned by Ralph Andrews. Seen over NBC, a short-lived attempt to air a high-stakes big-money quiz during the day.

T *Fun Factory,* emceed by Bobby Van. Seen over NBC, this variety-game show with a loose format aired briefly over the summer.

T,S *The Gong Show,* emceed by Chuck Barris. Seen over NBC from 1976 on. A syndicated version of *The Gong Show* first aired in 1977, first hosted by Gary Owens, later by Chuck Barris. Owned by Chuck Barris and Chris Bearde. See pages 264–269.

T *Hot Seat,* emceed by Jim Peck. Seen briefly over ABC during the summer. Owned by Heatter-Quigley. The game measured couples' emotional responses with a "galvanic skin response machine."

S *The $128,000 Question,* emceed by Mike Darrow, Alex Trebek. Owned by Steve Carlin. An effort to revive an unrigged *$64,000 Question.*

T *Stumpers,* emceed by Allen Ludden. Owned by Lin Bolen. Seen briefly over NBC in the spring.

1977

T *The Better Sex,* emceed by Bill Anderson and Sarah Purcell. Seen over ABC during the second half of the year. Owned by Goodson-Todman.

S *Hollywood Connection,* emceed by Jim Lange. Owned by Barry-Enright. Celebrity match game resembling *Match Game.*

T *It's Anybody's Guess,* emceed by Monty Hall. Owned by Hatos-Hall. Seen during the spring.

T *Knockout,* emceed by Arte Johnson. Owned by Ralph Edwards. Seen over NBC from the fall into early 1978.

S *Pro-Fan,* emceed by Charlie Jones. Pre-game sports quiz. See pages 273–276.

T *Second Chance,* emceed by Jim Peck. Owned by Carruthers Productions. Seen over ABC during the first six months.

T *Shoot for the Stars,* emceed by Geoff Edwards. Owned by Bob Stewart. Seen over NBC during the spring and summer. Celebrity-civilian riddle game.

T *To Say the Least,* emceed by Tom Kennedy. Owned by Heatter-Quigley. Seen over NBC from the fall through the spring of 1978. Celebrity-civilian word game.

1978

T *Card Sharks,* emceed by Jim Perry. Owned by Goodson-Todman. First seen over NBC during the spring.

S *The Cheap Show,* emceed by Dick Martin. Owned by Chris Bearde. This parody of a bluff game featured Truman Capote, Jill St. John, and Oscar the Wonder Rodent. Still running in 1979.

S *The $1.98 Beauty Show,* hosted by Rip Taylor. A Chris Bearde–Chuck Barris spin-off of *The Gong Show* with a guest celebrity panel that included Jack Ford, son of Gerald.

S *The Love Experts,* emceed by Bill Cullen, owned by Ralph Andrews. Panel advice to the lovelorn.

T,S *The New Tic Tac Dough,* emceed by Wink Martindale. Owned by Barry-Enright. First seen over CBS in the summer, the game entered syndication thirteen weeks later.

T *Pass the Buck,* emceed by Bill Cullen. Owned by Bob Stewart. Seen over CBS in the spring.

T *We Interrupt This Week,* emceed by Ned Sherrin. This comedy news panel show aired over Public Broadcasting stations in the summer and fall, and into 1979.

1979

T *ALL-STAR SECRETS,* emceed by Bob Eubanks. Owned by Bob Eubanks and Michael Hill. Seen over NBC in the spring. Contestants tried to guess which secrets belonged to which celebrities on the panel.

S *CELEBRITY CHARADES,* emceed by ventriloquist Jay Johnson. Owned by William B. Fein and Allan B. Schwartz with Mike Stokey as consultant. *PANTOMIME QUIZ* strikes again!

Even at the end of the decade, when game shows traditionally wane, there are these network pilots in the works as we go to press:

The Guiness Game, emceed by Bob Hilton. Owned by Hill-Eubanks.
Hollywood Smart Alecks. Owned by Hill-Eubanks.

Hoodwink. Owned by Hill-Eubanks.

Hotfoot. Owned by Heatter-Quigley.

In a Word, owned by Ralph Edwards.

Intuition, emceed by Alex Trebek. Owned by Allen Sloan Productions.

Joker! Joker!! Joker!!! Owned by Barry-Enright.

Three's a Crowd, owned by Chuck Barris.

and of course, Goodson-Todman always has a few dozen kettles on the back burner.

Rumored Syndicated Games, dates unknown

S   *Beat the Computer.* Owned by Aaron S. Bloom.

S   *By the Numbers.* Details unknown.

S   *TV Crossword Quiz.* Owned by Aaron S. Bloom.

About the Author

Maxene Fabe grew up in Cincinnati, Ohio, where in 1965, she graduated with high honors in English from the University of Cincinnati, then received her M.A. in English from the University of Pennsylvania.

A permanently transplanted New Yorker who spends her weekends in Vermont, Maxene Fabe has had a many-faceted career, working in publishing, driving a cab, and writing horror comics. Now a full-time writer, she is the author of a novel, DEATH ROCK, as well as BEAUTY MILLIONAIRE: *The Life of Helena Rubinstein,* and many articles. She is currently at work on her second novel.